The Economic
Development of Canada

The Economic Development of Canada

Richard Pomfret

⟨Π⟩ Methuen

Toronto   New York   London
Sydney   Auckland

Canadian Cataloguing in Publication Data
Pomfret, Richard, 1948–
    The economic development of Canada

Bibliography: p.
ISBN 0-458-94730-X (pbk.)

1. Canada - Economic conditions. 2. Canada - Economic
policy. I. Title.

HC113.P65   330.971   C81-094065-5

Printed and bound in Canada
1 2 3 4 5   81   86 85 84 83 82

Contents

List of Maps

Preface

The aim of this book is to provide an introduction to and interpretation of the development of the Canadian economy since European settlement. Easterbrooke and Aitken's *Canadian Economic History* has remained the standard work since its appearance in 1956. However, in the succeeding decades there has been considerable research on Canada's economic past, which has increasingly appeared inconsistent with their approach. The lack of an alternative framework has often made it difficult to assess the significance of new research for our wider understanding of Canadian economic development. I have attempted to bring together the results of recent research and to suggest a new framework which can accommodate further findings as they come along.

I have tried to keep the book concise rather than encyclopaedic, so that it can be read without loss of continuity or themes. Perhaps the main contrast between my view and previous interpretations of Canada's economic past is that, instead of emphasizing the continuity of Canadian economic development (with staple exports playing the leading role), I focus on the transition from the sparsely populated colonial economy of the early nineteenth century to the modern economy ranking among the seven largest market economies whose leaders now meet for economic summits. Thus, the emphasis is on the period since 1850, which I believe to be of greater relevance than the more romantic pioneer years for explaining the present nature of the Canadian economy. The relatively compact treatment of the fur trade in chapter 2 reflects this consideration and also its fairly straightforward economic impact, rather than any slighting of the fur trade's importance or length of dominance of the Canadian economy. Another consideration is the desire to report adequately the results of recent research, which has led, for example, to a long chapter on government policy whose length is in my view disproportionate to the importance of policy for Canadian economic development. Conversely, little space is given to the tertiary sector and, in particular, retailing, which has undergone huge changes affecting the economic life of all Canadians but has not been the subject of much academic research. Other omissions are due to my rather narrow definition of *economic* history, which leads me to skim over demographic and labour history.

There is no presumption of previous knowledge of either Canadian history or economic theory. All economic terms used are defined, although some of the theoretical points are more tersely dealt with than in economic principles texts. The history is economic, not political, and major political events such as the Conquest of New France or Confederation are not highlighted, despite their economic roots, because their economic consequences were not commensurate with their political significance.

My debts in writing this book clearly begin with all previous writers whose ideas and empirical work I have drawn upon. I have tried to acknowledge the source of each idea or figure which is not my own, but inevitably there will be some contributions which I have absorbed without remembering their origin, and I apologize to any slighted author. Most of the book's contents were given their first exposure to Concordia University students between 1976 and 1979. The first draft was written during the academic year 1977-78, and this and subsequent drafts were helpfully commented upon by academic colleagues and anonymous reviewers; among these readers I am especially grateful to Professor Bernice Wright for her acute criticisms of the whole manuscript. Financial and secretarial help in the book's preparation was provided by Concordia University and the Johns Hopkins University Bologna Center. I am also grateful to La Trobe University, whose visiting fellowship gave me the opportunity during the second half of 1979 to visit Australia, where I gained new perspectives on Canadian economic history from my discussions with Australian economic historians. In bringing the book through its final steps to publication I have been fortunate in the encouragement, helpfulness and efficiency of Peter Milroy, Herb Hilderley and Judith de Backer on the Methuen editorial team. Last but not least, my thanks go to Rosemary Prentice, whose identification of jargon, unclarity and inelegance helped to remove some of the evidence of an economist's poor literary style from this book.

RICHARD POMFRET
Bologna,
December 1980

Chapter 1
Introduction

No society is static at any point in time; it is the unique result of previous influences. In order to understand a present-day society it is necessary to know something about its past. The past, however, consists of a limitless number of events and forces which have directly or indirectly influenced the present. It is the purpose of this introduction to define our terms of reference—to limit the type of events and forces to be considered. The principal restriction is the concentration on economic phenomena, reflecting the belief that while economic phenomena are not the sole determinants of social change, they are of major importance.

The subject matter of economic history is the subject matter of economics applied to historical phenomena. A brief definition of economics would emphasize the questions which economists study—the production, allocation and expansion of resources, goods and services. Because economics deals primarily with the present as a point in time while economic history is more concerned with changes over time, the emphasis of the two disciplines differs. Two main issues have emerged as the dominant concerns of economic history: (1) the aggregate economic growth and/or decline of societies and accompanying structural changes in their economies; and (2) the relative economic welfare of society's component groups, i.e., consideration of what happens to people within the society during that growth and/or decline. In studying the Canadian experience we will focus on the question, "What factors influenced the rate of growth of the economy and the well-being of various segments of society as the economy grew?" It may be noted that some Canadian economic historians would consider the above summary of their discipline to be too restrictive; in particular, areas such as labour markets and business history, which have been studied on their own merits, are ignored in the present account, or at least only mentioned in their relation to the primary themes of growth and well-being.

In order to discuss meaningfully Canada's economic past we will use economic theory and historical data. All historical study has, either implicitly or explicitly, a theoretical framework; to draw some order from the anarchy of limitless facts it is necessary to have some notion of which facts are important and how the selected facts are related. In this book the hypotheses will be drawn from the body of theory most relevant to *economic* history, i.e., economic theory. Sometimes existing economic theories are unable to provide satisfactory hypotheses, in which cases we will have to search for alternatives. The decision as to whether a hypothesis is satisfactory or not is reached by testing it against the historical data, preferably using statistical techniques which have objective accepted criteria for rejecting hypotheses. The main problem in applying such

1

decision rules is that the historical data, especially for earlier periods, are often inadequate for rigorous statistical tests.

The study of Canadian economic history has passed through two fairly distinct phases. The "old" economic historians met the problem of inadequate data by foregoing rigorous hypothesis testing and supporting their arguments by verbal reasoning and descriptive evidence. The high points of the old economic history were a number of studies whose theoretical framework and presentation of empirical evidence were outstandingly appropriate to their subject; for example, the books by Innis (1940; 1930) and Creighton (1937) remain the classic studies of fish, fur and the St. Lawrence economy respectively. On the other hand, the absence of rigorous standards of proof led to sloppy, internally inconsistent and tendentious writing in the hands of lesser authors. In the late 1950s and the 1960s a new approach to economic history, reemphasizing the need for rigorous statement and testing of hypotheses, spread to Canada from the United States. The prime demand of the "new" economic history in the Canadian context appeared to be the improvement and organization of historical data to conform with the concepts of economic theory so that it could be used to test hypotheses drawn from economic theory. This data manipulation has taken much time and effort and is still far from completed. In consequence, the application of the new economic history to specific Canadian problems has been limited, consisting either of hypothesis tests run concurrently with the derivation of new macroeconomic figures (e.g., Bertram 1963) or of studies of microeconomic problems where the data requirements could be reduced (often by the use of economic theory) to fit the available information. Despite their restricted number, the studies by new economic historians have had a major impact in modifying acceptable interpretations of the Canadian past and rejecting unacceptable hypotheses. The approach adopted here is to combine the best of the old and the new to provide a synthesis of the present state of our understanding of Canadian economic development. The methodology, however, leans in favour of the new economic history; wherever possible the theoretical framework is made explicit, statistical tests of hypotheses are valued, and quantitative evidence is generally preferred to qualitative evidence such as the opinions of contemporaries.

A common characteristic of economic theories is their use of abstraction, focussing on key interrelationships and making the simplifying assumption that other things remain unchanged ("*ceteris paribus*"). This can be a powerful tool, but in making the *ceteris paribus* assumption it is as important to be correct about what is left out of the analysis as about what is included. When dealing with questions involving changes over time, a similar problem concerns specification of the counterfactual situation. The criterion for measuring the impact of an event is not to compare the situations before and after the event, but rather to compare the situation after the event with the situation which would have existed had the event not occurred. For example, the Reciprocity Treaty in force between 1854 and 1866 was accompanied by economic prosperity in Canada, but such contemporaneity provides no proof of a causal relationship. Many other factors contributed to the prosperity of these twelve years, and it is necessary to consider their impact before any conclusion about the causal role of one factor can be drawn. Most of the hypothesis testing in this book involves the use of time-series data to answer questions concerning the importance of individual events for Canadian economic development. Crucial to such tests is specification of the changes which would have occurred in the absence of the event, i.e., of a plausible counterfactual situation for the end date of the analysis.

Some of the terminology of economic growth and development will be so frequently used in this book that it should be clearly defined from the beginning. The term economic growth itself has two distinct meanings to economists. In popular usage, to say that a city or region is growing usually means that the number of people or the amount of business activity in that area is increasing. This phenomenon is captured by the economist's concept of *extensive growth*, i.e., an increase in the total amount of goods and services produced (an increase in Gross National Product, to use modern national accounting terminology). Extensive growth has sometimes been encouraged by governments to give their area greater power, political importance, etc., but it has no direct implication for the standard of living of the society's members. In this respect, the relevant concept is that of *intensive growth*, i.e., an increase in output per head of population. It must be noted, however, that the identification of intensive growth with increased living standards is not ideal; intensive growth only refers to an increase in the average standard of living, and if accompanied by changes in the distribution of income or a decline in non-material well-being then some members of society may feel worse off. With this caveat in mind we will use intensive growth as the best available measure of changes in material well-being. The distinction between extensive and intensive growth is an important one. Of course they often occur together, but one may take place without the other and the implications will differ depending on which type of growth has occurred. For example, if the hypothesis is accepted that the government's tariff policy after 1879 encouraged extensive growth at the cost of lower intensive growth, then evaluation of the government policy depends on whether a higher population or a higher average standard of living was more desirable.

A concept frequently used in the analysis of economic growth is the production function. The total output of goods and services (Q) is functionally related to the quantity of inputs employed, usually restricted to two factors of production, capital (K) and labour (L), i.e., $Q = f(K,L)$. The theoretical foundations of such a production function are a subject of furious academic debate, but it is perhaps more readily acceptable as a heuristic device. Since the effect on output of an additional unit of each factor of production can usually be assumed to be positive, any increase in the labour force will lead to extensive growth, but the effect on intensive growth may be positive, zero or negative. Increases in output can also be due to increased use of capital or to technical progress, defined as a change in the functional relationship leading to a larger output being associated with given combinations of capital and labour. Either capital accumulation or technical progress will normally be associated with both extensive and intensive growth.

Technical progress used to be seen as the key to economic growth. Economic histories of the leading economic nations stressed the innovations made there; the recipe for other countries was to adopt modern techniques, usually identified with industrialization, and economic growth would follow. This approach no longer has many proponents, primarily because in a world of more or less free technology many countries desiring economic growth are failing to experience it. Thus, technology cannot be the whole story. Attention shifted during the 1950s to capital formation. Investment is defined as the addition to the real capital stock and is that part of output used not for current consumption, but to increase future output. Total new capital formation is equal to gross investment, and net investment is the net addition to the capital stock after allowing for the replacement of capital consumed in the production process. Investment can take the form of buildings, machinery and equipment or additions to inventories, in which cases it refers to an increase in the stock of physical capital, or it can be in education and training, increasing society's human capital. There are several prerequisites for investment to take place: (1) the society must generate a surplus over its current consumption needs, either by production (perhaps combined with foreign trade), by borrowing or by conquest; (2) the people controlling the surplus must channel it to productive investment, either by force (e.g., government taxation) or voluntarily; voluntary investment may be in response to market incentives (usually involving intermediaries, e.g., banks); (3) there must be people willing and able to make the productive investment, whether government or corporation employees or individual entrepreneurs.

The emphasis on investment being productive has led some economists to discriminate between different forms of investment and to stress as most important, and that which must come first, investment in social overhead capital, i.e., the infrastructure of a modern society such as a transport network, a legal system, etc. In a country with Canada's geographical characteristics, investment in social overhead capital may be of especial importance and its scale so large that the government must necessarily be involved. A final point concerning investment is that it can be closely associated with technical change. For example, the introduction of mechanical grain harvesting in the nineteenth century necessarily involved investment in new machinery. When technical change is embodied in capital equipment, then mere availability of the new technology is insufficient to ensure its diffusion; it is also necessary to examine whether the prerequisites for the capital formation are present.

So far we have been concerned with economic growth, simply defined as an increase in the amount of goods and services produced by a society, measured either on a total or on a per head basis. Economic development is much more difficult to define, although it is not too difficult to recognize. There is general agreement concerning which countries are economically developed and which are not, but any quantitative measure (of which the most frequently used is per capita GNP) yields anomalies. Here, economic development will be considered as a process and will be rather loosely defined as involving structural change in the economy. Reference to Canada as becoming more economically developed appears to involve a favourable value judgement and will be used here to suggest greater control over man's economic environment. For most of the period under consideration such control may be summarized by the degree to which intensive growth is self-sustaining.

Having defined our subject matter and explained the methodology and most important terminology, the final task of the introduction is to limit the book's geographical and temporal boundaries. The geographical area of study is present-day Canada. After the border settlements of 1783 (in the east and centre) and 1846 (in the west) this is a clearly defined political entity, although before these dates the present boundary had no political, economic or cultural meaning and the whole North American situation must be considered (as in chapter 2). After 1783 care must be taken over the name Canada, which did not refer to the whole of British North America. The Province of Canada, created in 1791, contained only the present-day provinces of Quebec and Ontario, initially as the separate colonies of Lower and Upper Canada; and then after the 1841 Act of Union the names were changed to Canada East and Canada West. Confederation in 1867 added Nova Scotia and New Brunswick, and in 1870 the Hudson Bay lands to the west were transferred to the Dominion of Canada. British Columbia and Prince Edward Island joined Canada in 1871 and 1873 respectively, and additional provinces were created in the Prairies in 1870 (Manitoba) and in 1905 (Saskatchewan and Alberta). The political entity was completed only in 1949 when Newfoundland became the tenth province. .

Any historical study of economic development is faced by the ligation problem—the choice of beginning and end dates. Since economic change is a continuous process, any starting date must involve omission of relevant preceding events. Canadian economic development stretches back to the receding of the glaciers which covered the region some ten thousand years ago, and can be seen as a mixture of indigenous developments shaped by stimuli from within and outside North America. The beginning of European exploitation of Canadian resources for European consumption which followed Cabot's, and more especially Champlain's, voyages was the most significant of these stimuli so far as present-day Canada is concerned, and on this ground is selected as our starting point. Preceding developments within North America and within the European societies whence future settlers would come are left to anthropologists/ archaeologists and to other economic historians as part of the academic division of labour. The criterion of relevance to present-day economic conditions has also led to the identification of a second significant point of discontinuity in the mid-nineteenth century (the reasons for this choice are stated at the end of chapter 2.6), and the book's emphasis is weighted towards the years after this "turning point." The terminal point of our study is not a particular day or year, but is generally conceived as the Second World War. By that time the Canadian economy had most of its existing features, and the postwar era can be considered as a unit—as my conception of present-day Canada.

Map 1
Canada, 1873

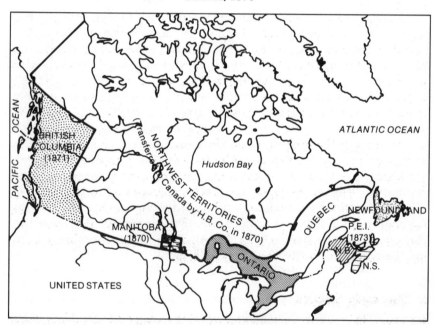

Source: From Canada, *Colony to Centennial* by D. Willows and S. Richmond, p. 199. Copyright McGraw-Hill Company of Canada Limited, 1970. Reprinted by permission.

Chapter 2

Economic Development prior to 1850

Man's first presence in the Americas can be traced back to the late Pleistocene period when hunters arrived from Siberia by way of a land bridge across the Bering Strait. Agriculture provided the basis for advanced civilizations in several parts of the preColumbine Americas, but not in the area of Canada. The only agriculture there was restricted to the St. Lawrence valley and southern Ontario and remained on a primitive level. The general picture of prehistoric Canada is of a sparsely populated area with perhaps less than a quarter of a million people spread in accordance with the abundance of edible wild life. Technological and social developments occurred in response to geographical and ecological conditions, and by the time of the arrival of Europeans the Canadian Indians had a material culture well-adapted to local conditions. The possibility of borrowing from this culture considerably eased the penetration of Canada by Europeans. In return the Indians received new goods, some improving their material living standards (e.g., metal axes, pots and firearms), others destroying them (e.g., alcoholic drinks and European diseases).

Passage from Europe to North America was always difficult. The earliest proven voyages were those of the Scandinavians. They maintained themselves in southwest Greenland for some five hundred years (starting in the tenth century), and from these bases sailed to Labrador and farther south along the North American coast. The extent and length of Scandinavian settlement in North America is unknown. They failed, however, to make any lasting impression. We may guess that the reasons for this were the failure to make the radical adaptations necessary to support themselves in the alien environment and the failure to find an export good which could be traded with Europe in return for goods which could assist the survival and improve the living standards of the settlers. The next Europeans to reach Canada found staples (exports with a high natural resource content) for which there existed a European demand, and it is with the exploitation of these staples, at first off the Canadian coast and then on land, that we move out of the prehistoric era and the economic "history" of Canada begins.

1. The Early Staples

It is probable that European fishing captains sailing off Iceland found the rich Newfoundland banks before Cabot's "discovery" of Canada in 1497. If they did, they kept the secret to themselves. The importance of Cabot's voyage was that he, as an explorer, had no reason to be reticent about his discoveries. His voyage was widely publicized and the accounts included

7

reports, often exaggerated, of the abundance of fish off Newfoundland.

The demand for fish was high in Europe, and now that Newfoundland's fish wealth was public knowledge an active fishery soon developed. The leading participants were the Portuguese, Basques from Spain and France, Bretons and Normans. Despite her financing of Cabot's voyage, the Newfoundland fisheries were unimportant to England before the 1570s; one reason for this being her shortage of salt, which was needed to preserve the fish on the return journey. The situation changed in the 1570s when the English government adopted a more active policy of encouraging Atlantic fishing as a breeding ground for sailors. From 1582 until the 1604 peace with Spain, England was very aggressive in seizing and destroying Spanish and Portuguese ships and in harassing French fishing boats. The English fishers maintained their competitive position by developing the technique of dry-curing their fish on shore before returning to Europe; at the cost of the time devoted to dry-curing, the need for salt was reduced. They thus preferred the banks close to the Newfoundland shore, while the French fishers, who continued wet-curing in salt until the mid-1600s, roamed in the Gulf of St. Lawrence and around northern Newfoundland.

The early fisheries were a form of economic activity characterized by the presence of many small units. The low capital requirements meant that entry into the industry was relatively easy and led to intense competition. The development of dry-curing introduced the possibility of realizing economies of scale. A division of labour between the fishers and land bases would increase economic efficiency, but the initial cost of establishing a colony in Newfoundland's inhospitable environment was high (Cell, 1969, chs. 4-5). Before the peace of 1604 English investors were not attracted to Newfoundland colonization projects because much higher returns were to be had from financing privateering ventures, and the first colony was not established until 1610. At first, settlement was slow because of the opposition of existing fishermen, who recognized that their competitive position would be destroyed. These westcountrymen used their power in the English Parliament and the "school for sailors" argument to hinder settlement and maintain free trade in the fisheries until the 1630s. During the 1640s there was a wider policy shift towards regulated trade, culminating in the Navigation Act of 1651. Government support moved in favour of chartered companies and was no longer given to the independent fishers. At the same time the fishers' need for regulation was increased by rising dangers from piracy during the 1640s and 1650s, which led them to request convoys for protection. The final blow was the French adoption of dry-curing, which yielded higher-quality fish upon arrival in Europe than did wet-curing, and their establishment of permanent bases on Newfoundland. The independent fishermen had nowhere to lobby against the French settlements and had to acquiesce to a general expansion of both English and French bases. Thus the economic factors favouring settlement triumphed over the opposition of vested interests and more substantial settlement began to take place in the second half of the seventeenth century, although restrictions on settlement unrelated to the fisheries continued until Newfoundland was finally granted colonial status in 1824.

Apart from the fisheries, European economic enterprises in Canada during the sixteenth century were marked by failure. The major goals of these enterprises, the discovery of routes to Asia or of rich kingdoms comparable to those of Spanish America, were not met. Cartier's expedition in 1540, which had the intention of establishing a colony as the base for conquest of the fabled Saguenay Empire, was an ignominious failure, and no settlement was founded. In the absence of riches to be traded or plundered, the mainland had nothing to offer Europeans.

For over sixty years after Cartier had claimed the St. Lawrence for France there was no serious attempt to establish a European settlement. The impetus which renewed interest was fur. Fishermen landing on the mainland came into contact with Indians and began to trade metal goods for luxurious furs such as marten. At first the fur trading was a sideline, and it remained incidental to fishing until the end of the century. The discovery which changed the nature and the scale of the Canadian fur trade came when European hat makers found that beaver fur made excellent felt hats. The popularity of these hats grew during the last quarter of the sixteenth century, and the beaver was ready to assume its lead role in the next two centuries of Canada's history.

Initially fur trading occurred around the Gulf of St. Lawrence, but the drainage basins of the coastal rivers were not extensive and were soon depopulated of beaver. Fur traders started to venture farther up the St. Lawrence. Tadoussac, at the mouth of the Saguenay River, became an important trading centre and the most westerly of the yearly rendezvous points between Indians and Europeans before 1600. Growing recognition of the possible profits from fur trading led in 1588 to the first attempt to obtain from the French government a charter granting monopoly rights. This was followed in the 1590s by a series of charters granting exclusive privileges, although nothing came of them beyond a short-lived settlement at Tadoussac in 1600. More important was the 1604 charter granting New France to the Sieur de Monts, who established a colony in Acadia which in 1608 was moved to Quebec City. The three, small two-storied buildings and a warehouse built under Champlain's command at Quebec mark the beginning of permanent European settlement in the St. Lawrence valley.

By the 1620s the French had well-established links with the Indians of the Great Lakes region. Lachine, at the first major barrier to navigation on the St. Lawrence, became a regular trading site on the island of

Montreal. The St. Lawrence and Ottawa valleys were a war zone where the Huron and their Algonquin allies faced the Iroquois, who had recently been driven south into what is now New York state. The two blocs had no economic contact and European trade had to be politically oriented. The Huron were the middlemen between the French and hunting Indians to the north and west, and Champlain's success in trading with the Huron stemmed from his willingness to form an alliance and to join in the fighting against the Iroquois. The Indian situation was, however, unstable, and with access to European weapons, which the Huron obtained from the French and the Iroquois from Dutch and English traders on the Hudson River and in New England, military activity escalated until the Huron were eliminated in 1649.

Deprived of the services of their Huron middlemen, the French fur traders had to make direct contact with the Indians farther west. Groseilliers and Radisson explored the Great Lakes area between 1654 and 1660 and realized the advantages of Hudson Bay as the approach to that area. Unable to gain French government backing for their idea of trading via Hudson Bay, they turned to England. After a successful trial voyage in 1668-1669, the Hudson's Bay Company was formed and received its royal charter in 1670. The Hudson's Bay Company's first permanent trading posts were built around James Bay during the 1670s.

Initially there was no direct conflict between English and French in Hudson Bay. The two nations were at peace in Europe during the 1670s, and in North America French attention was concentrated on the southwestern trade in the Mississippi Basin. In 1682 conflict in the Bay became open and the key posts changed hands several times before 1713 when France ceded exclusive rights to the shores of Hudson Bay to England. This was part of the peace settlement which ended Louis XIV's wars in Europe, but it also reflected Britain's naval supremacy and consequent ability to control the long sea route to Hudson Bay and the Bay's coastline.

The end of the conflict within Hudson Bay did not stop competition between the Hudson's Bay Company and the fur traders of New France, since their catchment areas always overlapped to a greater or lesser extent. At first overland competition was only felt by the Company's James Bay posts, while the posts on the Bay's western shores enjoyed freedom from competition. After Vérendrye's appointment as commandant of the postes du nord in the late 1720s, the French crossed the Height of Land west of Lake Superior and entered the Hudson's Bay drainage area. Trading posts built during the 1730s and 1740s as far west as the lower Saskatchewan River allowed the French to intercept many of the Indians who had previously voyaged to the Hudson's Bay Company's western posts. The Company's trade continued, but the value of furs traded at its posts dropped sharply during the 1740s and 1750s (Ray and Freeman, 1978, ch. 12).

At the middle of the eighteenth century the St. Lawrence remained by far the most important route for North American fur exports, despite the competition from the Hudson River route to the south and the Hudson's Bay Company to the north. For a brief interlude during the 1750s this dominance was interrupted as the deterioration of France's position in Canada led to the abandonment of her western trading posts, but even before New France had been officially ceded to Britain in 1763 British fur traders operating out of Montreal had taken over the French network. The French defeat had little impact on the fur trade's operation, and the events which would destroy Montreal's position in that trade still lay in the future.

The economic characteristics of the fur trade were quite different from those of the fisheries. It required large-scale organization for the conduct of trade over long distances by means of extensive transportation systems. Overhead costs were high because all costs incurred in collecting a shipload of furs had to be covered until the valuable cargo had been transported to Europe and sold. The industry was characterized by increasing returns to scale, i.e., the more furs which could be shipped out the lower the unit costs, and profits depended on high utilization of the administrative and ocean-shipping capacity. There were thus heavy pressures for expansion, which was bad news for the beaver and which explains why the fur trade routes spread rapidly. This was especially true of the Montreal fur traders, whose advantage lay in their water routes inland to the heads of the Great Lakes and who had the ideal means of transport in the canoe. Geographical expansion from Hudson Bay was slower because, rather than a single obvious inland route, there was an arc of non-competing bayshore posts which attracted Indians from a huge area; also the scarcity of birch around the Bay would have forced the Europeans to obtain canoe-making materials from far afield, and when the Hudson's Bay Company finally built a chain of inland posts in the 1770s it used the heavy York boat, suited to carrying larger cargoes along routes known to have few portages, rather than opening up new routes. The fur traders' exploration of Canada and the northwestern United States occurred in many regions long before permanent settlement. The legacy is the numerous French place names between the Great Lakes and the Rockies and the British, or rather Scottish, names of rivers flowing into the Pacific and Arctic discovered during the final post-1760 phase of the Montreal fur trade's expansion.

Besides being rapid, the growth of the fur trade was also uneven. In Europe the furs were sold by auction, the most important market-places being Leipzig, London, Moscow and Paris. Prices were determined by demand and supply. Furs were luxury items with inelastic demand, and beaver hats in particular were subject to abrupt shifts in demand due to the whims of fashion. These features of the market caused large price variations and hence large fluctuations in the fur sellers' profits. There is less agreement about the supply mechanism, and whether the market mechanism operated at all between the Indian suppliers and European traders. Rich claims that "in trade with the Indians the price mechanism did not work" (Rich, 1960, p. 23). This notion of trade being conducted by a fixed set of equivalences for non-economic motives has been expanded by Rotstein (1977) and attacked by Ray and Freeman (1978). Whichever view is accepted, there is no doubt that the quantity supplied did fluctuate independently of price changes because of intertribal politics or the opening up of new regions, and the ability of Europeans to elicit a quick supply response to changes in demand was limited. Thus, demand and supply conditions combined to make the profits from fur trading unpredictable and highly unstable.

A recurrent theme of the fur trade's history was the attempt to obtain and maintain a monopoly position, whether by the French chartered companies, the Hudson's Bay Company or the traders operating out of Montreal after the 1760s. The high fixed costs and the need to be large enough to weather bad times both contributed. Conversely, competition between fur traders was often disastrous; at the least it increased the companies' unit costs, and if the market mechanism worked competition would reduce the relative price of trade goods to furs. Evidence of the effect of competition can be seen in the falling profits of the Hudson's Bay Company's York Factory after the French entry into the northwestern fur trade during the 1730s, and again after the replacement of French by English traders in Montreal (Ray, 1974, pp. 52-3, 65).

Competition may also have accelerated the depletion of the beaver population. A monopolist would have an incentive to take conservation into account, but when beavers were a common property resource there was little point in self-restraint, for any beavers left to maintain the population would be taken by competitors. It is, however, unclear whether a monopolist would have behaved much differently than the actual Canadian companies; most of the trapping was done by Indians and the precise number killed was largely beyond the Europeans' control—and there always seemed to be new fur-rich regions to exploit until the west coast was reached. The only serious attention given to conservation was by the Hudson's Bay Company in the mid-nineteenth century when the fur trade had reached its last frontier.

A final economic characteristic of the fur trade was its antipathy to settlement. Establishment of the fur trade led to the founding of European settlements, which served primarily as the headquarters and shipment points for the fur trade. In addition to the fur traders there were religious orders, hoping to convert the Indians, and some subsistence farming. Beyond this the fur trading companies had little to gain and much to fear from permanent settlers. Any new settlers might provide competition in the trade with the Indians and reduce the companies' monopoly in providing European goods. The basic antagonism, however, was between the fur trade and agriculture. The latter required land-clearing, destroying the habitat of the fur-bearing animals. Finally the logistics of the fur trade were unsuited to immigration; because of fur's low bulk/value ratio the boats serving the trade were more heavily loaded (with trade goods) on the outward journey than on the return journey to Europe. Population growth remained slow, even after New France became a royal province in 1663 and the government tried to speed up settlement by encouraging ex-soldiers to stay and by shipping out a thousand marriageable women. In the entire century and a half of the French colony's existence not many more than ten thousand immigrants arrived. Attempts by English settlers to occupy the French fur traders' territory also provoked immediate opposition; when the Ohio Company was formed in Virginia with the intention of settling the Ohio Valley, and a fort built in 1752 to protect the Company's land grant, the French destroyed the fort and fortified the region themselves.

The fur trade was the heroic era of Canadian history, although the drama of individual achievements has been left out of the present account. The impact on the Indians is also ignored, although it must have been tremendous. Initially the opportunity to obtain European goods improved their material well-being, but the destruction of traditional values and the spread of new disease soon made contact with Europeans a mixed blessing; this cycle is well-documented for the Huron by Trigger (1977). For the Europeans, too, the fur trade was important; for two centuries its characteristics shaped the course of economic development in the area which was to become Canada.

2. Colonial Rivalries

From the beginning the raison d'être of the French colonies on the St. Lawrence was to channel the fur trade from as much of North America as possible through this route and hence through French hands. Almost immediately Champlain faced international rivalry from the Dutch based on the Hudson River, who in 1613 built Fort Nassau (later Albany). The next one hundred and forty-five years were to be characterized by wars between the European powers, their colonists and their Indian allies. At first the colonial rivalries in North America involved several European powers, but they soon focussed into a struggle between the two countries best endowed by location and economic power: France and England.

Although colonial rivalries were already strong in the seventeenth century, the outposts in present-day Canada were of secondary importance to the colonies of the Caribbean and Virginia—and to events in Europe. In 1629 English agents captured New France and a British company ran the St. Lawrence fur trade for the next three years, until Charles I restored the colony to France in return for payment of the outstanding part of his French wife's dowry. The next thirty years were difficult ones for New France as its inhabitants were terrorized and the fur trade routes were cut off by a revived Iroquois power. The centre of Anglo-French rivalry moved to Newfoundland, where French fishers were setting up an increasing number of bases for dry-curing their fish. In 1662 a fort was built to defend these bases, and the French fisheries flourished as the English ones declined. In the mid-1660s the situation in New France improved after the colony was converted into a royal province and an army sent from France checked the Iroquois threat, although the final defeat of the Iroquois was not until 1696. Thus, when war broke out in Europe between England and France in 1689, the French appeared to have the superior position in North America. Despite competition from the Hudson River route (under British control since 1664) and the Hudson's Bay Company (founded in 1670), the St. Lawrence remained the dominant route inland. In addition France had more bases on Newfoundland and better sugar-producing Caribbean possessions. The weakness of the French empire was that each part traded directly with France and there were no links between the colonies. This was in contrast to the English colonies, among which New England played an important role in shipping food to the West Indies and Newfoundland and in shipping fish direct from Newfoundland to the Caribbean. An additional advantage of the English mainland colonies lay in the larger populations which existed in areas not dominated by the fur staple.

When war broke out in 1689, New France's centralized leadership and her strategic advantages helped her gain a series of military victories. All of these were, however, set aside by the peace treaty of 1697 which primarily reflected European realities and imposed a general restitution of conquests. The renewal of hostilities after 1702 was accompanied by improved English fortunes in North America under New England leadership, but the only concrete success was the conquest of Acadia. The Treaty of Utrecht in 1713 again primarily reflected the European war, and as a result of Marlborough's victories it favoured England. Acadia and the Hudson Bay region were ceded by France, although their boundaries were not specified, and Newfoundland became British territory, although France retained fishing rights there. Despite the qualifications, the territorial concessions made by France significantly altered the strategic balance in North America.

After 1713 Europe and North America enjoyed a generation of peace. The situation benefitted all of North America, and was reflected in population growth. The rate of population growth was, however, more rapid in the British colonies and Acadia than in the fur-dominated colony of New France. Despite these thirty years of peace, the situation remained unstable. The New Englanders feared encirclement by the French along the Mississippi, which would both expose them to attack and block their natural route for expansion. New France in turn recognized the threat to its existence posed by New England's expansionist tendencies, and the

Map 2
North America, 1713

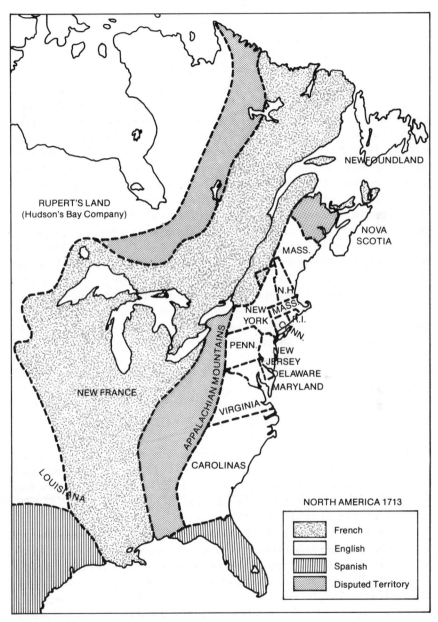

RUPERT'S LAND
(Hudson's Bay Company)

NEWFOUNDLAND

NOVA
SCOTIA

MASS.

N.H.

NEW
YORK

MASS.

R.I.

CONN.

PENN.

NEW
JERSEY

DELAWARE

MARYLAND

NEW FRANCE

APPALACHIAN MOUNTAINS

VIRGINIA

LOUISIANA

CAROLINAS

NORTH AMERICA 1713

French	
English	
Spanish	
Disputed Territory	

Source: From Canada, *Colony to Centennial* by D. Willows and S. Richmond, p. 72. Copyright McGraw-Hill Company of Canada Limited, 1970. Reprinted by permission.

French tried to strengthen their position by building a series of forts including the great stone fortress at Louisbourg on Cape Breton, which commanded the St. Lawrence estuary, and Crown Point on Lake Champlain.

The renewal of Anglo-French hostilities in 1744 was the prelude to a fight to the finish in the North American theatre of war. In 1744 the French enjoyed some success and almost captured Annapolis, but the tide soon turned and in the following year the British (in fact a New England army supported by a British naval flotilla) took Louisbourg. The next three years' fighting was inconclusive in North America, and at the Peace of Aix-la-Chapelle (1748) Louisbourg was returned to France in exchange for Madras. The peace was only a truce in Europe, and in North America semi-war persisted. In the Ohio Valley, open war between Virginia and France broke out two years before Anglo-French hostilities were officially resumed. Britain's position in North America, which had been improving steadily for many years, was now overwhelming; over a million British colonists were faced by only fifty-five thousand French Canadians, and British naval supremacy was almost total. Despite these advantages the winning of the war was slow. The period from 1754 to 1757 were years of disaster for Britain, but she finally managed to organize her forces, capturing Louisbourg in 1758 and Quebec City in September 1759. When the British navy was first to enter the St. Lawrence in 1760 all prospect of relief for the French defenders was gone, and Governor Vaudreuil surrendered. In the peace treaty of 1763 all French possessions in present-day Canada were ceded to Britain, although for the British government it was a fairly close choice between the extensive territory of Canada and the rich Caribbean sugar island of Guadeloupe.

The years between 1615 and 1760 were dominated by the struggle for colonial hegemony in North America. At first the North American struggle was ancillary to European conflicts, but indigenous forces, in particular the English colonists' desire to push the frontier of settlement westwards, played an increasingly important role. The conclusion was determined by the increasing British advantage both in global power and in the North American colonial situation. Although the British victory had significant political and cultural consequences, there was no dramatic change in Canadian economic development. The St. Lawrence economy was centred on the fur trade and the economic history of the period 1600–1760 is dominated by that industry's expansion. After the conquest of New France the focus of the economy was unchanged apart from the transfer of control from French to British merchants. The old methods were learned by the new masters and the characteristics of the trade continued to determine its monopolistic structure, lust for expansion and opposition to settlement. The economic conflict of the eighteenth century was between the St. Lawrence merchants in Montreal and the

Hudson's Bay Company to the north and the Albany traders to the south; the prizes were control of the fur trade at its new frontiers in the northwest and in the Mississippi Basin. In the latter area the fur traders faced additional competition for use of the land from potential settlers. The 1763 peace ended the imperial conflict for political control of North America but had little relevance to the economic conflict which would continue for another fifty-eight years.

3. American Independence

After the peace treaty of 1763 Britain was left with a large but diverse empire in America. The Caribbean sugar islands were run on the plantation system, often by absentee landlords who, together with the merchants who shipped the sugar, exerted strong political influence in London. In Virginia, tobacco was the important staple export, and elsewhere in the southern colonies indigo and rice were significant exports. The middle colonies were self-sufficient in food and financed their trade by food exports (New York, Pennsylvania and New Jersey) or by providing shipping services (New England). Quebec was a conquered territory with some subsistence agriculture, but whose economy was dominated by the fur trade. Newfoundland and Nova Scotia were small colonies, important for fish and with strong links to Britain.

An idea of the relative size of the North American colonies can be gained from looking at their populations. In the absence of a regular census this exercise is not as easy as it would be today, but people were sufficiently interested in sizes (measured by the simple concept of number of inhabitants) that several population estimates are available. For the time around 1770 they tell the following story for the northern colonies: Quebec 72,500, Nova Scotia 21,000 and Newfoundland 11,500. The northern colonies contained less than 5 per cent of the two and a quarter million people living in Britain's North American colonies.

We have little quantitative information on the standard of living in the colonies. Extensive growth had been taking place in the thirteen colonies which would form the United States; their population increased from some 330,000 in 1710 to over two million by 1770. There is some evidence that intensive growth, based on increased productivity in shipping and perhaps in agriculture, also occurred, although estimates of its average annual magnitude have been scaled down from "one per cent per capita or even a little higher" (Taylor, 1964, p. 429) to not "significantly more than 0.3 per cent" (Ball & Walton, 1976, p. 116) and perhaps even less (Anderson, 1979). For the northern colonies which would become Canada the picture is not as clear, and extensive growth was certainly slower. Prosperity remained linked to the fur and fish staples, and other activities remained of minor economic importance.

The one economic magnitude for which we have good data during this period is trade. Because it was relatively easily supervised, trade was the major tax source and records of trade transactions were kept. Shepherd and Walton (1972) have reconstructed the current accounts of the colonies' balance of payments for 1768-1772. Their estimates clearly reveal the relatively high export-orientation of the three northern colonies, whose average annual exports of £1.98 per head of population were considerably higher than the £1.37 average for all the North American colonies. In spite of their export orientation, the northern colonies ran a substantial trade deficit. In 1772 their estimated total commodity exports were £229,000, and commodity imports £417,000. Invisible earnings, from shipping for example, amounted to £16,000, leaving a current account deficit of £172,000. The deficit was covered by military expenditures and capital inflow, public and private, from Britain. The trade deficits of the other mainland colonies were, in contrast, almost covered by invisible earnings.

If the thirteen southern and middle colonies were enjoying intensive and extensive growth within the British Empire, why did they decide to unilaterally declare their independence in 1776? The conventional wisdom used to be that the costs of being a colony now exceeded the benefits, especially after the departure of the French when the protection services provided by Britain became less valuable. Recently, however, this view has come under attack in a number of studies which raise the counter-factual question of how well off the thirteen colonies would have been between 1763 and 1776 if they had been independent. The tobacco producers would certainly have benefitted because, although their main markets were in continental Europe, the tobacco had to be shipped via Britain where middlemen took a cut. The transactions costs in Britain had, however, been declining throughout the eighteenth century, and the real problem of the tobacco producers lay in the slow growth of markets for their staple export. Indigo and rice producers might have been worse off with independence, because they exported to Britain and benefitted from Imperial preference. Although the American shipping interests complained of British restrictions on their activity, they would have suffered from independence because they would then have been in no trading bloc and the navigation laws of all important trading nations would have worked against them. Attempts to quantify these and other costs and benefits suggest that the magnitudes are small, and that independence would have yielded little net economic benefit between 1763 and 1776, especially if the costs of fighting an independence war are included.

Explanation of American independence by economic phenomena is thus not so easy as it once seemed. Nevertheless, some good arguments with economic bases can be made: (1) it is possible that the revolutionaries thought they would be better off economically, even though they were mistaken. For example, much of the protest in the years before 1776 came from shipping interests who thought that independence would remove the irksome restrictions placed on them by the British navigation acts and that they would then capture the world's shipping business; (2) war is not declared by referendum, and even if independence had a net cost, it did benefit some sectors of the economy which perhaps had sufficient political power to declare war (George Washington, for example, was a Virginian tobacco producer); (3) the revolutionaries may have been looking to the future rather than narrowly at the present. The third argument centres on the British government's solution to the problem of what to do with the area west of the Mississippi tributaries, land which she had acquired from France under the 1763 peace treaty. An Indian reserve was established west of the Appalachians, and then in 1774 the territory north of the Ohio River and west of Pennsylvania was annexed to Quebec. This policy alienated colonial land speculators and fur traders in the middle colonies and placed Britain in the role, previously occupied by France, of curtailing western settlement.

Consideration of the economic bases of American independence sheds light on the northern colonies' position. They did not join the revolt because they had nothing to gain. The small Newfoundland population relied on its function as land support for the English fisheries, and the profits from the fisheries were outside its hands whether within or outside the Empire. Nova Scotia had a thriving sideline providing naval supplies and also profited from the garrison retained at Halifax after 1763. The merchant class was small and could not compete on equal terms with New England—a consideration which made the prospect of New England outside the British Empire while Nova Scotia remained within appear the best possible outcome. The Quebec population, a conquered people with no tradition of self-government, was apathetic. The fur traders of the St. Lawrence were content with the 1774 territorial settlement and considered the imperial government to be the guarantor of their rights in the southwest fur trade. In sum, the northern colonies gained economically from the British connection, as clearly indicated by the size and financing of their trade deficit. Sectional interest groups who might gain from independence did not exist, and the northern colonies did not see their future expansion in terms of western settlement.

To agree that there are good economic-based explanations for the revolt of the thirteen colonies and the loyalty of the northern colonies is not to say that economic forces were the only ones at work. The early establishment of state legislatures in the middle colonies previewed their independent tendencies, although this too had an economic basis. The economic activities in the middle colonies were suited to the liberal democratic mentality, and in general, the economic structure of the thirteen colonies did not fit into the eighteenth-century idea of empire. In contrast, the economy of the northern colonies continued to fit this imperial ideal into the nineteenth century, even after it had been abandoned by Britain.

Map 3
Quebec, 1774

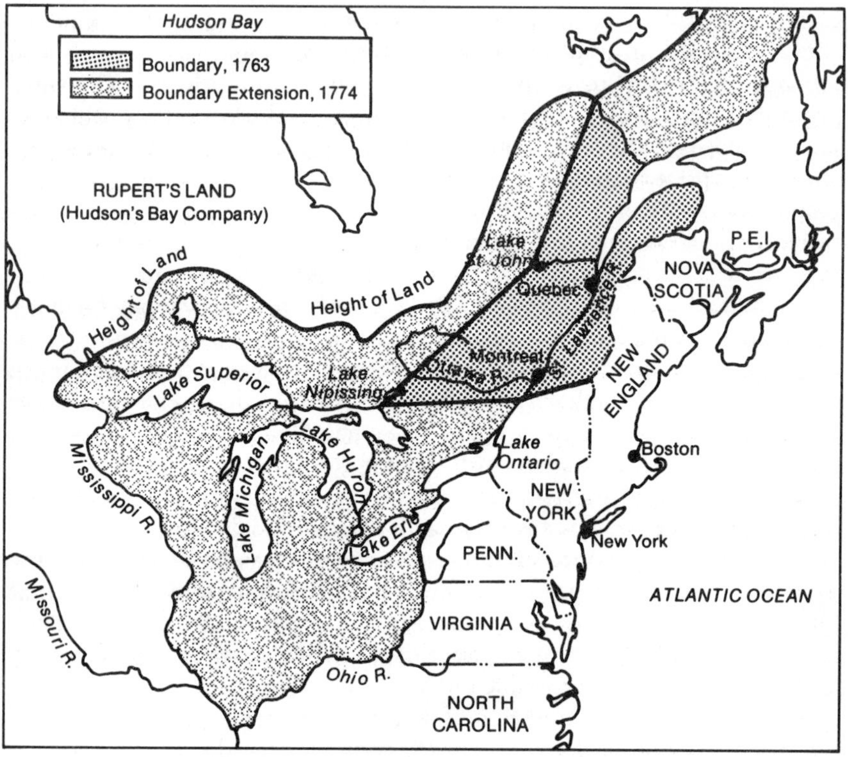

Source: From J.B. Brebner, *Canada: A Modern History*, University of Michigan Press, 1960, p. 78. Reprinted by permission.

4. The Aftermath of 1783

Two major forces influenced the economies of the British North American colonies in the decades following 1783: the existence of an independent United States and the French Revolution of 1789 with the ensuing British involvement in the revolutionary and Napoleonic wars. The economic history of British North America between 1783 and 1820 largely concerns her reaction to these new forces, although as previously, the local capacity for shaping events was limited by decisions taken in London. During this period the British colonies were still separate entities, and the impact of the new forces was felt in different ways; for Newfoundland and agricultural Quebec the impact was minimal, but in the Maritimes and in the St. Lawrence fur trade decisive changes resulted.

For the Maritime colonies (now divided into Nova Scotia, New Brunswick, Cape Breton and Prince Edward Island) the major economic consequence of the War of American Independence was that the thirteen colonies were no longer part of the same imperial economic system. The New England merchants now faced the same restrictions as any other foreigners as far as trade with ports of the British Empire was concerned, and they still faced restrictions in trading with other European nations and their colonies. Thus, although U.S. shipping increased from the very low levels of the early 1780s, by 1793 it had still not returned to pre-1776 levels. On the British side of the border it was hoped that Nova Scotia would take over New England's former role in Britain's American empire. Lumber and shipbuilding industries were encouraged in the expectation that commercial expansion would soon follow.

The principal obstacle to attaining the goal of replacing New England was the Maritimes' lack of self-sufficiency in food. Even with the inflow of loyalist farmers from the south, the Maritime colonies could not produce enough food to feed themselves, let alone to trade with the West Indies. Food was therefore imported from New England and paid for with fish, which the New Englanders traded with the British West Indies. In spite of the British navigation acts which legislated against this trade, the more-experienced New England merchants started to win back the Caribbean trade from the Nova Scotians. Their victory became complete after 1793 when Britain became involved in war with France and her navy was too busy to enforce the navigation acts. During the next thirteen years the United States experienced an economic boom based especially on her shipping industry, which now enjoyed a near monopoly of the world's carrying trade as the only important neutral in a world at war. The warring nations were not completely happy with this state of affairs, and there were some seizures of U.S. boats and, especially after 1802, attempts to limit U.S. shipping activity. President Jefferson responded in 1807 with the Embargo Act, forbidding U.S. trade with all foreign countries.

The Embargo Act achieved for Nova Scotian shipping what the navigation acts alone had been incapable of. Although the Embargo Act was intended to hurt Britain, it instead provided an ideal opportunity for Nova Scotian and New Brunswick merchants by granting them a monopoly position in North American international trade. The effect was immediate. In 1808 the number of ships landing in the British North American ports exceeded the number landing in U.S. ports. The Maritimes became a centre for reexports to the Caribbean, finally fulfilling the hope that they would take over New England's old role in the British Empire.

The years between 1808 and 1815 were difficult ones for New England, but they saw a tremendous boom in the Maritimes. The boom had been initiated by a political decision, which would be reversed when peace returned. It might therefore only be a temporary phenomenon, but the important point was not so much the immediate profits as the opportunity which had been provided for the Maritimes' merchants to establish a shipping industry undisturbed. If they could use the time gained to build up an efficient shipping industry, then they would be able to stand on their own in peacetime. After 1815 this was in part achieved, although the prize was of diminishing importance as the West Indian market declined in significance during the nineteenth century.

For Quebec the impact of the American and French revolutions on international trade relations was of secondary importance to two other consequences of the 1783 settlement in North America: the emigration of Empire Loyalists from the United States and the determination of the international border. The loyalists who settled west of Montreal were mostly experienced frontier farmers and therefore desirable immigrants, but they were used to the social and political institutions of the thirteen colonies. The British government met the potential tension between the newcomers and traditional Quebec society by creating the provinces of Upper and Lower Canada in 1791 (roughly equivalent to Ontario and

Map 4
British North America, 1783–1825

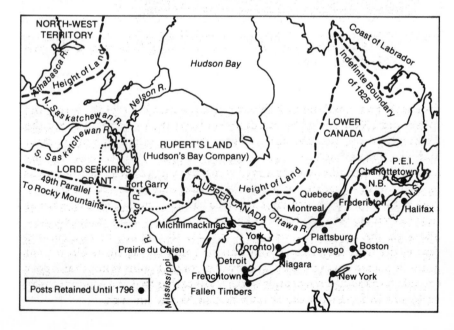

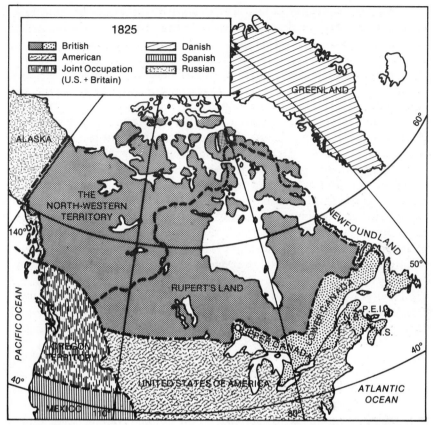

Sources: From W.L. Morton, *The Kingdom of Canada* (1963), p. 203, reprinted by permission of McClelland and Stewart Limited, Toronto; *National Atlas of Canada* (1974, 4th ed.), p. 83.

Quebec). The population of Upper Canada expanded rapidly during the 1790s and 1800s, fueled by immigration from the United States. For the new immigrants, the international boundary was relatively unimportant and the prime motive was economic; Upper Canada was on the agricultural frontier and possessed some advantages over frontier areas farther south—peaceful Indians, cheap land and relatively good transport links. The rapidly growing province had an economic base which was new to Canada. Already by 1794 Upper Canada was a net grain exporter, although the importance of wheat exports should not be exaggerated during the next fifty years when Canada could still be turned into a net grain importer during lean years. The important point is not that Upper Canada had found a new staple export, but rather that she was more self-sufficient in food than the rest of British North America.

The expansion of agricultural settlement in Upper Canada was not a welcome tendency for the St. Lawrence fur traders, but its impact paled behind the disaster of the 1783 border settlement. As with all eighteenth-century peace treaties affecting Canada, the decisions were taken in London. The British government adopted a policy of generosity towards independent America in the hope of maintaining good trade relations. This policy of valuing reconciliation above mere territory was most clearly seen in the determination of the American northern border. Quebec lost the vast territory between the Ohio and the Mississippi Rivers, which as recently as 1774 had been confirmed as hers. Every important fort, depot and trading post serving the St. Lawrence fur trade was now on American territory (Niagara, Detroit, Michilimackinac, Grand Portage), and even part of the water communications from the Great Lakes to the northwest was lost. The Montreal traders fully recognized the extent of the catastrophe. They delayed implementation of the treaty and they cherished the hope of border revision for thirty years, but when Britiain failed to take up the issue after the War of 1812 the situation had to be accepted.

Having lost the southern fur trade, the Montreal fur traders' need for expansion drove them into a program of rapid establishment of posts beyond the Great Lakes. In a last, great burst of exploration, Mackenzie reached the Pacific Ocean in 1793, after a false turn in 1789 had taken him to the Arctic Ocean by the river later named in his honour. Before that, however, the conflict between the Montreal traders and the Hudson's Bay Company had become keener. The challenge for the northwest fur trade, which had begun in the 1730s, had by the 1770s forced the Hudson's Bay Company to establish its own inland trading posts. Once the Hudson's Bay Company had become more aggressively competitive, its superior geographical position relative to the western fur areas (foreseen by Groseilliers and Radisson over a century earlier) was decisive. The length and vulnerability of water communications from Montreal were emphasized with the founding of the Red River Settlement by Lord Selkirk in 1812, which blocked the Montreal route and provoked open violence. By 1821 the struggle was over; the Montreal fur traders were absorbed by the Hudson's Bay Company and Canada's first transcontinental economy broke up; west and east would now go their separate ways until after Confederation.

5. The Timber Trade

During the first half of the nineteenth century fur was replaced as Canada's leading export by timber. Both England and France had imported North American pine for ships' masts as early as the seventeenth century, but despite their large demand for wood and dislike of being dependent on Baltic supplies, no large-scale trans-Atlantic timber trade developed before 1800. The reason lay in timber's high bulk/value ratio; shipping costs accounted for a large part of the total price of imported wood, and thus only pine of especially high quality could be shipped profitably across the Atlantic.

The Napoleonic Wars, with their accompanying high demand for timber and the cutting off of Baltic supplies, brought on a timber crisis for Britain. In order to encourage firms to export timber from British North America the imperial government placed heavy duties on foreign timber, thus giving a large price advantage to colonial timber which paid no duty. The price advantage was sufficient to stimulate a flourishing export trade centred on Quebec City and Saint John, New Brunswick.

The economic characteristics of the timber trade differed from those of the fish and fur staples. Firstly, entry costs were low and there was little tendency toward monopolization. Secondly, the timber trade was not antagonistic towards settlement. There were several possible sources of complementarity between lumbering and agriculture: land had to be cleared before the commencement of farming; lumber camps provided a market for food products; and the two activities were seasonal, with the busy period in one coinciding with the slack period in the other. In practice, however, this complementarity did not work well. Along the Ottawa Valley—the main lumbering area—the land was unsuitable for agriculture. In New Brunswick the lumber camps and shipbuilding offered sufficiently higher wages relative to agriculture so that farming activities were mostly abandoned. Only in Upper Canada did farmers make supplementary income from lumber while maintaining their farms. The third and most significant characteristic of the timber trade was the high bulk/value ratio of its product, which led to problems in filling the timber ships returning from Europe. Some brought salt for the fisheries, but there remained substantial overcapacity. The problem was solved by offering cheap voyages to a new life for those who had suffered from the industrial revolution in Britian. The push of pauperism in Great Britain and in Ireland (especially during the potato famine of the 1840s), coupled with the availability of cheap transportation, led to a huge increase in emigration to British North America during the 1820s, 1830s and 1840s. The largest numbers found their way along the St. Lawrence to Upper Canada, but the populations of Lower Canada, Nova Scotia and New Brunswick also grew substantially (see Table 2.1).

The victory of free trade in British economic policy marked the beginning of the end for the trans-Atlantic timber trade. The British tariff on timber imports was reduced in 1842 and then at intervals until its elimination in 1860, thus eroding the British colonies' preferential tariff edge over their European competitors. Canadian timber exports to Britain continued, but the advent of the steamship and increased use of

Table 2.1
Population of British North American Colonies, 1825 to 1850

Year	Upper Canada	Lower Canada	Nova Scotia	New Brunswick
1825	157,923	479,288	104,000	74,176
1840	432,159	716,670	—	156,162
1851	952,004	890,261	276,854	193,800

Sources: Urquhart & Buckley (1965), p. 14; Easterbrook & Aitken (1956), p. 239, p. 274.

iron and steel for construction hastened the effective end of this trade in the 1870s. The end of tariff preference in Britain did not immediately end the timber trade's importance in Canada, because just as it was starting to lose the British market it gained a new market in the United States. The economic boom and rapid urbanization in the United States during the 1840s and 1850s increased the demand for timber for construction. At the same time, the coming of the railway reduced the timber trade's reliance on waterways for transportation and lowered the costs of north–south trade. Exports to the United States grew rapidly, and the lumber industry was the leader in changing the orientation of the Canadian economy away from Britain to the United States. Representatives of the industry were prominent in lobbying for free trade with the Americans, and after the signing of the Reciprocity Treaty in 1854 they made further gains in the U.S. market.

Although timber was the major Canadian export in the first half of the nineteenth century, it did not dominate the economy to the extent that fur had earlier. The waves of immigrants, although partly a consequence of the timber trade, were involved in agriculture rather than lumbering, and the commercial agriculture sector in Upper Canada was growing rapidly. The main outlets for the trans-Atlantic timber trade were Quebec and Saint John, and the related industries (e.g., shipbuilding) were also concentrated in these ports, while timber played a relatively less important role in the largest commercial centre, Montreal. The history of the Montreal merchants and the Upper Canada farmers is a separate story, to which we will now turn.

6. The Struggle for the Second Empire of the St. Lawrence

The economic history of Quebec during the seventeenth and eighteenth centuries can be understood largely as a struggle to direct the trade of continental North America along the St. Lawrence. A glance at a map illustrates the geographical basis for Montreal's claim to be the natural capital of the inland empire; the St. Lawrence–Great Lakes system is the only direct link from the Atlantic to the Mississippi Basin and beyond.

Montreal's geographical disadvantages—the rapids upstream and the ice which closes the port for half the year—are not revealed on a map. In the days of the fur trade, the disadvantages were unimportant because portages were relatively easy and trans-Atlantic voyages infrequent with a low bulk/value staple. By the end of the French regime, Montreal was the clear centre of the fur trade, the capital of the First Commercial Empire of the St. Lawrence. The disastrous boundary settlement of 1783 spelt the end of this empire; despite a rearguard action, the Montreal fur trade was squeezed between its old rivals from Albany and from Hudson Bay, and expired within forty years. The reaction of the Montreal merchants was to try to reestablish their hegemony on the basis of the new staples of the Great Lakes area and to build the Second Commercial Empire of the St. Lawrence (Creighton, 1937).

In order to gain an advantageous position as the shipment point for the whole of the Great Lakes region, the Montreal merchants demanded from the British government a mixture of free trade and protectionist policies. They wanted free entry of U.S. goods into Canada but imperial preferences for goods shipped to Britain from Canada, whatever their origin. These policy goals, while consistent in themselves and reasonable within eighteenth-century views of political economy, stood little chance of success in the nineteenth century. For a brief period after 1815 they were almost realized, but thereafter the situation gradually deteriorated as the United States adopted protectionist trade policies and Britain moved towards universal free trade, culminating in the repeal of the corn laws in 1846.

In the absence of an artificial advantage, Montreal's natural disadvantages were decisive. New York, with her superb harbour and rich hinterland, had already outdistanced her U.S. rivals. The opening of the Erie Canal in 1825 provided a direct link between New York and Lake Erie, and feeder canals brought Lake Ontario into the network as well. In contrast, the route from the Great Lakes to Montreal was disastrously slow. The imperial government completed the militarily inspired Rideau Canal from Kingston to Bytown (Ottawa) and the Ottawa canals in 1832, thus providing a continuous, but rather tortuous, route to Montreal. The more substantial project of canalizing the St. Lawrence was not begun in earnest until 1833 and not completed until 1848. For a quarter of a century New York enjoyed a superior link to the Great Lakes, and even after 1848 the St. Lawrence route had difficulty in competing with the Erie Canal and the new challenge of the railways. More important than these difficulties, however, was Montreal's ultimate disadvantage of not being an ice-free port. The continuous shipping season and advantages of scale economies meant that charges were lower and service more frequent from New York.

While the merchants of Montreal were fighting their American rival, they had to face opposition at home in the assemblies of Upper and Lower Canada. Continually outnumbered in the Lower Canada assembly by French-Canadian representatives antipathetic towards merchants and intent on preserving their traditional society, the Montreal merchants pressured for union of the two provinces in the hope that the support of "progressive" elements from Upper Canada would give them control. Failure to achieve union during the 1820s and the beginning of mass immigration changed the political balance, and led to the most turbulent decades of Canadian history. As agricultural settlement in Upper Canada grew, radical leaders emerged who shared the habitants' dislike of commercial and financial men. The latter's control of the state machinery and use of public funds, for personal enrichment as well as for the canal projects, were the centre of controversy. When reformist majorities in the assemblies were ineffective and short-lived, discontent turned to open revolt in 1837. Although the revolt was defeated, its political consequences, union of the Canadas in 1841 and responsible provincial government in 1848, created institutions which the mercantile classes would not succeed in dominating. Just as they were losing the struggle with New York, the merchants were losing the struggle for power within Canada. The trend was not clear immediately, but by 1849 the failure of the Commercial Empire of the St. Lawrence was apparent to all. The Annexation Manifesto of 1849, a primarily urban movement for union with the United States, was the final frustrated reaction to the collapse of Montreal's imperial aspiration.

The middle of the nineteenth century represents a watershed in Canadian economic development. In politics, commerce, agriculture and industry the years around 1850 witnessed significant changes. The granting of responsible government permitted the adoption of indigenously determined policies for economic development. The defeat of Montreal by New York meant that the basis of the Canadian economy could no longer be considered commercial, centred on the transshipment of U.S. goods. In agriculture the Ontario wheat economy was about to enter two decades of rapid expansion in response to increased overseas demand, accompanied by the adoption of new farm technology. In industry, previously restricted to flour and saw mills, factory production was heralded by new establishments opened along the Lachine Canal in the late 1840s. Such far-reaching changes do not occur overnight, but the end of the Commercial Empire of the St. Lawrence was the prelude to the development of the modern Canadian economy.

Appendix: Meanwhile in the West

After the demise of the Montreal fur trade in 1821 the development of the areas east and west of the Great Lakes went their own ways. The west, under the control of the Hudson's Bay Company, showed a continuity in strong contrast to the economic changes in the east. Settlement continued to be discouraged by the fur traders, and apart from the small Red River Settlement started by Lord Selkirk in 1812 the population of the Prairies remained small until the 1860s. (There is dispute over the exact numbers (Urquhart & Buckley, 1956, p. 4), but the majority were undoubtedly Indians and Métis.) The situation west of the Rockies was slightly different, and it is to the economic history of this area that we will now turn.

In the initial European conquest of the Americas, the Pacific coast was designated as a Spanish zone of influence. The northern part of the coast had little attraction until the fur resources of the region were recognized in the eighteenth century. Russian fur traders moving eastwards across Siberia reached the northwest coast of America and started to exploit the fur there during the first half of the eighteenth century. The possibility of a sea-borne fur trade became publicized after Cook's contact in 1778 with Nootka Indians on what is now Vancouver Island. The first permanent base in the Pacific Northwest was established by Russian fur traders in 1783, and this induced the Spaniards to extend their presence northwards along the coast until they made contact with the Russians in 1788. Although the coastline was now partitioned between Russia and Spain, neither was in a position to dominate the region effectively. An important announcement of this impotence was the Nootka Sound incident of 1789, when Spain tried to evict English fur traders from Vancouver Island and seized four of their ships. The British government threatened war and the Spanish government backed down, agreeing that the whole region should be open to all traders.

The 1789 agreement left a power vacuum on the northwest coast. Russia continued to dominate the most northerly part and laid claim to the coastline north of the 51st parallel, but their hold was not very strong. The weakness of the Russian position lay in their inadequate supply system, which forced them to depend on U.S. or British bases farther south. Britain's initial advantage was not followed up, because her primary naval interests were around Europe (in the war against France) and in India. The United States became the dominant power in the region from the 1790s onward, partly by default, but more importantly because the Boston merchants had some advantages, such as their local shipbuilding industry, and they had lost ground in their traditional trading areas since independence. American trade was interrupted, however, by the War of 1812 and was not vigorously renewed in the northwest. Partial reasons for this were fears of sea otter depletion and increased Indian aggression, but the main cause was the westward movement of overland fur traders who attracted the furs of the interior Indians, cutting off their links with the coast. Once a northern overland route to the Pacific had been established in 1811, the coastal fur traders found their competitive position increasingly difficult.

Although the Pacific area now became part of the eastern-based fur trading region, it was not an important area at the time of the Hudson's Bay Company's monopolization of the trade in 1821. The main reasons for its unimportance were high transport costs, political uncertainty (the United States, Britain and Russia laid conflicting claims to sovereignty) and pessimism over fur conditions. A survey in 1821 indicated that the final reason was unfounded, so the Hudson's Bay Company through the offices of the British government set about clearing up the political uncertainty. Agreement was reached in 1825 with Russia, setting the southern boundary of Russian Alaska at latitude 54°40′, but there was no agreement with the United States beyond the establishment of a condition of "joint sovereignty" in the northwest.

The economic characteristics of the Pacific fur trade were similar to those in the remainder of the continental fur trade, including the discouragement of permanent settlement. A major reason why the Hudson's Bay Company wanted an early solution to the sovereignty question was the imminent arrival of (American) settlers in the Oregon region, which would strengthen the U.S. claims and exclude the Hudson's Bay Company. In the uncertain situation of the 1820s and 1830s the Hudson's Bay Company hoped that the border would be set along the Columbia River, and they therefore concentrated on cleaning out the fur resources south of the Columbia. When the settlers started to arrive in increasing numbers during the late 1820s and the 1830s, the pressure for fixing the border was accompanied by a rise in expansionist sentiment in the United States. Polk won the 1844 presidential election on the slogan "54–40 or Fight," meaning the U.S. border should be with Russian Alaska to the exclusion of Britain, but in 1846 a compromise was reached at the 49th parallel. The future boundary of Canada was thus finally established, although it was not seen in that light at the time and, as with the eastern boundary, was set by a British government at best partially acquainted with the geographical reality.

The Hudson's Bay Company shifted its main Pacific base from Fort Vancouver (opposite present-day Portland) to Fort Victoria and concentrated on keeping its shrunken domain free of agricultural settlement. In this aim they were opposed by the Westminster Parliament, where the border negotiations and threat of British exclusion from the Pacific Northwest had excited demands for the establishment of a British colony. The Hudson's Bay Company tried to ensure that the colony would be under their control and succeeded when Vancouver Island was ceded to the Hudson's Bay Company in January 1849 for a rent of seven shillings per year, subject to a colony being established within five years. The first governor appointed by Britain, Blanchard, was independent of the

Hudson's Bay Company, but finding himself without authority he resigned in 1851. His successor was James Douglas, the Hudson's Bay Company's chief factor in the Pacific area. The Company gave no positive encouragement to immigrants, and the colony's inaccessibility and the high price of land there ensured that settlement remained low during the early 1850s.

The fur traders were thus successful in excluding permanent settlement from at least part of the northwest during the first half of the nine-

Map 5
British Columbia in the Early 1860s

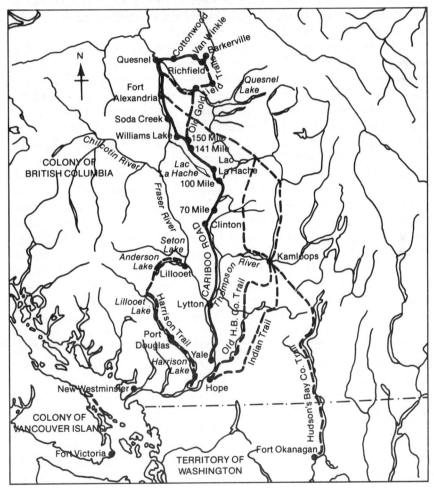

Source: From Art Downs, *Wagon Road North*, Northwest Digest Ltd., Quesnel, British Columbia.

teenth century. The discovery of gold by the Fraser River in 1856–1857 changed the situation. Gold was in many ways similar to fur as a staple, but differed crucially in being more labour-intensive. Although the Hudson's Bay Company could discourage agricultural settlement, it could not prevent a gold rush. Between April and August of 1858 twenty-five to thirty thousand prospectors arrived at the Fraser River. Making the best of the event, Douglas tried to establish a trading monopoly for the Hudson's Bay Company on the mainland, although the area was outside his official jurisdiction. The British government reacted to the chaotic situation by opposing the monopoly and creating the new colony of British Columbia in August 1858. With time at a premium Douglas, the man on the spot, was appointed governor, but on condition that he severe his ties with the Hudson's Bay Company. Thus ended the fur trade's rule over the west coast.

The gold rush moved farther inland after 1858, reaching the Cariboo district by 1861. To accommodate the geographical change, the government was involved in financing transport improvements. The Cariboo Road, for example, from Yale to Barkerville was completed in 1864 at a cost of one and a quarter million dollars. The importance of gold in the colony was already falling after 1859. Few other economic activities were generated by the rush and local reinvestment of profits was minimal. As immigration ceased in the mid-1860s and gold output dwindled, the colonial government was left with large debts and declining revenues.

British Columbia and Vancouver Island were united as an economy measure in 1866, but this did not solve the problems of the isolated colony. The year 1867, with the U.S. purchase of Alaska and Canadian Confederation, clearly posed British Columbia's options. Many B.C. inhabitants were American-oriented, having come from the United States. Nevertheless, the Canadian prime minister, John A. Macdonald, was determined to secure Canada as a transcontinental nation, and in this goal he had the support of the British government. A pro-Confederation governor was appointed to the colony in 1869, negotiations with Canada were concluded the following year and British Columbia officially joined in 1871.

Chapter 3

Alternative Approaches
to Canadian Economic Development

The preceding account of Canada's early economic development may at first sight appear to contradict the idea that facts can exist without theories. This is not the case. Behind the apparently descriptive account, there is an implicit but clear theoretical framework. This framework is the staple theory, which asserts that the pace and nature of an area's economic growth is determined by the characteristics of its staple product. The staple theory has been the most common approach to Canadian economic development, both before and after 1850. The validity and usefulness of this approach to the earlier period is generally accepted, but during the last twenty years there has been growing criticism of its applicability to the later period. The present chapter will examine the staple theory and some alternative approaches to Canadian economic development.

1. The Staple Theory

The staple theory has dominated the study of Canadian economic history; it has even been adopted in studies of other countries' economic development, which has led one economist to state that "it is Canada's most distinctive contribution to political economy" (Watkins, 1963, p. 141). Extensive application has given the theory a richness of variety, in that it has been developed to explain a wide range of phenomena from economic growth to cultural change. Some of the more influential variants are examined below. In view of the differing approaches taken within the staple framework, we may expect some inconsistencies, but in practice these have been minimal, at least in the work of the best theorists.

For Harold Innis, the Toronto economist whose monumental study *The Fur Trade in Canada* first appeared in 1930, the major problem for settlers in a new country is the working out of new cultural traits suitable to the environment. The problem is severe because people who have become accustomed to one set of cultural traits find it difficult to work out new ones, as evidenced by the high death rates of the earliest European settlements in North America. The severity of the transition process can be reduced by continuing dependence on the mother country. On a material level the migrant is unable immediately to supply all his needs, and if these needs are to be met he will be forced to rely on goods obtainable from the mother country. Some of these goods may have been brought with the migrant, but the most important device for obtaining them is by trade. Here lies the basis for the importance of the staple export in colonial life. As Innis states:

> The migrant was consequently in search of goods which could be carried over long distances by small and expensive sailboats and which were in such demand in the home country as to yield the largest profit. (Innis, 1956, p. 384)

Innis's contention is that the economic characteristics of the specific staples which were available for export determined the evolution of Canadian culture. Several cultural and institutional changes related to the economic characteristics of the early staples have already been identified in chapter 2, but we can also take note of some other phenomena which Innis related directly to the fur trade: (1) Canada has had few serious problems with her native peoples, unlike the United States where conflict between settlers and Indians was frequent; (2) the creation of an extensive, but centralized, financial organization by fur traders led to the establishment of the Bank of Montreal in 1817. Although other banks were founded later, the Canadian banking system has remained one with a small number of eastern-based banks, unlike the American situation with its large number of geographically diffused banks.

Innis's research in this area was primarily concerned with the cod and fur staples. Other writers have continued to apply the staple theory to later periods in Canadian history. For most of the nineteenth century, timber was a thriving staple export, and its economic characteristics affected immigration, agricultural development and commercial policy. The period between 1873 and 1896 is characterized by the lack of an export staple and is therefore considered by staple theorists to have been a time of "secular depression" in Canada. After 1896 rising wheat prices led to the emergence of a new staple as the rapid development of the agricultural potential of the Prairies led to booming wheat exports in the first decades of the twentieth century. Also, in the present century a variety of minerals, newsprint and hydroelectric power have emerged as new staples in response to the changing demands of industrialized countries. These developments have led some economists to believe that "it is still true that the pace of development in Canada is determined fundamentally by the exports that enable Canada to pay its way in the world. And among these exports the staple trades, particularly the new staples, the products of Canada's twentieth-century resource industries, hold pride of place" (Aitken, 1961, p. 74).

Since all of the staples are based on the availability of exploitable natural resources, an important element of the staple theory is the significance of geographical factors for economic development. This was emphasized by Mackintosh when comparing the western expansion of the United States and of Canada. Both countries had large expanses of relatively easily exploitable land as far west as the Rockies, but the pace of western expansion differed greatly. In the United States the period 1783–1854 was the great age of westward expansion; settlers crossed the

Appalachian Mountains and the frontier shifted west with each new wave of immigrants. Large-scale migration to the Canadian Prairies did not take place until after 1896. In Mackintosh's view, it is the earlier start in exploiting western lands and exporting the new staple, wheat, which explains the more rapid economic development of the United States during the nineteenth century. The reason for faster western settlement in the United States is the absence of major geographical barriers west of the Appalachians. In Canada the Laurentian Shield bordered the north shore of the upper Great Lakes so closely that movement into the Prairies was blocked. The frontier moved west through the United States and only reached the Canadian Prairies after Minnesota; until that time "the New West of the Canadians was the American North West" (Mackintosh, 1923, p. 23).

Emphasis on geographical factors has also led staple theorists to emphasize the significance of government policies in overcoming geographical disadvantages. The Erie Canal which linked Lake Erie to the port of New York in 1825 was important for U.S. western development in providing a direct route from the Great Lakes to an all-year port, as well as settling the long conflict for preeminence among eastern North American cities. In Canada the construction of the Canadian Pacific transcontinental railway (1880–1885) reduced the barrier posed by the Laurentian Shield. Even after the frontier reached the Prairies, settlement would not have been so attractive had transport costs on staple exports been higher. The CPR reduced these costs by providing a direct link between the Prairies and the Atlantic, most critically by bridging the difficult portage between Winnipeg and Lake Superior. As the North American frontier reached Manitoba and as the transport links between the Prairies and the east were improved, the stage was set for a new export boom based on wheat. The upturn in the world price of wheat in 1896 is seen as the trigger for the wheat boom; in the words of one economic historian, "Canada's hour had struck" (Skelton, 1913, p. 191) and most staple theorists date Canada's modern prosperity from that hour.

So far we have seen why settlers turn to staple production, the importance of geographical factors in determining the availability of an exploitable staple and the ways in which the economic characteristics of the particular staple exert a strong influence on cultural and institutional development. If the staple theory is to be used as a theory of economic growth and development, it is necessary to specify the economic consequences of staple exploitation. In a simple colonial economy staple exports are the leading sector of the market economy setting the pace of economic growth, but if growth is to be sustained after staple exports decline it will be necessary to have shifted resources into more diversified economic activities. Crucial to economic development are these spread effects, and the central point of a staple theory of economic development is that the spread effects are determined by the technology of the staple production.

The most rigorous attempt to classify the spread effects of staple production is that of Watkins (1963). The linkages between staple production and other branches of the economy take three forms. Backward linkages occur when staple production increases the demand for domestically produced inputs; for many staples the construction of transport facilities for shipment to ports is a particularly important backward linkage. Forward linkages arise when increased availability of a staple stimulates the expansion of branches using the staple as an input. Final demand linkages are a consequence of the increased income generated by staple production leading to increased demand for consumer goods; the extent of final demand linkages depends on how much of the increased income goes to domestic consumers and also on the income distribution associated with the staple. In addition to these increased demands for goods, Watkins identifies three supply-side linkages: the nature of the staple will affect the level of entrepreneurship, the rate of immigration and the amount of capital in the economy.

The relationship between the technology of a staple and the extent of its spread effects can be illustrated by comparing the impact of fur and wheat on the Canadian economy. The backward linkages from the fur trade were small because there were no domestic inputs; even the extensive transport network required no new construction activity because fur's low bulk/value ratio permitted efficient use of existing (Indian) technology. The Prairie wheat economy required a much more expensive transport network to take its product to the port, and the backward linkages included railway construction, grain elevators and rolling stock manufacture, as well as reaching to the agricultural implement industry. Forward linkages from the fur trade were small because the staple was exported in an unprocessed state and further stages of processing (e.g., hat manufacture) took place in Europe. Wheat, too, had few forward linkages for the same reason, although there may have been some induced increase in the number of flour mills. The final demand linkages from fur were minimal because the income remaining in Canada largely accrued to a few merchants, leading to no broadly based increase in demand for domestically produced consumer goods. (Hamelin (1969, p. 55) estimates that between 1675 and 1760, 72 per cent of fur revenue stayed in France, 5 per cent went to the Crown, 14 per cent to New France fur merchants, i.e., twenty or so families, and the remaining 9 per cent was spread more widely in the colony.) The Prairie wheat economy, being based on the family farm, had the opposite effect, greatly increasing the domestic market for consumer goods and having no bias in favour of imports. The same feature of the Prairie wheat economy may have stimulated self-reliance and other features helping to increase the number of potential entrepreneurs in Canada. No such consequence could be expected from the monopolistic fur trade. With respect to international flows of labour and capital, fur and wheat had opposite impacts. The fur trade was antipathetic to immigration and provided no incentive for capital inflows; in fact, repatriated profits from the fur trade constituted a net outflow of capital. The wheat boom with its promise of free land and profitable investment opportunities provided an incentive for large inflows of both labour and capital. In sum, the fur trade had few linkages and negative effects on the inflow of factors of production, whereas the wheat economy had extensive linkages and positive effects on factor inflows. Thus it is not surprising to staple theorists that the fur trade was not associated with diversification and economic development, whereas the wheat boom was.

Until the late 1950s it was generally accepted that the staple theory was the most useful approach to Canadian economic history. This is typified by Easterbrook and Aitken's 1956 textbook, in which the staples fish, fur, timber and wheat occupy centre stage, determining the selection of material and the way in which the material is ordered. Since then, doubts have arisen about the relevance of the staple theory as applied to some phases of Canada's economic history.

The first widely publicized statement of scepticism was made by Buckley in 1958, and the statement perhaps had added force coming from someone whose own research had been set in a staplist mold. The theme of Buckley's paper is that, although the staple theory throws much light on early Canadian economic development, it is no longer valid because the present-day Canadian economy is too diversified to be influenced greatly by the export of a single product. The question raised by this contrast between early development and the present-day economy is, "When does the usefulness of the staple theory cease?" Buckley's answer was the 1820s, after the shift of the fur trade's commercial centre from Montreal to Hudson Bay. Commenting on Buckley's paper, Aitken shows fundamental disagreement, not surprisingly in view of his belief in the continuing validity of the staple approach, and the most he is prepared to concede is that there could be dispute over the post-1914 era:

> It would seem beyond dispute that the staple trades remained the dominant factor in Canadian economic growth at least up to 1914. (Aitken, 1958, p. 251)

Neither protagonist provides convincing support for his case, but they did set the chronological limits within which the debate over the staple theory has been centred.

The controversy over the staple theory has been virulent and will be referred to in later chapters. Before trying to evaluate the validity of the staple theory, three aspects of the debate should be emphasized. Firstly, the conflict is not over the internal logic of the staple theory. Although some individual economists' use of the staple framework may have had theoretical weaknesses, the general reasonableness of the approach is not seriously in doubt. Buckley raised the criticism that the staple theory is too imprecise, merely stating relations between the staple and economic development while not specifying how large the relations will be; but the Watkins model shows that the staple theory can be specified rigorously enough to say what linkages will exist and to predict orders of magnitude; this is perhaps as precise as a general theory of economic development can be expected to be.

The question therefore is an empirical one: for which periods is the staple theory as an explanation of Canadian economic growth and development consistent with the facts? The relevant empirical tests of the staple theory would try to answer the following more specific questions. Firstly, did the pattern of Canadian economic growth follow changes in the value of her staple exports? In this context argument has focussed on the years 1873-1896, which in the absence of rising exports have been characterized as a depression by staple theorists. Secondly, were the expanding sectors during boom periods the ones with linkages to the export staple, and was the degree of sectoral expansion related to the strength of these linkages? The first of these questions, concerning the macroeconomic relationship between staple exports and aggregate economic activity, will be examined in chapter 4.6 after the available macroeconomic data have been evaluated. The second question, concerning the microeconomic effects of the staple, will be addressed in later chapters as the various aspects of Canadian economic development are analyzed, but in particular in the appendix to chapter 7.

Finally, the debate is over an important issue. If the validity of the staple theory to all Canadian economic history is agreed upon, then we accept a specific interpretation of Canada's past which emphasizes the following points: (1) Canadian economic development is highly vulnerable to shifts in overseas demand and lacks internal strength; thus there is a need for government intervention to ease social distress during depressions and, indeed, to hold the country together in those times; (2) government activity in the economy is also justified by the need to overcome geographical obstacles to economic development; (3) industrial development, except where there are linkages to the staple export, is unnatural and can only take place with government assistance, e.g., by restricting the entry of competing imports. Those who accept the validity of the staple theory with respect to the present day are therefore pessimistic about Canada's economic prospects: the economy is vulnerable because of concentration on staple production, and diversification into industry can only be done inefficiently.

2. A Marxian Approach

An alternative approach to Canadian economic history, based on Marxian dialectical materialism, has been proposed by Stanley Ryerson. He emphasizes the role of class struggle as the driving force behind economic development, although in the Canadian case the impact of domestic class relations was modified by conflicts between French and English Canada and by the imperial connection with Britain. While agreeing with staple theorists that geographical and technical factors were of crucial importance for Canadian economic development, he criticizes the staple approach for its omission of the social relations amid which the staples are prepared. Although the technical characteristics of the staple products provide the material basis from which changes in social relations evolve, it is the latter changes and in particular the conflict between established and emerging classes which are the important development; preeminence is given to the genesis of changes in the class structure and to political events which reflect changes in the balance of power between classes.

Karl Marx identified the ancient, feudal and capitalist modes of production as the epochs of the prehistory of human society, i.e., of the era of class struggle preceding the establishment of socialism. Since the Europeans in Canada started at the second stage and since socialism has not yet been established, the central question for Ryerson is the transition from feudalism to capitalism.

New France before the Conquest had many aspects of a feudal economy. In particular a seigneurial regime of landholding existed, under which the land was held by the Church and seigneurs while the farmers were subject to a large array of feudal dues. In principle feudalism involved a sharing of rights and duties, where the lord's main duty was the provision of protection, but in New France as in Europe earlier the community of interests became submerged by the antagonism between rich and poor. The tenure system was reaffirmed after the Conquest and in the Quebec Act. Colonial politics were dominated by a coalition of merchants and landholding interests, supported by the imperial government. This last aspect made the 1791 constitution, which granted representation without power, amenable to the merchant-landowner oligarchy.

For Ryerson, the important dates in nineteenth-century Canadian economic history are not related to changes in British timber tariffs or American demand, but to the stages of the bourgeois revolution. The timber industry was important as one of the stimuli to early industry and in the creation of wage labour; timber-related activities, especially sawmills and shipbuilding, were in the vanguard of industrial development during 1825 to 1840, and returning lumber ships provided cheap transport for immigrants. But there were other factors too. Early industry was also stimulated by the technological innovations of the British industrial revolution (e.g., the Molsons' manufacture of ships' engines in

Montreal) and by the increasing domestic demand which led to the development of small-scale consumer goods industries (e.g., distilleries, hat-makers, potteries, carriage-makers) in more fertile areas like the Richelieu valley. The new activities led to the emergence of new classes, and it was these classes which provided the pressure for political change culminating in the Rebellion of 1837–1838. The rebellion was defeated because the forces for democracy were insufficiently developed, and the 1841 Bill uniting Upper and Lower Canada did not grant responsible government to the new Province of Canada.

Political discontent remained in both Canada West and Canada East, although now under more moderate leadership, and economic events were on the side of the reformers. Ryerson dates the birth of the factory system in Canada to 1846, and thereafter industrial development was particularly accelerated by the new railway technology. An important feature of the railways was the need for large amounts of capital beyond the means of indigenous entrepreneurs, which increased the importance of financiers (often merchants acting in conjunction with foreign finance). A new oligarchy of industrialists and railway financiers was growing in significance, and they felt handicapped by the absence of responsible government. Nevertheless, the immediate cause of the first responsible Canadian government—the Baldwin-LaFontaine administration of March 1848—was not domestic pressure but a policy change by the British government. The policy change was no doubt affected by international events, e.g., the Year of Revolutions in Europe (although the decision concerning Canada was taken before open revolution occurred in Europe), and the fear of U.S.–Canada union. Its main cause, however, was the shift in political power in Britain following the defeat of mercantile interests by industrial interests (symbolized by the repeal of the corn laws in 1846) which led to a change in official attitude towards the colonies. As Ryerson puts it:

> The transition from an economy dominated by the old mercantile-landowner, "Family Compact" ruling group to that of the new industrial-railroad oligarchy is the main content of the bourgeois revolution in British North America. It is a revolution effected "from above," the armed popular struggles having met defeat. (Ryerson, 1968, p. 281)

Once responsible government was installed in Canada it worked clearly in the interests of the capitalist classes. The major acts provided for massive railway subsidies from the public purse (e.g., the Guarantee Act of 1849), the replacement of feudal tenure relations by the cash nexus (1854) and a protective tariff for manufactured goods (1858–1859). Most elements of the older elite accepted their fate: the landowners received generous compensation for relinquishing their feudal powers and some merchants became financiers or even involved in industry.

Some discontented merchants put out the Annexation Manifesto in 1849, and there seemed grounds for believing that U.S. Manifest Destiny (to rule all of North America) might prevail; but the new elite were determined to reserve the Canadian market for themselves and with the support of the imperial government they succeeded.

Ryerson's theory highlights many aspects of Canada's past which are left in the dark by the staple theory. A striking example is the staple theorists' neglect of the seigneurial system, even though it involved most of the Canadian population until the nineteenth century, was abolished only in 1854 and the last feudal dues were not paid off until the 1940s. The argument can be made that, despite employing few people, the fur trade was the dynamic sector of the economy of New France. If the staple theorist rests on this argument, however, he must be taken to account for ignoring the industrial developments of the nineteenth century. Although still small in total employment, by 1900 the industrial sector was the dynamic sector of the economy, and yet this is ignored by the staple theory until the twentieth century.

There are some serious problems with Ryerson's approach. Firstly, rigid application of Marx's stages is not completely appropriate to Canada. The economy of the early nineteenth century had one feudalistic aspect, the land tenure system in Lower Canada, but in other aspects it bore few resemblances to European feudalism. It is also questionable whether the elite of the 1840s was a capitalist class. Industrial development by that date was minor and railway construction by 1850, given so much prominence by Ryerson, amounted to sixty-six miles in the whole of British North America. A second problem arises from Ryerson's attempts to integrate the two nationalities aspect of Canada into the Marxian framework. This enables him to adapt the Marxian theory to explain specific Canadian phenomena, including the economic disparity between French and English Canada, which is primarily ascribed to the British bourgeois revolution having happened prior to British migration to Canada whereas a French bourgeois revolution before the settlement of New France had not occurred. These adaptations are not very successful. For example, if the timing of the bourgeois revolutions in Britain and France is critical to explaining economic development in the component parts of Canada, of what significance is a Canadian bourgeois revolution? A final problem, which does not reflect on the approach itself but does influence our ability to accept or reject its relevance to Canada, is that a theory emphasizing class relations rather than changes in quantifiable variables is difficult to test.

3. Rostow's "Stages of Economic Growth"

Although the difficulties in constructing a universal theory of economic development are immense, this has not deterred writers from attempting it. The desire to construct such a theory stems from a belief in the existence of universal uniformities in the process of economic development. If this view is correct, there is a large payoff to explaining these uniformities, both for understanding past economic development and for clarifying the options open to less-developed countries today. Considering the size of the difficulties and of the payoff, we should not judge these general theories too harshly and expect complete explanatory power—if they can find any patterns it will be useful, but unfortunately many have not done even that.

The most popular variant of general development theories is the stages approach—the idea that every country must pass through a series of sequential changes during the process of economic development. Stage theories have a long history, and the stages have been defined in a variety of ways, for example, from primary to secondary to tertiary activity or from consumer goods to capital goods. Most of the theories, however, while having some success in classifying past patterns of economic development, have possessed little explanatory power. The major exception is the Marxian approach which does contain a dynamic mechanism for moving within and between stages, and partly for this reason it has been the most influential stage theory. An ambitious attempt to develop a competing stage theory in recent years is that of Rostow, whose book *The Stages of Economic Growth: a Non-Communist Manifesto* presents a stage theory without the class conflict basic to Marxian theory.

Rostow specifies five stages through which all nations must pass in the process of economic development, although he acknowledges that the details within the stages and the timing of individual stages could vary between countries:

1. In *traditional society* land is the basis of wealth. There is a low level of productivity in agriculture and a large part of the population works in that sector. The social system is hierarchical with little mobility; political power is decentralized and the value system reflects these social and political traits. The level of investment is low.

2. The *preconditions period* is a transition period, usually triggered off by an exogenous shock. Fundamental social and political changes, including changes in income distribution in favour of more commercially oriented classes, lead to the emergence of a new elite willing to invest for future gains. Increased agricultural productivity enables a smaller proportion of the population to feed the whole population or even to produce a surplus, permitting the release of labour and capital for other sectors.

3. The *take-off* is a short period of twenty to thirty years when the pace of intensive growth rises to new levels. It may be triggered by a political revolution, a technical innovation, the opening of new markets or some other external shock. The important point is not the nature of the stimulus, but rather that the economy is at the point where the effects of

the stimulus will be felt throughout the economy (because of changes during the transition period). Rostow identifies three conditions of a successful take-off: (a) an increase in the investment/output ratio from 5 per cent to 10 per cent; (b) the development of one or more leading sectors; and (c) the emergence of a political and social framework which exploits opportunities for economic growth.

4. The *drive to maturity* follows take-off. The higher investment/output ratio and the new social and political framework make economic growth self-sustaining. New sectors emerge to take over from the old leading sectors, and a more diversified economy is the result.

5. The *age of high mass consumption* is the culmination of the drive to maturity.

The ideology of Rostow's manifesto is clear: less-developed countries must be patient (because they have to pass through all the stages) and should be grateful for aid (because investment is a key variable), after which they will reach the desideratum of a high mass consumption society (not unlike the United States). The ideological bias of Rostow's approach has led some people to reject it, just as the Marxian approach is dismissed by people at the other end of the political spectrum. This is no grounds for rejection. We should ask whether the approach is theoretically viable and whether it fits our empirical knowledge.

Two major theoretical criticisms can be leveled against Rostow. Firstly, his stages are not logically distinct. For example, the critical preconditions and take-off stages are both characterized by social and political change, and there is no distinction between the types of change in the two stages. The take-off period is also identified by a leading sector or sectors, but this is empirically meaningless because there will always be some sectors ahead of others. Secondly, the mechanism whereby an economy moves from one stage to the next is not specified. Thus the model is not dynamic, which is a prerequisite for a theory of economic development.

The applicability of Rostow's stages has been tested against the experience of developed countries, and the conclusions have been mixed. In particular the condition that the investment/output ratio increases from 5 per cent to 10 per cent during take-off has not been supported by the empirical evidence. Developed countries are characterized by investment/output ratios greater than 10 per cent and less-developed countries by ratios below 5 per cent, but the increase typically occurred after the take-off period (identified by changes in the rate of intensive growth) and took longer than twenty to thirty years. Also Rostow's dating of take-offs has been disputed (e.g., in the case of Germany) or in some cases there is dispute over whether a twenty to thirty year take-off existed at all (e.g., France and the United States). Nevertheless, Rostow's stages continue to be used by economic historians with some frequency. This is because Rostow seems to have captured some of the uniformities of economic development, and in particular the idea that a take-off period occurred in most developed countries' histories appears valid, even if for some countries Rostow selected the wrong dates.

In sum, Rostow's model is not acceptable as a theory of economic growth and development, but it does have some validity as a classificatory device for comparing the economic development of different countries. If Canada could be fitted into this framework, it would imply that Canadian economic development was not very different in its broad outlines from that of other developed countries, and therefore doesn't require a special approach (as with the staple theory).

The dates assigned by Rostow to the stages of Canadian growth, and accepted by the only Canadian economic historian to use this framework (Firestone, 1969, ch. 11), are:

1. The traditional society, 1605–1867.
2. The preconditions period, 1867–1896.
3. Take-off, 1896–1914.
4. The drive to maturity, 1914–1950.
5. The age of high mass consumption, 1950 onward.

As Firestone points out, the preconditions period should more plausibly start at an earlier date to include the move to responsible government in the 1840s. A more important question concerns the take-off dates, since this is the most clearly identifiable stage in the model and the pivot upon which all else turns. The appropriateness of the 1896–1914 dating can only be examined seriously in the next chapter, but the influence of the staple theory on the choice of dates can be noted already. When Rostow wrote his book in the late 1950s the staple theory dominated Canadian economic history, and whichever account Rostow may have referred to would have emphasized the wheat boom of 1896–1914 as the beginning of modern economic growth (see chapter 4.6). Yet Rostow's approach is in some ways in conflict to the staple theory, and the world seen from the staple theorist's perspective may differ from that according to Rostow's approach. Specifically, Rostow did not appear to have agriculture in mind when he talked of leading sectors, and furthermore there was little social or political change during this period. Thus, in evaluating the relevance of Rostow's approach to Canada we should be prepared to be flexible with respect to the dates he gives.

4. Other Approaches

Attempts to construct non-stage theories of economic development with universal applicability have been made, but with little success. The problem is that if non-stage theories try to explain all aspects of economic development, they tend to become too diffuse. Thus writers dissatisfied with stage theories have usually focussed on one aspect of economic development.

One such writer is Gerschenkron, who explains variations in the speed and nature of industrial development by the relative backwardness of a country when its industrial development begins. Thus he is not trying to explain why industrialization occurs, but rather the more limited question of why it has taken different forms. A feature of his explanation is the rejection of the stages concept of a preordained path of economic development which must be followed by all countries. The path will be different for a less-developed country today than it was for England in a world composed only of less-developed countries, or for Russia in a world with a few more-developed and many less-developed nations. Gerschenkron postulates direct relationships between the degree of backwardness and the following variables:

- the speed of industrial growth, with a high probability of industrialization starting discontinuously as a "great spurt,"
- the stress on bigness of plant and enterprise,
- the percentage of producers' goods in total output,
- the reliance on borrowing technology, and perhaps capital,
- the pressure on per capita consumption,
- a passive role for agriculture,
- the importance of banks and state budgets in industrialization.

The only attempt at empirically testing Gerschenkron's theory gave it some support; on the basis of six countries' experience, the first relationship was confirmed, the third vaguely confirmed and the sixth neither confirmed nor rejected (Barsby, 1969).

The relevance of Gerschenkron's thesis to Canada lies in the fact that, although preindustrial Canada was less economically backward than the main subjects of Gerschenkron's studies (Germany and Russia), she was backward relative to her two main points of reference, Britain and the United States. Thus once industrialization had begun, Canada enjoyed many of the advantages of latecomers (e.g., the access to technology and capital) and her industrial development took on some of the characteristics predicted by Gerschenkron. The most apparent of these characteristics were the role of the government and foreign capital (compared to Britain or the United States in earlier periods). In later chapters we will try to test Gerschenkron's other predictions. This will largely involve breaking new ground, as Gerschenkron's theory has not been previously applied to Canada. Its influence, however, is to be seen in Naylor's thesis concerning Canadian industrial development, examined in chapter 6.

5. Conclusions

The most common framework in which to analyze Canada's economic development has been the staple theory. Since the late 1950s the relevance of this theory to the years after 1821 has been questioned, and this has encouraged the application of alternative theories of development. Which is the best approach. The theories discussed in the present chapter were proposed when there was little quantitative data on the Canadian economy before 1926, so they could flourish without being subjected to rigorous tests and possible rejection. Now our empirical knowledge, although still far from good, is better than it was, and some tests of the competing theories are possible. Before doing that we must examine what data are available and which are reliable—or rather which are more reliable, less reliable, or worthless.

Chapter 4

The Statistical Evidence
on Canadian Economic Growth

The Dominion Bureau of Statistics (DBS—now called Statistics Canada) began the systematic collection of economic data only in 1919, and the first DBS-produced set of national accounts is for 1926. Statistical testing of economic hypotheses concerning the period before 1926 is thus much more difficult than for recent years. A major part of Canadian economic historians' research during the 1960s and 1970s has consisted of attempts to organize the earlier historical data into national accounting categories so that they can be used to test hypotheses drawn from economic theory. For some concepts this was relatively easy (e.g., foreign trade data were quite good), but for aggregates like total output of goods and services (GNP) there are large gaps. In order to assess the reliability of historical estimates it is necessary to have some knowledge of the quality of the primary data and to judge the appropriateness of the gap-bridging assumptions. In this chapter we examine first the major source of primary data, the censuses, and then the available estimates of important economic magnitudes. The aim is twofold: to provide a quantitative summary of Canadian economic growth and development since the mid-nineteenth century and to consider the implications of the quantitative data for the various approaches described in the previous chapter.

1. The Quality of Canadian Census Data

Censuses have existed for over three hundred years in Canada. The first census, taken in 1666, was followed by thirty-six censuses during the French regime. Under British rule censuses continued to be taken, at first less frequently than by the French, but in 1824 Upper Canada introduced an annual census which was retained until the 1841 Act of Union. During this period five censuses were taken in Lower Canada, seven in the Assiniboine and Red River district (Manitoba) and several in the Atlantic colonies. In addition, population estimates based on surveys exist for many non-census years. The Province of Canada passed census acts in 1842 and 1851 providing for regular decennial censuses, and this practice was extended to other provinces after Confederation.

It is impossible to measure the degree of accuracy of the census figures. All economic data based on enumeration are likely to be inaccurate in absolute terms; even today we cannot expect the census population figure to be correct to the last digit. The problem is that the size of the discrepancy cannot be predicted from looking at the census data themselves. The practice today is to check the census returns against independent estimates, for example, the Canadian Labour Force Surveys, and it appears that the census data are consistent with the outside checks. Such checks are more difficult for earlier censuses, but there is some evidence to suggest that the nineteenth century censuses are less reliable than those of the twentieth century and that some of the nineteenth century censuses are worse than others.

The 1851 and 1861 censuses underenumerate; the DBS later suggested that the population figure was too low by about 100,000 people. The main problem was that the enumerators and clerical staff were untrained and, especially in Upper Canada, not conscientious. The introduction to the 1851 census deplored "the negligence and ignorance displayed" by the enumerators in Upper Canada (which is strong language for an official document) and also noted the existence of "a very general feeling ... that the census had ... reference to taxation.... Enumerators were frequently received most ungraciously, and the information sought was, not only partially, but, in some cases, altogether withheld." The latter problem might be expected to have applied particularly to the figures on farm sizes, livestock, equipment, crops, etc. Similar criticisms were made of the 1861 census.

Under the direction of Taché, the censuses of 1871 and 1881 were conducted more efficiently. Some months before the census began, thirteen census officers were appointed to assist in preparation and later to supervise the enumerators, who all received instruction before commencing field-work. The system was improved in subsequent censuses until the establishment of a permanent census staff in 1905.

Individual censuses have continued to have their critics, and that of 1891 was particularly controversial. The fundamental legal reason for the census is to determine representation in the federal House of Commons, and the returns can have political significance. The 1891 census was bitterly attacked by the Liberal opposition on the grounds that people who had emigrated or died were counted in some areas, presumably where the Conservatives were represented. The charged overenumeration was in the range of 250,000 to 300,000 people. Overenumeration is also apparent in the inflated number of industrial establishments appearing in the 1891 census (the figures for specific industries are inconsistent with those in previous and succeeding censuses). Whether the overestimates were due to a Conservative conspiracy or whether they followed from the 1891 practice of paying enumerators according to the number of establishments reported is unclear. In either case we have no means of knowing the extent to which the true figures are overstated.

From an international perspective Canada, with its long history of frequent censuses, is relatively well endowed with quantitative historical data. The coverage and quality of the data deteriorate, however, as we go back in time. Before 1851 the censuses were irregular (on a Canada-wide basis), covered little more than population and agriculture, and the coverage varied. After 1851 the coverage broadened and became more standardized between censuses, but the collection process left much to be desired. The quality improved in 1871, but modern standards were only approached after the Census and Statistics Office of Canada was established in 1905. Thus, serious problems with the nineteenth-century censuses must be acknowledged; all the figures are subject to some degree of error and for some years figures appear to be biased, but the worst of it is that the degree of error and extent of bias are unknown. This is not cause for discarding the census data. In most cases the figures are useful indicators of the order of magnitude of the true figure, but they cannot be regarded as accurate cardinal measures and must be used with caution.

2. Population

The most reliable aggregate data are undoubtedly the census population figures. The concept of an area's population is a simple one leaving little to the enumerator's interpretation, and it has not changed over time (although the enumerators' competence has improved). The only exception in Canada has been the treatment of the indigenous population, for whom little effort was made to obtain accurate figures during the nineteenth century; a factor important for the Northwest Territories and British Columbia.

The census estimates of Canadian population since 1851 are given in Table 4.1. The rapid increase between 1820 and 1850 (cf. chapter 2.5) continued during the 1850s, under push pressures in Europe and the pull of cheap land in Upper Canada, aided by cheap transport. Population growth then slowed down during the 1860s and slow growth continued until the turn of the century. The wheat boom of the 1900s was accompanied by rapid population growth, but the rate of increase declined continuously during the next three decades. Another period of rapid increase occurred during the 1950s.

Changes in the rate of population growth can be due to changes in the birth rate, the death rate or net immigration, or a combination of these three factors. For Canada the most volatile of these components of population growth has been migration. The decades of rapid growth, 1820–1860, 1900–1910 and 1950–1960, are characterized by high rates of immigration, while slower growth is associated with low or even negative net immigration. Mortality and fertility patterns have been more stable, both showing downward trends over the past century. Fertility has been examined by Henripin (1968), who found high levels up to 1871 followed by a rapid decline until 1941 and then a slight rise from

Table 4.1
Population of Canada[a] at Census Dates, 1851-1971 (thousands)

	Canada	Que.	Ont.	N.S.	N.B.	P.E.I.	B.C.	N.W.T.	Man.	Alta.	Sask.	Yukon	Nfld.
1851	2,436	890	952	277	194	63[b]	55	6	—	—	—	—	—
1861	3,230	1,112	1,396	331	252	81	52	7	—	—	—	—	—
1871	3,689	1,192	1,621	388	286	94	36	48	25	—	—	—	—
1881	4,325	1,359	1,927	441	321	109	49	56	62	—	—	—	—
1891	4,833	1,489	2,114	450	321	109	98	99	153	—	—	—	—
1901	5,371	1,649	2,183	460	331	103	179	20	255	73	91	27	—
1911	7,207	2,006	2,527	492	352	94	392	7	461	374	492	9	—
1921	8,788	2,361	2,934	524	388	89	525	8	610	588	758	4	—
1931	10,377	2,875	3,432	513	408	88	694	9	700	732	922	4	—
1941	11,507	3,332	3,788	578	457	95	818	12	730	796	896	5	—
1951	14,009	4,056	4,598	643	516	98	1,165	16	777	940	832	9	361
1961	18,238	5,259	6,236	737	598	105	1,629	23	922	1,332	925	15	458
1971	21,568	6,028	7,703	789	635	112	2,185	35	988	1,628	926	18	522

Notes: [a]excluding Newfoundland before 1951; [b]1848.
Source: Canadian censuses.

1941–1961; the last phenomenon appears to be a compensatory reaction to the low birth rates of the 1930s depression and war, rather than a reversal of the long-term trend.

Canada West (Ontario) became the largest "province" just before 1850, and its population continued to grow rapidly during the remainder of the century. The population gap between Canada West and Canada East (Quebec) continued to widen, until the difference in population between the two provinces was some half a million by the 1880s. The gap then remained more or less constant until the 1950s, reflecting a slightly faster rate of population growth in Quebec. The trend was drastically reversed after 1950, when Ontario experienced a far larger population increase.

The Maritime provinces experienced rapid population growth during the 1850s and 1860s, but the decline of the timber trade and obsolescence of sailing ships during the 1870s were a severe blow to the region. The population figures clearly reflect the subsequent relative economic retardation, at least with respect to extensive growth. The population of Nova Scotia and New Brunswick has grown consistently more slowly than that of central and western Canada, while the population of Prince Edward Island, afflicted by its own problems, actually fell in the late nineteenth and early twentieth century to the extent that its peak was not reached again until the 1960s.

British Columbia's population fluctuated widely in the mid-nineteenth century and only started to grow continuously after the 1880s. Clearly her importance was increased by the construction of the first trans-Canada railway in the 1880s and the opening of the Panama Canal on the eve of World War I. Manitoba's population grew continuously and rapidly from the establishment of the province until the depression of the 1930s, during which period growth slowed noticeably. Saskatchewan and Alberta are included in the Northwest Territories population figures before 1901, and no separate estimates are available. Their population was small before 1900 and then increased very rapidly in the next three decades. The two provinces were affected by the 1930s depression in opposite ways; Alberta's population continued to grow as she became Canada's fourth largest province in the postwar era, while Saskatchewan's population declined by almost 10 per cent between 1931 and 1951. During the wheat boom the Prairie provinces became to a great extent synonymous with the agricultural sector, and their experience will be considered in that context in chapter 7.

Changes in the size of the labour force have closely followed the increase in population, apart from the early twentieth century. This is reflected in stable participation rates, i.e., the proportion of total population in the labour force, 1881–1901 and 1921–1951 (Table 4.2). Unfortunately, data do not exist for years before 1881 and the method of

Table 4.2
Labour Force Data, 1881–1951

	Total Labour Force (millions)	Percentage of population over 10	Percentage of population over 14	Percentage of total in: (a) agricultural pursuits	(b) non-agricultural pursuits
1881	1.4	44%		48%	52%
1891	1.6	44%		46%	54%
1901	1.8	44%		40%	60%
1911	2.7	49%	55%	34%	66%
1921	3.2		53%	33%	67%
1931	3.9		54%	29%	71%
1941	—	—	—	—	—
1951	5.3		53%	16%	84%

Note: Northwest Territories and Yukon excluded; Newfoundland only included in 1951. Data for 1941 omitted because of war.
Source: Urquhart & Buckley (1965), p. 59.

measurement was changed in 1911. Nevertheless, a sizeable increase in participation in the 1900s, partially offset by a reduction during the 1910s, is discernible. This change appears closely related to the high immigration of the 1901–1911 decade, as immigrants tend to contain a higher proportion of males and of people under sixty-five than do sedentary populations. In Canada the fifteen to sixty-four age group increased from 60.6 per cent of the total population in 1901 to 62.4 per cent in 1911 and the male-female ratio for that age group rose from 1.06 to 1.20 (Green & Urquhart, 1976, p. 229). The importance of the constancy of participation rates is that, with some allowance for 1901–1921, we can use population figures both to convert extensive to intensive growth and as a measure of the size of the labour force.

The composition of the labour force since 1881 has changed continuously in favour of non-agricultural pursuits, even during the wheat boom of the early twentieth century (Table 4.2). It is unfortunate that we do not have comparable pre-1881 data, but it is at least clear that the decline in the relative importance of agriculture had started by the 1880s. The same trend is revealed in the rural–urban distribution of population (Table 4.3). Such data suffer terribly from definitional problems, especially in the era of suburban sprawl, but the continuity of the shift from rural to urban residence is clear. This shift can be dated back to at least 1871; unfortunately the rural–urban distinction was not made in censuses before 1871. In sum, the period since the mid-nineteenth century has been one in which the importance of agriculture as a source of employment has continuously declined, while non-agricultural employment associated with urbanization has increased.

Table 4.3
Population[a], Rural and Urban[b] (millions)

	Urban	Rural
1871	0.7	3.0
1881	1.1	3.2
1891	1.5	3.3
1901	2.0	3.4
1911	3.3	3.9
1921	4.4	4.4
1931	5.6	4.8
1941	6.3	5.3
1951	7.8	5.8

Notes: [a]excluding Newfoundland;
[b]urban population defined as all inhabitants of incorporated cities, towns and villages.

3. Output

The most important aggregate magnitude for the study of economic development is total output. Unfortunately, the principles of national accounting were not well developed before the present century, and the data required for constructing national accounts were only systematically collected in Canada after the establishment of the Dominion Bureau of Statistics. The first comprehensive national accounts did not appear until the end of World War II, but the DBS later constructed fairly reliable annual estimates back to 1926.

The measure of total economic activity is gross national product, i.e., the market value of all final goods and services produced by Canadian residents during a given period of time. Since any transaction simultaneously represents expenditure (by the buyer) and income (to the seller), the sum of all transactions measures total expenditure (GNE) and total income (GNI) as well as total output (GNP); i.e., GNP ≡ GNE ≡ GNI. Thus total output can be measured either by summing expenditures or by summing incomes, both approaches producing an estimate of a common magnitude (Y):

Expenditure Approach	Income Approach
Personal consumption expenditure (C)	Wages and salaries
Gross private investment (I)	Rent and interest
Government purchases of goods and services (G)	Profits
	Net national income
+	+
Net exports (X-M)	Capital consumption (depreciation) Indirect taxes
GNE ≡ Y≡ C + I + G + (X-M)	GNI ≡ Y

Some economic activities are omitted from the national accounts; in particular, non-market and illegal activities may be significant omissions from some of the estimates quoted below. It is also worth recalling that GNP or net national income are not measures of human welfare, but at most a guide to the level of material well-being; although it should be borne in mind that for most people in most ages increased material well-being has been an important aspect of total welfare.

In 1979 Canadian GNP was $260 billion, which represents a large increase over the 1926 figure of $5 billion. This increase reflects partly the expansion of real output in the last fifty years, and partly the higher prices existing in 1979. In order to isolate the former component, temporal comparisons are made in terms of GNP in constant dollars or "real output," i.e., the GNP estimates are deflated by a price index. Constant dollar GNP series for the years since 1926 also indicate rapid extensive growth interrupted only by a major recession during the 1930s, less serious recessions in the immediate post-World War II years and the mid-1970s, and other minor recessions during the postwar era.

Before 1926 there are no DBS-prepared national accounts, but many of the data sources for the early DBS accounts are available for earlier years. Some economists have used these sources to construct retrospectively pre-1926 GNP estimates. The method is to fill as many as possible of the component parts of GNP from the available data, following either the expenditure or the income approach. The remaining components are then estimated, usually by constructing an index for a proxy variable and then finding absolute values from a benchmark year. For example, the construction component of I is estimated using an index of the production and net import of construction materials, and C is estimated from the behaviour of a "representative" bundle of consumption goods for which data exist. An assessment of the reliability of such estimates will depend on the extent (and reliability) of available data and on the validity of the assumptions used in filling gaps.

For the years 1900–1926 several estimates exist. The censuses were put on a fairly sound basis at the beginning of the century, and much of the primary data required for national accounts began to be gathered under reasonable standards of collection. In consequence, there is some agreement as to the general movement of GNP and that its 1900 level was approximately $1 billion. There were, however, sufficient data gaps so that the need to make bridging assumptions led to variations in the individual estimates, which become significant when precise magnitudes are desired (cf. Bertram's (1973) contribution to the debate summarized in the appendix to chapter 7).

The only estimates of nineteenth-century Canadian GNP are those of Firestone (Table 4.4). These figures have been widely criticized, but also extensively used. The main problem is that Firestone's figures are diffi-

Table 4.4
Firestone GNP Estimates, 1851–1900

	1851	1860	1870	1880	1890	1900
Total ($ million)						
current dollars	169	319	459	581	803	1057
constant (1935–9)						
dollars	406	582	764	982	1366	1877
Per capita ($)						
current dollars	68	98	125	135	167	197
constant (1935–9)						
dollars	164	178	208	228	283	350

Source: Firestone (1960), p. 222.
Note: The estimates given in Firestone (1958) and Firestone (1969) differ slightly from the ones given here (Firestone, 1969, p. 276).

cult to reconstruct from the descriptions given in their published versions (although Green (1971, Appendix B) appears to have managed a replication). This is a criticism of Firestone's work, but not necessarily of the results. Criticisms of individual post–1900 figures leading to construction of revised estimates have not produced substantial alterations to Firestone's numbers, but this reveals little about the reliability of his pre–1900 estimates. Better assessment of the latter will only be possible when alternative estimates for those years have been made. A start in this direction is contained in the investment estimates described in the next section, which indicate that Firestone's 1870 estimate is too high and his 1890 and 1900 figures too low by 10 to 25 per cent. This suggests that substantial revisions of Firestone's estimates may be in order, but it must be remembered that investment is perhaps the most difficult component of GNP to estimate accurately. Even without alternative estimates with which to judge Firestone's figures, we know that they can be only rough orders of magnitude. Critics of Firestone's method have centred on his gap-bridging assumptions, but even if these were perfectly appropriate the raw data do not permit reliable estimates, especially for 1851 and 1860 when the data are worst and have the most gaps. In sum, Firestone's figures for 1851–1900 must be used with great caution. They have been and continue to be used, however, because they are the only figures we have and they do have some basis in the data which are available for this period. They represent educated guesses and are to be preferred to uninformed guesses or anecdotal references to economic conditions.

Firestone has combined his and the DBS estimates to calculate growth rates for the Canadian economy during the century following Confederation (Table 4.5). Extensive growth averaged 3.5 per cent per annum, and was fastest during the wheat boom and postwar eras, two periods of large scale immigration. The intensive growth rates show a different pattern. The postwar era has the fastest increase in per capita real output, but the wheat boom period has the slowest. The years 1867 to 1896, when population growth was slow, enjoyed rapid intensive growth. The 1914 to 1950 period shows a relatively poor economic record in terms of both extensive and intensive growth, but hides a diversity of subperiods covering two world wars and their aftermath, the roaring twenties and the depression of the 1930s; the interwar years will be studied in greater detail in chapter 9.3. Both the intensive and extensive growth rates in Table 4.5 are high by international standards; the result has been not only high living standards for Canadians, but also the sixth largest GNP among the world's non-communist countries and the grudging assumption of economic power status.

Table 4.5
Economic Growth in Canada, 1867–1967
(GNP in constant dollars; annual averages)

	1867–1967	1867–1896	1896–1914	1914–1950	1950–1967
Real output	3.5%	3.3%	3.7%	3.0%	4.5%
Real output per capita	1.7%	2.0%	1.3%	1.5%	2.1%

Source: Firestone (1969), p. 123.

4. Capital Formation

The level of investment figures prominently in most theories of economic growth, and economic historians have thus shown particular interest in this component of GNP. Attention has centred on the behaviour of the investment/output ratio which provides an indicator of the proportion of GNP not for immediate consumption. In quoting investment data it is necessary to define the measure carefully, distinguishing between gross and net and between domestic and national (i.e., financed by Canadian savings) capital formation. For our purposes we would usually prefer measures of net domestic capital formation (NDCF), i.e., additions to the physical capital stock in Canada, but will have to be content with gross domestic capital formation (GDCF) data. The reason is that GDCF (total expenditure on construction, machinery and equipment and changes in inventories) is the simpler to measure, while NDCF requires not only GDCF data but also knowledge of the proportion of GDCF used for replacement.

Estimates of GDCF for years before 1926 are bedevilled by the same problems as the GNP estimates quoted above—only more so. The primary data gaps which require bridging assumptions are relatively larger than they were for GNP estimates, especially with respect to the most volatile (inventory changes) and the largest (residential construction) components of GDCF. An example of the pitfalls surrounding attractive but inappropriate assumptions is provided by Pickett's estimates of residential construction, 1871–1921. Noting that there was no domestic manufacture of window glass and that the trade statistics therefore gave excellent annual data on Canadian use of window glass, he assumed that window glass expenditure represented a constant proportion of the total value of residential construction and was able to calculate annual construction estimates. The problem with this approach is that if the window glass data are compared to the number of houses built in census years, we find that window glass imports per thousand houses varied from six dollars in 1870 to twenty-seven dollars in 1890, suggesting that Pickett's constant proportion assumption, although at first sight reasonable, is in fact not so. For this reason Pickett's estimates have not been generally used, but his paper, which has the great merit of clearly describing how the estimates were reached, remains a warning of the need for care in making assumptions upon which historical estimates are based. Other investment estimates have taken a more disaggregated approach and tried to use a greater variety of primary data in order to limit the significance of the assumptions.

The twentieth-century behaviour of capital formation in Canada is well documented. Since 1926 GDCF has averaged 20 to 25 per cent of GNP, with slightly lower ratios for the 1930s and higher ratios after World War II, while NDCF has been somewhat over 10 per cent of GNP. The early twentieth century is not so barren in useful data as the nineteenth century, and fairly reliable investment data exist for the period 1900–1926. These indicate GDCF/GNP ratios of over 20 per cent between 1900 and 1920, reaching a peak in the decade 1905–1915, when the ratio has been estimated at 27 per cent (Buckley, 1955) and 29 per cent (Caves & Holton, 1959). The estimates by Firestone (1958) for 1910 and 1920 are similar, 26 per cent and 23 per cent respectively, corresponding to NDCF/GNP ratios of about 10 per cent or more. Firestone's 1900 GDCF estimates are smaller, and in this respect they are consistent with those of Buckley (1955) and give a GDCF/GNP ratio of 13 per cent and a NDCF/GNP ratio below 5 per cent. The overall picture, then, is one of a sharp increase in investment/output ratios during the first decade of the twentieth century, a movement seen in both gross and net figures, with GDCF rising above 20 per cent of GNP and NDCF increasing to over 10 per cent of GNP—ratios which have persisted ever since.

The nineteenth-century estimates are more flimsy and go back only to 1870, but the availability of two independent sets of estimates permits a cross check which was not possible with the GNP data. Firestone's estimates show a doubling of GDCF between 1870 and 1900, but a slight decline in the investment/output ratio. More recent estimates, drawing upon research done since Firestone's work (in particular the estimates of manufacturing output described in the next section) indicate a trebling of GDCF over these decades and a significant upward shift in the investment/output ratio during the 1870s (Table 4.6). The differences between the two series come at both ends, with Pomfret's higher 1900 GDCF estimate shifting some of the drama of the early 1900s back into the nineteenth century and his lower 1870 estimate implying an increase in the investment/output ratio during the 1870s. Support for Firestone's extremely high values of residential construction in the early 1870s (not repeated until the twentieth century) is provided by Pickett's estimates, although as mentioned above their foundations are shaky. Support for Pomfret's less dramatic 1871 peak comes from Buckley's (1952) national index of urban building activity derived from the value of building permits issued in major cities, which peaks in 1871 but has a new peak in 1887.

Table 4.6
Investment/Output Ratios, 1870–1920

	GDCF : GNP		GDCF : GNP	NDCF : GNP
	Firestone		Pomfret: Firestone	Firestone
	a			a
1870	12%	15%	12%	4%
1880			18%	
1890	14%	16%	18%	5%
1900	12%	13%	16%	3%
1910	18%	26%		8%
1920	18%	23%		11%

Note: a, excluding changes in inventories
Sources: Firestone (1958), pp. 65, 100, 112, 114; Pomfret (1981).

The picture that emerges from the capital formation data is fairly clear for the twentieth century, and rather indistinct for the late nineteenth century. Despite the absence of quantitative data it seems safe to assume that investment averaged less than 5 per cent of GNP before Confederation—a typical ratio for a premodern economy. This ratio had risen above 10 per cent by 1910 and has remained at that level since. A substantial upward shift occurred between 1900 and 1910, but there is controversy about the magnitude of this shift and as to whether it was preceded by an earlier upward shift in the investment/output ratio during the 1870s.

The composition of GDCF also changed during the late nineteenth century, with accumulated inventories becoming less important and fixed capital formation (construction plus investment in machinery and equipment) more important, reflecting the improved transportation network and other social overhead capital formation permitting a smoother functioning of the economy and reducing the need to hold stocks. Also the share of machinery and equipment in GDCF tended to increase after 1880, an additional sign of economic modernization. These trends in GDCF composition may have begun earlier, but pre-1870 estimates are needed before this hypothesis can be tested.

Despite their weaknesses, estimates of investment in physical capital are available and are useful. When we turn to human capital, the picture is almost completely blank, being limited primarily to data on formal education. Universal elementary education was achieved in the middle of the nineteenth century, although the average daily attendance was still only about 50 per cent at the time of Confederation (Firestone, 1969, p. 264). Higher education institutions were also well established by then, but their economic significance is difficult to measure. Society's commitment in financial terms to formal education remained small before 1900; the ratio of educational expenditure to GNP has been estimated at 1¼ per cent in 1896, 2 per cent in 1914, 3 per cent in 1956 and 7.3 per cent in 1967 (Firestone, 1969, p. 185), indicating that it is only since the 1950s that a rapid expansion in the resources devoted to education has occurred. Such quantitative data do not tell the whole story; the quality of education may not have changed concurrently with expenditures, and the economic impact of education may be discontinuous (e.g., the attainment of universal elementary education may be more critical for economic growth than the expansion of secondary education). Moreover formal education is not the only source of improvements in human capital; migration, learning by doing and a host of other forces influence the accumulation of skills and the complex of attitudes and values which may be included in a broad definition of human capital. In sum, the concept of human capital may be important for understanding economic growth, but at present it cannot be operationalized easily in studying the Canadian past.

5. Other Data

Population figures suggest that the last century has been a period not only of rapid extensive growth but also of substantial structural change in the Canadian economy. The declining relative importance of agriculture indicates the significance of other sectors in Canada's economic development, and in particular attention has been directed to the growth of the manufacturing sector. Estimation of manufacturing output is not easy, because the early census data do not follow modern classifications of branches, but some of the problems associated with other sectors (e.g., the non-marketed output which occurs in agriculture) are avoided.

The best early estimates of manufacturing output showed an average annual growth rate of 4.2 per cent between 1870 and 1957

(Bertram, 1962). The noteworthy feature of these estimates was the steadiness of the growth rate which only deviated widely below the trend in the 1930s and above the trend in the late 1920s. This relative steadiness applied to the pre-1914 era, when the growth rate was 4.6 per cent for 1870–1890, slowed down during the 1890s and then showed a rapid increase for 1900–1910 (6 per cent per annum). Bertram's conclusion regarding the late-nineteenth century is that:

> . . . development in the three decades of the nineteenth century has frequently been regarded as disappointing and depressed. Growth rates estimated from the revised manufacturing series give quite a different impression of the period. (Bertram, 1962, p. 96)

In sum, Bertram found that modern rates of industrial growth date back at least to 1870.

McDougall's more recent estimates for 1870–1915 confirm Bertram's conclusion. He found that real manufacturing output increased from census year to census year throughout the period of study. The most rapid growth in real manufacturing output per head of population was during the 1880s, probably followed by the 1870s and 1900s, while the 1890s were "an interval of stagnation" and 1910–1915 showed slow real growth per capita because 1915 was a year of cyclical recession compared to 1910 (McDougall, 1971). Although the increase in output was rapid and uneven, McDougall found some constancy in the structure of manufacturing output between 1870 and 1915. An interesting aspect of his structural breakdown is the category "producer durables," whose behaviour provides a check on the investment data of the previous section. McDougall's ratio of producer durables to total manufacturing output is fairly stable for the census years 1870–1900 (12.5 per cent, 12.4 per cent, 13.3 per cent and 13.2 per cent), with increases after 1900 (16.9 per cent in 1905, 17.1 per cent in 1910 and 13.7 per cent in the recession year 1915) similar to the pattern seen for GDCF/GNP in section 4.4. In 1973, however, McDougall published additional estimates of total domestic use of manufactured commodities (i.e., domestic output minus exports plus imports) and these give a different picture with respect to producer durables. The ratio of producer durables to all manufactured goods increases more steadily than when measured by domestic production and starts to speed up noticeably as early as the 1890s. The implications of this result are twofold. Firstly, Firestone's GDCF estimates which do not make the adjustment from domestic output to domestic use are biased. Secondly, foreign trade played an important role, especially around the turn of the century, in permitting Canada to import investment goods which she did not produce. International trade meant that when Canadian demand for investment goods increased rapidly, structural change in domestic production could respond more slowly; to reverse the argument, desired increases in investment ratios were not thwarted by bottlenecks in the domestic producer goods industry. Producer goods imports rose from a third of total imports in the 1850s to two thirds of the (much larger) total in 1910 (Vickery, 1974).

Most of the foreign exchange needed to pay for increased imports came from Canada's exports, but they did not cover all her imports. Between 1870 and 1914 Canada's balance of trade was consistently negative, and even during the wheat boom decade, 1900–1910, it was negative in more years than it was positive (Table 4.7). The unrequited imports were covered by large net inflows of capital.

Table 4.7
Foreign Trade, 1870–1960 ($millions)

	Domestic Exports	Total Exports	Total Imports	Trade Balance
1870	59	66	67	−1
1880	73	86	70	+16
1890	85	94	112	−17
1900	169	183	173	+11
1910	279	299	370	−72
1920	1268	1298	1337	−39
1930	864	883	1008	−125
1940	1179	1193	1082	+111
1950	3118	3157	3174	−17
1960	5256	5387	5483	−96

Note: These selected figures are good indicators of the growth of foreign trade but poor indicators of trends in the trade balance. Between 1868 and 1893 the balance was negative in all years except 1880 and 1881; between 1894–1903 it was positive in all years, and between 1904–1914 negative in all years; between 1915–1949 it was positive in all years except 1920 and 1929–1931.
Source: Urquhart & Buckley (1965), p. 173.

The estimated volume of foreign capital in Canada at the time of Confederation was $200 million of which over 90 per cent was British and some 80 per cent of the total was in government and railway bonds. The net inflow 1868–1899 was $1000 million, still primarily British and portfolio investment (Hartland, 1960, p. 723). The pattern started to shift from securities sold in the London market towards direct investment, primarily from the United States, during the 1890s, and these trends have continued in the twentieth century (Table 4.8). At first direct investment in Canada consisted mainly of American activity in railways and lumber (to some extent reciprocated by Canadian firms, e.g., the Canadian Pacific Railway's purchase of feeder lines south of the border) and of British and U.S. insurance companies moving into the Canadian market. During the twentieth century, however, foreign investment has increasingly been in the manufacturing sector and has been characterized by the phenomenon of "branch plant" production by multinational corporations. The extent of foreign ownership and the deleterious consequences in terms of lost sovereignty and possible economic dependence have made this a hotly debated topic in current economic policy. The causes and effects of foreign investment will be examined in chapters 5.1 and 6.5. For the moment, we can note the significance of foreign investment in Canadian GDCF from an early date; Hartland estimated that the net capital inflow contributed about 30 per cent of GDCF in 1870, 25 per cent in 1900 and as much as 50 per cent in 1911–1915.

Table 4.8
Foreign Capital in Canada, 1900–1960

	Direct	Portfolio	Total	UK	US
	(billion dollars)			(percentages)	
1900			1.2	85	14
1905			1.5	79	19
1910			2.5	77	19
1913			3.7	75	21
1920			4.9	53	44
1926	1.8	4.2	6.0	44	53
1930	2.4	5.2	7.6	36	61
1939	2.3	4.6	6.9	36	60
1945	2.7	4.4	7.1	25	70
1950	4.0	4.7	8.7	20	76
1960	12.9	9.4	22.2	15	75

Source: Urquhart & Buckley (1965), p. 169

6. Testing Theories of Canadian Economic Development

Having presented the available macroeconomic data on Canadian economic growth since 1850 we are now in a position to test some of the hypotheses proposed in chapter 3. The appropriate methodology is to examine a hypothesis against independent data to determine whether or not the hypothesis should be rejected. Before doing this, however, we should ask to what extent the data are independent of the theories. The staple theory in particular has influenced the compilation of historical economic statistics in Canada.

The staple theory was developed before much quantitative information on nineteenth-century Canada was available. Data did exist on wheat production, exports and prices, and the beginning of Canadian prosperity was identified with the upturn in world wheat prices in 1896. The only other quantitative information available to early Canadian economic historians concerned population and foreign trade, both of which were thought to support the staple theory by showing a depression before 1896 and a boom thereafter. The negative net immigration between 1860 and 1900 was taken as evidence of "secular depression" in the absence of exploitable staples; it is suggestive of a depression, but not proof of one. Firstly, net emigration may indicate the existence of superior economic opportunities in the United States without precluding economic expansion in Canada; and, secondly, population continued to increase rapidly in Ontario, indicating that the aggregate population data hide regional variations. Staple theorists also saw evidence of secular depression in the horizontal trend of real exports per capita 1870–1895, but stagnant exports do not provide an independent test of the absence of economic growth. An alternative theory could postulate a negative relationship between exports and growth (e.g., if increased home demand diverted exports to the domestic market), and the export data only support the view of 1870–1895 being years of depression if the staple theory is accepted first. Whether the tests were valid or not, the staple theory was widely accepted and believed to be supported by the facts, so that attempts to reconstruct further quantitative data were sometimes based on the preconception that the important turning points were already known (e.g., Buckley's capital formation series starts in 1896). Most recent studies have avoided this pitfall, mainly because their reliance on decennial census data has determined the years for which estimates are made, but the staple approach permeates interpretations often to a degree unjustified by the data (e.g., Firestone's dating of Rostow's stages and Bertram's test of Rostow's model, where the preconceptions show through clearly; Firestone (1969), Bertram (1963)).

The output estimates given above cast serious doubt on the hypothesis that 1870–1914 was a period of depression followed by boom. Although the average annual rate of extensive growth was higher for 1896–1914 than for 1867–1896, the latter period's average of 3.3 per cent is not indicative of a depression (Table 4.5). Moreover, the rate of intensive growth was lower for 1896–1914 than for any other period since Confederation, while the 1867–1896 rate was above the century average. These growth rates have been criticized on the grounds that Firestone's estimates are unreliable, but successive estimates of manufactured output have supported the view that the late nineteenth century, at least up to 1890, was a period of growth. These estimates not only conflict with standard staple theory interpretations of post-Confederation economic development, but are also inconsistent with the dates assigned to the Rostovian take-off in Canada. The onset of self-sustaining intensive growth must be set before 1870. Firestone's GNP estimates point to the 1850s and 1860s when growth was rapid from a low base (Table 4.4), but the 1851 and 1861 figures are Firestone's weakest. (As well as reflecting the less adequate census data, they also encounter the problem of non-marketed output.) The evidence is consistent with Ryerson's focus on the late 1840s, but provides no positive support. There is no evidence of Gerschenkron's predicted big spurt, but this could have occurred before the useful data are available.

Increased investment has an important role in both the staple theory, where social overhead capital is a prerequisite for realizing the potential gains from the wheat boom, and in Rostow's model, where the NDCF/GNP ratio rises from 5 per cent to 10 per cent during take-off. The evidence points to such an increase in the investment/output ratio between 1900 and 1910, or perhaps starting in the 1890s, which is too late to fit the staple theory or a revised take-off date. An earlier increase in this ratio perhaps occurred around 1870, which might coincide with the end of a revised take-off period, but could not have involved an increase from 5 per cent to 10 per cent as predicted by Rostow. It is interesting to note, however, that a lag between the onset of modern intensive growth rates and increased investment/output ratios has been consistently found in other developed countries' histories (Kuznets, 1961), implying that a high investment/output ratio is a feature of the self-sustaining growth period rather than the initial stimulant for economic development. (Note that investment may still be important without any change in the investment/output ratio; for example, if the composition of physical investment changes or if investment is in human rather than physical capital.) Gerschenkron's hypothesis that the investment/output ratio is higher in latecomers is not supported by the Canadian data, although the predicted reliance on foreign capital is evident.

In sum, the staple theorists' characterization of 1896 as a critical turning point in Canadian economic development should be rejected. Intensive growth was already rapid by Confederation, as was the structural change associated with economic development. Firestone has suggested that Canada experienced an industrial revolution in the 1860s and 1870s (Firestone, 1960, p. 230), while Ryerson dates the event from the late 1840s; an attempt to identify these beginnings will be made in chapter 6.

Apart from the question of timing, tests of the approaches outlined in the previous chapter require disaggregated data. The staple theory's predictions concerning the impact of the wheat boom will be examined in the appendix to chapter 7, where the (still debated) conclusion appears to be against the staple theory. On the other hand, we will find in chapter 6 that changes in staple exports from Ontario were important for Canadian economic development in the second half of the nineteenth century—an area and period neglected by staple theorists in the past. The same evidence casts doubt on Gerschenkron's prediction of the unimportance of agriculture, although other Gerschenkron hypotheses (e.g., large enterprises and high capital inflows during the drive to maturity) will be found to have some validity. Rostow's model fares less well; his take-off dates must be moved into the nineteenth century, but then the predicted increase in the investment/output ratio occurs after take-off. The occurrence of significant political and social change during the pre-conditions and take-off stages is scarcely testable because "significant" changes can be identified at many dates, but the leading sector hypothesis suffers the opposite fate in the absence of a clear leading sector at any point after 1821. Ryerson's approach is given some support by the pushing back of the onset of modern economic development, but otherwise the validity of his approach is difficult to test.

The data summarized in this chapter provide a fairly reliable idea of the contours of Canadian economic growth and development since the mid-nineteenth century. The data contradict the staple theory scenario of late nineteenth-century depression followed by the wheat boom with its spread effects promoting general economic development in the twentieth century. The stages approaches of Marx and Rostow have found few Canadian disciples and, at best, need considerable refinement if they are to be useful in the Canadian context. This leaves modern (post–1850) Canadian economic history without a generally accepted analytical framework. Given this absence, the remaining chapters will be organized on a topical basis: government policy, the manufacturing, agricultural and financial sectors, and temporal and spatial variations in Canadian economic growth. Although no unifying analytical framework is used, the final chapter will address the question of whether the topical analyses can be brought within a general approach.

Appendix: The "Sources of Growth" in Canada

The estimates of total output and of labour and capital, two factors of production considered to be major determinants of the output level, raise the question of the empirical relationship between factor inputs and extensive growth. One approach to this question is the "sources of growth" technique, developed by a number of American economists during the 1950s. The technique is based on the concept of the aggregate production function, which relates the level of output to the quantity of labour and capital employed. To quantify the contribution of growth in the labour force and in the capital stock to extensive growth, it is necessary to specify the exact form of the aggregate production function. There is no unanimity on the appropriate specification, but the most popular has been the Cobb-Douglas form:

$$Y = AL^aK^b \qquad \text{where } a + b = 1$$

where A is sometimes defined as "technical change" but is more appropriately called the residual because it picks up the effect of all variables other than L and K and of any errors in specifying the form of the production function. The superscripts a and b are the output elasticities of L and K respectively, and any change in output can be decomposed into three parts:

$$\Delta Y/Y \equiv \Delta A/A + a\Delta L/L + b\Delta K/K$$

where $\Delta Y/Y$ is the percentage change in output, etc. The three terms of the right hand side of this identity can be identified as the contribution of the residual ($\Delta A/A$) and of the two factors L and K to extensive growth.

Lithwick has applied the "sources of growth" technique to Canada for the period 1926–1956. He used a Cobb-Douglas production function, and having knowledge of $\Delta Y/Y$, $\Delta L/L$ and $\Delta K/K$ could calculate $\Delta A/A$ as the residual. The elasticities a and b were found by assuming that each factor of production is paid its marginal product, in which case a and b are the shares of wages and profits (i.e., the return to labour and to capital) in GNP. Although we will not enter into theoretical issues here, the assumptions underlying the sources of growth technique, the appropriateness of the Cobb-Douglas specification or even the permissibility of using aggregate production functions in this manner are all open to question. Lithwick's estimates of the sources of growth in Canada for 1926–1956, and comparable figures for the United States, are given in the first two columns of Table 4.9. In Canada the contributions of capital and labour to extensive growth were of almost equal importance, unlike in the United States where labour was the more important (perhaps because of significant improvements in labour quality due to education). The total contribution of the two factors was higher in Canada than in the United States. A further reason for Canada's faster extensive growth was a higher residual; Lithwick attributes this to the shift from low productivity to high productivity activities, which had occurred earlier in the United States.

Table 4.9
The "Source of Growth" in Canada and the United States

	Canada, 1926–56	U.S.A., 1929–57	Canada, 1910–26	Canada, 1891–1910
Average annual rate of extensive growth (%)	3.89	2.95	2.46	3.38
Contribution of:				
—labour	0.58	0.41	0.98	1.82
—capital	0.61	0.23	0.31	0.81
—the residual	2.70	2.31	1.16	0.75

Note: labour and capital data were adjusted for quality changes and utilization rates.
Source: Lithwick (1970), pp. 53-4.

Lithwick also applied the "sources of growth" technique to the pre-DBS era. The output, labour and capital data are all less reliable before 1926, and factor shares data are non-existent, a problem which Lithwick overcame by assuming that a and b remained constant before 1926. Lithwick's estimates for 1891–1910 and 1910–1926 (columns 3 and 4 of Table 4.9) indicate that labour's contribution was more important than that of capital before 1926, and that extensive growth was primarily due to increases in factor inputs. These results are what we would expect for a period of rapid population increase and substantial capital accumulation, but leave open the interesting question of whether the increasing importance of the residual is a secular trend or whether 1891–1926 was an exceptional period of factor augmentation.

Lithwick's study is interesting in that it illustrates one approach which could be used to throw light on the Canadian growth experience if we had adequate data. His analysis of the years since 1891 suggests that increased factor productivity, reflecting structural or technical change, has been the primary source since 1926, but that increases in the quantity of factor inputs was more important between 1891 and 1910. If this finding is accepted, it provides a useful signpost as to which direction research on extensive growth in a specific period should follow. The usefulness of Lithwick's study for Canadian economic historians is, however, severely limited by the inadequate pre-1926 data; in particular the assumed constancy of factor shares in GNP is unrealistic in a period of significant structural change.

Chapter 5

Government Policy

A new factor in Canadian economic development after 1848 was the existence of a Canadian government capable of pursuing an independent economic policy. This presents a sharp contrast to earlier years when policy decisions were taken in Paris or London with little understanding or regard for Canadian problems. The three main elements of Canadian government policy affecting economic development have been commercial policy (i.e., the foreign trade regime), policy towards social overhead capital formation and land policy. The shape of the first two policies was already determined in the 1850s and remained consistent until after World War II, while land policy assumed greatest importance after Confederation and its significance diminished when the Dominion lands were ceded to the Prairie provinces in 1930.

1. Commercial Policy

Commercial policy has always been an important factor in Canadian economic development. Firstly, the level of foreign trade is high even today; in 1968, for example, Canada's ratio of international trade to GNP was higher than that of any other economically developed country (compare Canada's 36 per cent with 8 per cent for the United States) and foreign trade per capita was almost 50 per cent greater in Canada than in the next country by this measure (Grubel, 1977, p. 125). The share of foreign trade in total economic activity was even higher in earlier times. Moreover some economists—staple theorists, for example— argue that foreign trade is even more important than is indicated by GNP shares, because exports have been a leading sector in economic development. Secondly, restrictions on foreign trade are one of the most strategic development variables under government control in a capitalist economy. The political significance of commercial policy is reflected in the tariff being the major issue in the elections of 1878, 1896, 1911 and perhaps 1930, and it was also debated in the 1874, 1921 and 1935 elections, despite there being no great distance between the Conservative and Liberal positions since the late nineteenth century.

The Evolution of Commercial Policy

Until the 1840s the British North American colonies were part of an imperial trade network, just as New France had been before 1760. Tariffs were closely monitored by the imperial government, existed primarily for revenue purposes and were preferential. The other major restriction on trade was the raising of transport costs by the navigation acts, under which foreign ships were not permitted to use Canadian ports. On balance, the system worked well for the Canadian economy of the time. The British movement towards free trade marked the end of the old system. The repeal of the corn laws (1846) initially allowed for a three-year adjustment period for the colonies' benefit, but famine in Ireland speeded up the process and most preferences were abolished by January 1847. The years 1847-1849 saw a severe depression in Canada, particularly in the towns. It is not clear that the end of British preferences was a major cause—recession in the United Kingdom and changes in U.S. transport policies may have been more important—but it was an easy scapegoat. The Canadian reaction was twofold, part towards free trade and part towards trade restrictions. Without imperial preferences the shipping restrictions had no compensating advantage, so the navigation acts, which had been amended in 1846 to allow foreign ships into Quebec City and U.S. vessels from the Great Lakes into Montreal, were suspended through 1847 and repealed after the 1848 shipping season. The Canadian legislature also abolished all previous tariff acts and introduced new duties with a general rate of 7.5 per cent and no preferences.

The tariffs established in 1847 were introduced rather hurriedly, as a reaction to British policy changes and in response to a depression, and the tariff structure was fairly simple. Most items were subject to a zero or minimal tariff or to the general rate. Although the tariff rates were amended in 1849 and 1855, this structure was retained throughout most of the 1850s. Of the 353 classified items in the tariff schedule existing in 1858, 97 were duty free, 70 faced minimal rates ($\leqslant 5$ per cent), 184 were subject to the general rate (15 per cent) and only 2 faced other rates (Table 5.1, column 1).

The first tariff schedule designed by Canadian ministers and tailored to Canadian needs was introduced by Cayley and Galt in 1858-1859. The immediate pressure for upward revision was the 1857 depression, with its increased unemployment, but there were other longer-term pressures. Government revenue was still heavily dependent on customs duties, and the 1850s railway boom increased government expenditures and pointed a need for increased revenues. Requests for protection came from the growing manufacturing sector; for example, in March 1858 manufacturers in the Hamilton-Toronto area petitioned Cayley to "protect" their interests. Cayley and Galt probably responded to all of these pressures; the unemployment, revenue and protection motives are not inconsistent, as long as the tariff reduces rather than eliminates competing imports and demand for the dutiable items is not highly price elastic in the relevant range. There were, however, good political reasons for emphasizing the revenue motive. Canadian tariff changes still had to be officially sanctioned by the British Parliament and several U.K. manufacturers petitioned their Parliament claiming injury from the proposed tariff. The

Table 5.1
Province of Canada Tariff Schedules before August 1858
and after March 1859 (number of items by tariff rate)

Nominal Tariff Rate (%)	All Items		Primary		Intermediate		Tertiary	
	Before	After	Before	After	Before	After	Before	After
0	97	113	56	75	26	35	15	3
2.5	55	—	10	—	35	—	10	—
5	15	—	—	—	9	—	6	—
10	—	57	—	1	—	50	—	6
15	184	1	10	—	24	1	150	—
20	2	175	—	—	—	8	2	167
25	—	4	—	—	—	—	—	4
30	—	3	—	—	—	—	—	3
Total	353		76		94		183	
Average Tariff Rate (%)	8.54	12.11	2.30	0.13	5.24	7.18	12.81	19.62

Note: excluding edibles (71 items), natural products (34), specific duties (27) and special
items (settlers' effects, etc.).
Source: Barnett (1976), pp. 393-5.

Canadian government could hope for a smoother passage if they emphasized the revenue aspects and claimed that any protection was "incidental,"
than if they expressed a desire to protect Canadian manufacturers.
British exports to Canada were almost entirely manufactured goods and
the industrial lobby at Westminster was strong, but the tariff changes
passed the House of Lords after a stormy debate and the principle of
independent tariff-fixing in Canada was upheld.

To understand the aims of the Cayley-Galt tariff we cannot rely on
the official pronouncements, but must look at the tariff schedule actually
implemented. The average tariff rate increased from 8.5 per cent to a
little over 12 per cent, which is consistent with either a revenue or a
protective tariff. The structure of the tariff was altered so that differen-
tiations according to the stage of production became more pronounced.
Whereas the old tariff had allowed most primary and intermediate
imports to enter at minimal rates while tertiary items paid 15 per cent,
the new schedule eliminated the duty on primary items, set a 10 per cent
tariff on intermediates (with a substantial free list) and subjected almost
all tertiary items to a 20 per cent rate (Table 5.1). In consequence the
effective rate of protection on manufactured goods increased by a far
greater extent than is indicated by the change in the average nominal
tariff.

The effective rate of protection (ERP) is the rate of protection on value-added, and is therefore the relevant measure of the protection enjoyed by a domestic producer. Measures of ERPs are difficult to construct in the absence of detailed knowledge of industries' input structure, and we do not even possess rough estimates of ERPs in nineteenth-century Canada. The concept can, however, be illustrated with Cayley-Galt tariff rates. In the leather industry (boots, shoes, harnesses, saddlery, etc.) the pre-1858 tariff on inputs was 15 per cent and on outputs 14 per cent; the former remained unchanged, but the latter was raised to 25 per cent in 1858–1859. Consider a foreign saddlemaker whose output price consisted of $50 worth of material inputs and $50 value-added; ignoring transport costs his product would sell in Canada for $114 before the 1858–1859 tariff, and for $125 after. Now consider the position of his Canadian competitors, whose inputs cost (at most) $57.50. Under the old tariff he could undercut the imported good by charging no more than $56.50 for his value-added (i.e., ERP = 13 per cent), but under the new tariff he could charge up to $67.50 (i.e., ERP = 35 per cent). Thus an increase of the nominal tariff from 14 per cent to 25 per cent would lead to an increase in ERP from 13 per cent to 35 per cent. Of course, this calculation is hypothetical; if the share of value-added in total output were less, the increase in ERP would be even more, and vice versa. The general point remains, however, that if the spread between tariffs on inputs and those on outputs is widened, then ERPs will increase. This is what happened in 1858–1859.

There has been considerable debate among Canadian economic historians over whether or not the Cayley-Galt tariff was purely a revenue tariff (Barnett, 1976). The consequences of any tariff change are complicated by other forces working on import levels, tariff revenue and domestic production, but in this case they seem fairly clear. Noting that some tariffs were in fact cut and that the increases tended to involve rises in ERPs, reducing imports of higher duty items, we would not expect a substantial increase in tariff revenue. This was in fact the case; although revenues increased in comparison to the 1857–1858 recession, they were only marginally higher than in 1856 (Table 5.2). On the other hand, the composition of imports was greatly affected as the share of semi-manufactured and manufactured products fell; the ratio of imported inputs to imported final products increased by 31 per cent between 1856–1858 and 1860–1862 in the leather industry, and by 150 per cent in textiles. In general, changes in the ratio of imported inputs to imported outputs were positively correlated with changes in ERPs. Judged by its consequences, the intent of the Cayley-Galt tariff appears to have been protection of manufacturing rather than revenue.

The pre-Confederation tariff history of the Maritime colonies is similar to that of Canada, although their tariff levels were on the whole

Table 5.2
Net Tariff Revenue Collected, Province of Canada,
1856–1861 ($millions)

Year	Net Tariff Revenue
1856	4.5
1857	3.9
1858	3.4
1859	4.4
1860	4.7
1861	4.7

Source: Barnett (1976), p. 396.

lower. Customs duties were the main source of revenue, but protection was not absent from the design of tariff schedules. As early as the mid-eighteenth century Nova Scotia's main revenue duty, on spirits, yielded incidental protection for local distillers. In the 1820s and 1830s there was growing pressure for more systematic protection of agriculture and, especially in Nova Scotia, of flour milling. By the 1840s, protectionist forces were strongest in New Brunswick, and after the granting of colonial autonomy the Assembly explicitly recognized that the tariff structure should protect domestic producers and admit their raw materials duty free. Tariff rates were, however, below those of Canada; in 1851 the general rate was 5 per cent in Prince Edward Island, 6.5 per cent in Nova Scotia and 7.25 per cent in New Brunswick, compared to Canada's 12.5 per cent, and the free list was broader in the Maritimes (McDiarmid, 1946, p. 120). The Maritimes' tariffs rose during the 1850s and 1860s to raise revenue for railway projects, and by 1866 the 15.5 per cent general rate in New Brunswick was higher than the 15 per cent of Canada, while a 10 per cent rate existed in Nova Scotia and Prince Edward Island. In the absence of such a thoroughgoing reform of tariff structure as Canada underwent in 1858–1859, the protective effect of Maritimes' tariffs was still less than that of Canada on the eve of Confederation.

Although Britain's 1846 Enabling Act empowered colonies to remove all preferences, the colonial office from time to time urged the British North American colonies to form a customs union. In 1847 Nova Scotia offered to remove duties on imports from any British North American colony which would reciprocate, and in the following year New Brunswick offered Canada reciprocal free trade in all goods except spirits. As Prince Edward Island held back and Canada was unwilling to accept reciprocity in manufactured goods, negotiations stalled; and when preferences were introduced in 1850 they were restricted to free admission of a list of foodstuffs and raw materials. A complete free trade area was postponed, and the colonies pushed forward negotiations for preferential trade with the United States, culminating in the Reciprocity Treaty of 1854.

By the end of the 1850s Canada was ready for full free trade with the Maritime colonies, just as she was introducing the Cayley-Galt tariff to protect her manufacturers from other suppliers. The 1858-1859 tariff was one of the forces contributing to the United States' refusal to renew the Reciprocity Treaty in 1866—a decision known several years before the expiry date. Thus a reorientation of British North American trade relations was indicated; but opposition to a customs union came first from Britain and then from the Maritimes over the possibility of the latter's customs duties being averaged up to the Cayley-Galt rates in a new union's common external tariff. After 1864, however, events moved quickly towards full economic and political union, while the conflicts over the common external tariff level were lessened by rising Maritimes' tariffs and an 1866 reduction in Canada's tariffs.

The 1867 British North America Act gave the federal government of the new Dominion of Canada unrestricted control over customs matters. In the immediate post-Confederation boom little attention was paid to commercial policy. Negotiations for a new Reciprocity Treaty with the United States broke down in 1874, and in the same year there was a small upward revision in Canadian tariffs. Protectionist pressures were, however, stronger than in the 1850s as the growing manufacturing sector was being exposed to stronger American competition. A severe depression from the mid-1870s provided the scene for the Conservatives to win the 1878 election, with tariff protection as their main campaign promise.

The "National Policy" tariff of 1879 involved a substantial increase in tariff levels (duty collected rose from 14 per cent of total imports in 1878 to 20 per cent in 1880) and a revision of the tariff structure to distinguish between semi-finished goods and industrial materials (subject to 10 to 20 per cent duty), manufactured equipment (25 per cent duty) and finished consumer goods (30 per cent duty). The greater tariff spread meant that effective rates of protection rose by more than the increase in nominal tariffs. Between 1879 and 1887 continuous refinement and extension of the National Policy tariff, adoption of the bounty system of subsidizing domestic iron and steel production, and tightening of customs procedures confirmed the protective nature of Canadian commercial policy. Indeed, despite some reductions in duties on manufactured goods in 1894 to appease farmers during an agricultural depression, by the century's end both major parties accepted the protective tariff as the basis of Canada's commercial policy.

In the twentieth century the biggest upward revision in Canadian tariffs came with the Bennett tariffs of 1930-1933, which were a reaction to U.S. tariff increases and high unemployment in Canada. These retaliatory tariff hikes were, however, annulled by a series of trade agreements, and between 1935 and 1939 Canadian tariffs returned to their 1920s level. Since 1945 Canada has been moving away from her high tariff policy and has participated in the various rounds of international negotiations to reduce tariffs on a multilateral basis. Despite postwar tariff cuts, Canadian tariffs remain among the highest in the industrialized world.

In addition to protection by tariffs, Canada has had an array of non-tariff barriers to trade (NTBs), although these have generally been introduced for reasons other than protection and have been less important than in other countries. Customs valuation procedures have been used as a tool of commercial policy. For example, the practice of valuing imports at their point of origin has been followed in order to favour British over American goods, and valuations were increased in the early 1930s to protect Canadian producers. The various subsidies and buy-Canadian clauses adopted in particular to promote the iron and steel industry (see chapter 6.7) are other examples of measures favouring domestic products over imports. More recently the proliferation of safety, technical, language and other requirements have imposed NTBs, although it is doubtful whether these are serious impediments to trade. More significant is the increasing resort since the mid-1960s to specific NTBs, such as quotas and voluntary export restraints on products as varied as textiles, clothing, footwear, bicycles and canned tomatoes. Thus the postwar trend towards lower tariffs has been accompanied by an off-setting increase in non-tariff barriers, in particular to support declining manufacturing industries.

Preferential Trading Arrangements

A frequent issue in Canadian commercial policy debates has been whether imports from particular countries should enjoy access to Canadian markets at lower rates of duty than the general tariff. By history and geography Canada has had two obvious partners for preferential trading arrangements (PTAs) since the 1840s: the United Kingdom and the United States. Agreements have been reached at various times with France and other European countries, but their scope has been limited. During the 1970s Canada, in common with other industrialized countries, adopted a policy of granting general preferences to less-developed countries; but the Canadian scheme adopted in July 1974 is sufficiently restrictive that, although individual trading partners have benefitted, the scheme is of little economic significance to Canada because the total resulting increase in imports is not substantial.

The PTA with the United Kingdom which existed until the 1840s was on the whole successful, because the two economies were complementary. There was little cost to the colonies of permitting U.K. goods easier access to their markets; they were not yet interested in protecting infant industries, and because the United Kingdom was the most efficient world producer of practically all manufactured goods, the colonies suffered little diversion of trade from cheaper import suppliers. At the same time, the North American colonies' export trades, especially timber, benefitted greatly from preferential access to the large British market. The effects were not so totally favourable for the United Kingdom, because in some products the North American colonies were not the lowest cost suppliers and Britain suffered some trade diversion. Nor were the gains from free access to the colonies' markets so great, for the markets were small and at that time Britain could undersell her competitors without preferential treatment. These considerations provide an indication of why British policy moved towards free trade, although the movement was far broader than the narrow area of North American trade.

At the end of the nineteenth century Canada tried to revive the PTA by granting preferential access to imports from Britain and her colonies. Imperial preference could, however, have little success as long as Britain retained her free trade policy, and in particular without significant duties on grain there was no room for preferences on Canada's major export. The preferences became more substantial in the early 1930s when amidst international economic chaos Britain abandoned free trade and extended preferences to her dominions. This twentieth-century episode of imperial preference had little impact on the Canadian economy. Some exporters benefitted from reciprocal PTAs with the other dominions, but the PTA with Britain herself had little to offer Canada, who by the 1930s was competitive in her major exports to Britain. The influence of imperial preference was soon eroded when in the late 1930s Canadian tariff levels were reduced and the United States was granted most-favoured nation status by Canada. In the postwar era the last vestiges of a U.K.–Canada PTA have disappeared, and since Britain's accession to the EEC, Canada is disadvantaged in the U.K. market vis-à-vis EEC producers.

After Britain's adoption of free trade in the 1840s British North America turned towards the United States for a PTA. After eight years of negotiations the Reciprocity Treaty was signed in 1854. Free Trade was allowed in a comprehensive list of natural products. Manufactured goods were excluded from the PTA. Here, unlike the previous U.K. relationship, the treatment of manufactured goods was favourable to Canadian producers in that they were not forced to compete with the more efficient U.S. industrial sector on equal terms. Omission of manufactured goods, however, raises the question of the purpose of a PTA in natural goods in which British North America and the United States had similar resource endowments offering few opportunities for increased specialization.

From the colonies' point of view the Reciprocity Treaty provided a one-way option; little concession was made on the import side, but there were potential export opportunities. Before the treaty 75 per cent of the items covered entered Canada at a tariff of 2.5 per cent or less, and the average tariff on all freed imports was 6 per cent. The average U.S. tariff on Canadian exports freed by the treaty was 21 per cent. The Americans were in fact not very interested in a PTA in natural goods, but they were persuaded to accept it by concessions with respect to U.S. fishing rights off the Maritimes and by a promise from the Canadian Minister of Finance (Hincks) that the tariff on manufactured goods would not be raised. In sum, the Reciprocity Treaty involved a limited commitment by both sides with hopes of small gains for Canada from the PTA.

Until recently, evaluation of the Reciprocity Treaty was positive. Writers emphasized the great increase in Canada–U.S. trade during the operation of the treaty. Canadian exports to the United States, for example, increased by 365 per cent between 1853 and 1866. Later writers (e.g., Masters, 1969; Officer and Smith, 1968; Ankli, 1971) have, however, been more cautious in interpreting such figures, stressing the data problems and the need for correct specification of the counterfactual situation.

Before the Reciprocity Treaty there was "a large clandestine trade in butter and eggs across the Niagara River and into Buffalo" and also a "notoriously large illicit trade in horses and cattle" (Officer and Smith, 1968). Undoubtedly smuggling activities were not limited to these goods. Tariffs provided the incentive to smuggle, and customs supervision of the long U.S.–Canada border was difficult under mid-nineteenth century conditions. Lake Erie was particularly suited to smuggling because of its narrowness and the large number of natural harbours and inlets along its shores. Free trade in natural goods removed the incentive to smuggle these goods and hence led to an increase in reported trade. By its nature the size of the illicit trade is unknown; we can be sure that the actual increase in trade under the Reciprocity Treaty is overstated by the official trade statistics, but we do not know by how much.

Many forces independent of the Reciprocity Treaty were working to increase Canadian exports during this period. In the 1850s the midwest was being settled rapidly and the U.S. economy was booming. Aggregate demand was rising rapidly, in particular demand for lumber products which were used by the construction and railway industries and demand for food products. Thus, almost all Canadian natural product exports would have expanded during the 1850s even in the absence of the treaty. During the early 1860s the American Civil War was accompanied by rapid inflation with prices rising by 25 per cent per annum between 1861 and 1865. Meanwhile the annual increase in Canadian prices between 1861 and 1865 was 7 per cent, giving an increasingly greater incentive to export to the United States. This was especially true of war-related goods such as horses, but was applicable to a greater or lesser extent to all Canadian exports. Extensive railway construction during the 1850s reduced the costs of moving natural products, which are normally bulky. Turning from general to specific considerations, one of Canada's fastest growing exports to the United States was barley, and it indicates the problem of isolating causal relationships. Large-scale German immigration to the midwest in the 1850s and the imposition of an internal revenue duty on whiskey in the early 1860s led to a rapid increase in U.S. beer consumption (Jones (1946, pp. 218-9) cites an estimate of a sixteen-fold increase between 1860 and 1865) and hence to increased imports of Canadian barley which was considered particularly suitable for good beer. Removal of the 20 per cent U.S. tariff on imported barley under the Reciprocity Treaty undoubtedly helped Canadian exports, but how important was this relative to the other explanatory variables?

Evaluation of the Reciprocity Treaty's impact is thus more complicated than a simple perusal of the increase in Canada–U.S. trade. The exercise, in fact, requires full explanation of the determination of trade in all the affected products, and nobody has yet attempted this. In the most complete recent evaluation of the treaty, Officer & Smith are sceptical as to how much trade creation resulted. They argue that there was a small once-and-for-all boost to Canadian exports in the mid-1850s and thereafter little effect. They also indicate two negative consequences of the treaty. Increased shipments to the United States led to a decline in Canadian transport revenues and difficulties for Montreal as her main port, while the government was unable to provide assistance because of the reduced tariff revenues. Some infant industries (e.g., brewing and cheese) which could have grown up in Canada with protection from U.S. competitors did not do so until after the abrogation of the treaty in 1866. Both of these consequences imply that Canada suffered from the loss of foregone opportunities. There has been no comparable evaluation of the treaty's impact on the Maritime colonies; both exports to and imports from the United States rose substantially (Masters, 1969, p. 148), but how much of this was due to reciprocity is not clear.

On the American side, once the United States had received the fishing rights there was little benefit from the Reciprocity Treaty. Relations with Canada worsened when Galt reneged on Hinck's promise and raised the tariff on manufactured goods. Political relations further deteriorated during the Civil War, and the United States declined to renew the treaty.

After 1866 pressure for reciprocity continued from the Canadian side and was almost agreed upon in 1874 when several manufactured goods were included to make it more attractive to the Americans. Failure to obtain U.S. government assent to the 1874 draft treaty was perhaps a significant turning point in Canadian commercial policy, which turned away from free trade with the United States and raised the ERP on manufactured goods five years later. Reciprocity was embraced by the Liberals as an election issue in 1891 and 1911, but in both years they were defeated at the polls. Opponents may have recognized the limited contribution of the Reciprocity Treaty to Canadian prosperity. More importantly, the growth of Canadian industry behind protective tariffs in the second half of the nineteenth century created an increasingly powerful pressure group for which reciprocity had little attraction.

In the postwar era there has been a revival of interest in a PTA with the United States, partly in reaction to the emergence of trade blocs such as the EEC. The only concrete step towards U.S.–Canadian free trade has been the 1965 Auto Pact. This has some similarities to the Reciprocity Treaty, in that it was not aimed at promoting general free trade but rather at realizing a limited but positive gain for Canada. Again, Canada received the better economic concessions because the United States agreed to the pact partly for other reasons, and Canadian exports under the agreement were helped by favourable exogenous events as well (e.g., the increased demand for compacts which were strongly represented in the product lines located in Canada). The Auto Pact is not a good example of a PTA, because it involves no more than rationalization of a single industry. Some economists continue to advocate a full free trade area, but the historical experience of limited U.S.–Canada PTAs provides little evidence for or against such a proposal.

The Revenue, Infant Industry and Employment Effects of Canadian Commercial Policy

Soon after Canada had responsible government with an independent tariff-making capacity, she imposed protective tariffs. With some revisions, of which the national policy increases in 1879 were the most substantial, Canada remained a high tariff country until after World War II. Despite frequent attempts to establish PTAs with either the United States or Britain, preferential tariff reductions have had little impact. Thus, evaluation of Canadian commercial policy essentially concerns the costs and benefits of high tariffs.

The basic cost of any trade restriction stems from its distortion of the allocation of global resources. Whenever opportunity costs differ among countries, specialization according to comparative advantage will permit increased world output. The gains will be reinforced if economies of scale or learning-by-doing occur, that is, if specialization itself further reduces opportunity costs. Since it is difficult to imagine all outputs having identical opportunity costs in any two countries, the gains from trade are pervasive, and economists have usually presumed that free trade is the optimal commercial policy. The only undoubted exception is the case where a country is able to use its market power to affect world prices, in which case the "optimal tariff" (from the country's viewpoint) may be greater than zero. This argument cannot apply to "small" countries (such as Canada is in most world markets), and yet we rarely observe such countries pursuing a free trade policy. What, then, are the arguments in favour of trade restrictions?

The economic benefits of tariffs to a nation arise from their revenue, infant industry and employment effects. Historically, tariffs have often been imposed as a source of government revenue. Especially in an economy where self-sufficiency and barter are more common than monetary transactions, income and sales taxes are difficult to collect. Taxes on imports and exports, which typically pass through a small number of ports, are much more easily assessed and collected. Tariff revenues represented about 60 per cent of the Province of Canada's ordinary revenue in the 1850s and 1860s, and after 1867 they accounted for as much as 75 per cent of the federal government's income. Assuming the desirability of some government expenditure (e.g., on social overhead capital) and the inferiority of other sources of revenue (e.g., because of high collection costs), there is a strong case for the existence of tariffs in the nineteenth century. With increasing monetarization and improved administrative capabilities, other sources of revenue have become more important in the twentieth century, with tariff revenues falling to 40 per cent of the total in 1929 and less than 10 per cent since 1945.

In sum, the revenue aspect of tariffs was important in Canada at least until after the First World War, when the income tax was introduced. This is not to say that revenue was the motivation for *changes* in the tariff schedule. Revenue considerations may suggest a desired average tariff level or an emphasis on taxing imports with inelastic demand, as embodied in the fairly uniform 1847-1849 Canadian tariff which had higher rates on spirits. The tariff changes in 1858-1859 increased effective rates of protection with little impact on revenue, and the National Policy tariff of 1879 probably had the same effect. Thus, changes in Canadian commercial policy after 1850 did not yield revenue benefits.

Any restriction on imports provides protection to existing or potential domestic producers. In some cases the protective element of a tariff may be incidental to its revenue purpose (early Canadian tariffs on brandy, for example, were in practice no more than a sales tax, as there were no potential Canadian producers), but the level and especially the structure of tariffs are usually intended to grant some degree of protection against competing imports. One motive for granting protection is the "infant industry" argument. If learning-by-doing is important in an industry, a new firm may be unable to match established international competitors under a laissez-faire trade regime, even though the home country may have a potential comparative advantage in the product. If the infant industry is protected by a tariff, it may establish itself and become efficient, to the extent that the later benefits to society offset the gains from trade foregone in the short-run. This is to some degree a problem of capital or entrepreneurial deficiencies rather than of trade, because if the future benefits really do offset the short-run costs, then a foresightful entrepreneur with access to effective capital markets should undertake the project even under a laissez-faire system. Even allowing for these domestic distortions, tariff protection is not the best means of infant industry promotion; the tariff taxes consumers of the particular good in order to promote an industry with positive long-run social benefits. A more efficient policy would be for the government to subsidize the firm, thus tackling the problem at its production-side root without distorting consumption patterns. A subsidy has the added advantage of being more visible and more easily removable than a tariff; it is thus simpler to assess the cost of the policy, and there is less likelihood of protection surviving into the industry's adulthood. In practice, however, governments have found it politically and administratively easier to grant tariff protection than to subsidize infant industries; an interesting exception is the bounties granted to the Canadian iron and steel industry (chapter 6.7).

A related argument in favour of protection is often made for "senescent" industries. As comparative advantage patterns change, some previously competitive industries find it increasingly difficult to compete with imports, often with hardship to affected workers. If the adjustment problems appear severe—for example, if the industry is geographically concentrated in areas with few alternative employment opportunities— then the government may grant temporary tariff protection to lengthen and thus ease the adjustment process (although again a subsidy to affected workers or a retraining program would be preferable to a tariff). This argument has not had much relevance to Canada with its young and growing economy, although it has sometimes been applied where regional problems were severe and in the post-1945 era has become more common (e.g., the textiles industry's seeking protection from developing countries' exports).

The senescent industry argument suggests that tariffs can reduce redundancies in specific industries and hence regional unemployment. Trade restrictions can also be used at the macroeconomic level as an anti-unemployment policy. The ensuing reduction in imports increases aggregate demand for domestically produced goods and services, stimulating output and employment. The negative aspect of this method of reducing unemployment is that the reduction in imports is simultaneously a reduction in other countries' exports. In these countries the decreased demand for their products will lead to increased unemployment; that is, the initial unemployment is exported from the tariff-imposing country. A likely consequence is retaliation by the affected countries, who will raise their own tariffs to export their unemployment until the result is loss of the gains from trade and no net employment benefits. This is essentially what happened during the early 1930s. Before that time, Canada as a "small" country could hope to export her unemployment by trade restrictions without provoking widespread retaliation; but in the postwar era Canada is a more significant economic power, and such "inconsiderate" policies are under close international watch and approbation.

Other economic arguments in favour of tariff protection are fallacious; at most, tariffs are only second best (or worse) methods of achieving economic goals. It may, however, be accepted that tariffs involve economic costs but are desirable on other grounds. For example, trade in military goods is often restricted in order to encourage industries considered essential to national security. Other restrictions may aim to protect indigenous culture or morals: the regulation of U.S. magazines or TV broadcasts in Canada or prohibitions on importing pornographic literature. Such arguments are difficult for the economist to evaluate, although at least an attempt to assess the economic costs of imposing tariffs for non-economic objectives can be made.

The employment benefits from tariff increases have been viewed as a short-term goal. As seen above, this was a feasible and effective countercyclical policy for the Canadian government before the 1930s. The employment effects may help to explain why tariff increases were introduced at times of depressed economic activity, but they cannot explain the continuous retention of high tariffs.

The long-term goal of Canadian commercial policy has been the fostering of manufacturing industry. The theoretical case for infant industry protection was outlined above, and the empirical question centres on whether high ERPs did in fact bring new industries into existence. Examples can be found of infant industries emerging as a result of the Cayley–Galt and National Policy tariffs. It is not known whether the eventual economic benefits from these industries outweighed the loss of gains from trade during their infancy. Since the protective tariffs remained at high levels for much longer than normal expectations of maturity, it seems probable that the net economic effects were negative. In cases where firms became internationally competitive, they were shielded from competing imports and were able to exploit monopoly positions in the Canadian market. In other cases, inefficient firms could remain in business behind the protective tariff wall. The presumption of net economic costs from the protective tariff is generally accepted by supporters and opponents of the tariff policy alike. Supporters argue, however, that these costs are outweighed by the benefits of having a Canadian manufacturing sector. This position raises the questions of whether manufacturing industries would have developed in Canada without protection (as the agricultural machinery industry did) and whether there are superior government policies, such as subsidies, for achieving the same purpose. Canadian commercial policy has also been attacked on the grounds that the tariff increased regional inequality within Canada and protected manufacturing rather than Canadian manufacturers, exacerbating an undesirably high level of direct foreign investment.

The Costs of Protection

The welfare loss from a tariff on a good with an upward-sloping domestic supply curve is illustrated by Figure 5.1. In the absence of the tariff OE units are sold in Canada at a price P; of these, OA are produced in Canada and AE are imported. After imposition of the tariff, the Canadian price rises to P + T and sales fall to OC, of which OB are domestically produced and BC are imported. Consumers suffer a welfare loss from the increased price and reduced consumption. This loss in consumers' surplus can be measured by area I + II + III + IV. Other groups gain from the tariff in the form of increased prices received by domestic producers and the tariff revenue accruing to the government. The gains in producers' surplus and tariff revenue are represented by areas I and III respectively. The net result is a loss to society because those parts of the lost consumers' surplus represented by area II and IV are not offset by compensating gains to other members of society. These two welfare triangles, representing the

Figure 5.1
Static Welfare Loss from a Tariff

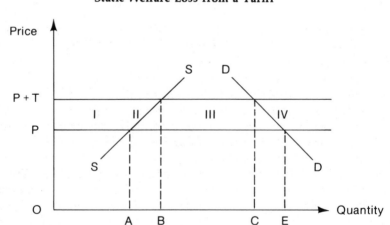

Note: P = price of competing imports before duty, T = tariff paid per unit imported, SS = Canadian domestic supply curve, DD = domestic demand curve.

cost of replacing more efficient foreign suppliers by domestic producers (II) and the cost of consumers' being unable to purchase units of the good which they would buy at price P but not at price P + T, are thus known as the deadweight loss from the tariff.

The different impact on various groups suggests why a tariff may be imposed despite the resulting net social cost. The losers—consumers—have had much weaker lobbying power than the gainers—producers and government. Figure 5.1 also illustrates why the government may justify a tariff as being in the national interest. Under the tariff both domestic production and government revenue are higher than they would have been in its absence. If either or both of these are desirable and if the cost of alternative policies is greater than the deadweight loss from the tariff, then the tariff can be justified. Finally, Figure 5.1 indicates why a subsidy is a superior means of promoting infant industries. Increased domestic production from OA to OB can be realized under free trade by a government subsidy equal to area II. The static welfare loss from this policy is less than the deadweight loss from the tariff by the value of area IV.

The size of the annual welfare loss due to tariff-induced resource misallocation had been estimated for 1956 by John Young (1967). He calculated the loss at $1 billion, or 4 per cent of GNP, using an approach similar to Figure 5.1. This approach ignores the further gains from specialization which are possible if economies of scale exist. Taking account of this further source of gain, Wonnacott and Wonnacott (1967) estimated the annual welfare loss at around 10 per cent of GNP during the early 1960s. In view of the higher levels of protection before World War II it is possible that the loss was even higher between 1859 and 1939. Since the loss recurred continuously, the total foregone welfare resulting from the tariff has been substantial.

It can be argued that the above analysis of the costs of the tariff does not tell the whole story because it is static, whereas the important economic forces are dynamic. A hypothesis concerning the long-term effects of the tariff on GNP has been propounded by Dales (1966). The essence of his argument is that, if the inflow of commodities is restricted by a tariff but factors of production can move freely into or out of the country, then extensive growth will be encouraged and intensive growth will be hindered. Dales' argument can be summarized as follows. The immediate effect of the tariff was a welfare loss and emigration to the United States in response to lower Canadian living standards. The existence of a protected industrial sector provided an incentive for increased investment, including an inflow of capital, to realize the potential profits. The increased demand for labour led to immigration, more than offsetting the initial emigration and consisting of people from lower income European countries (whose citizens' entry to the United States was restricted). Increased supplies of capital and labour led to faster extensive growth than would have existed with free trade, but was not accompanied by more rapid intensive growth (compared to the free trade situation). Three main forces hindered intensive growth: (1) the recurring static welfare loss discussed above; (2) the turnover of labour being associated with a lower quality of labour; (3) the higher ratio of capital costs to wages leading to less rapid scrapping of old equipment. Dales concludes that the full cost of the tariff in terms of foregone intensive growth has averaged 8 per cent per year and that the tariff can explain most of the U.S.-Canadian income differential once allowance has been made for the differing resource bases.

As evidence in support of his hypothesis Dales quotes the Canadian–U.S. ratios of several variables, primarily for the period 1926–1955. In the case of both GNP and population, the ratio increased, whereas for per capita GNP the ratio did not rise and perhaps even fell. Although Dales' hypothesis is consistent with these trends, an adequate test of the hypothesis would require more rigorous analysis of the relationships involved; Dales' treatment of labour movements has been particularly criticized. If Dales' hypothesis is accepted, then assessment of Canadian commercial policy requires a value judgement. Dales believes that the promotion of extensive growth at the expense of intensive growth was consciously pursued by the government as part of a "Big Canada" policy; was this emphasis on size at the expense of current living standards desirable or not?

In addition to its economy-wide costs, a high tariff can have adverse effects at the industry level. A recurring observation in studies of Canadian industries is that production costs are higher than they would be if current best practice technology were used. The cause appears to lie in the small domestic market, but the fundamental reason for the excess production costs is the tariff. The tariff has two implications in this context. Firstly, it *permits* inefficient production; without the tariff firms would have their price limit set by competing imports. Secondly, it *induces* behaviour which leads to inefficient production. By reducing and isolating the domestic market the tariff encourages an oligopolistic market structure (i.e., an industry with a small number of sellers) in which market shares are predetermined and price competition avoided. The situation is illustrated in Figure 5.2 for a good with an assumed Canadian market of 2000 units and a landed price for competing imports of $1. In the absence of a tariff there would have to be a single large plant to be competitive with imports (assuming transport costs are small), but with any ERP over 25 per cent there can be two Canadian firms with suboptimal plants each producing 1000 units. The two firms may tacitly agree to hold 50 per cent of the market each, rather than try to expand and inaugurate a mutually harmful price war. Eastman & Stykolt (1967) studied sixteen Canadian industries in the late 1950s and concluded that this model

Figure 5.2
Production Below the Minimum Efficient
Scale of Operations

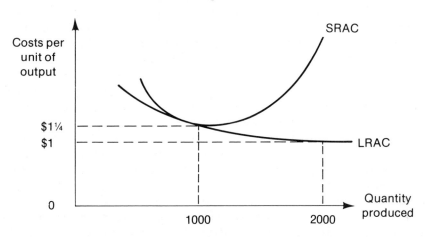

Note: LRAC = long-run average cost curve (assuming all inputs can be varied), SRAC = short-run cost curve (for a given plant).

explained their behaviour well. They argue that a reduction in protection would increase the Canadian market, facilitating the realization of scale economies, and it would also reduce the possibility of collusive behaviour to obstruct construction of plants of efficient scale. It should be noted that this is not necessarily an argument for free trade; the point is that if the Canadian tariff had been lower (but not necessarily zero) there would have been gains in productive efficiency. The high tariff also may have affected productive efficiency indirectly; if it encouraged direct foreign investment (see below) and the firms from an American industry all established plants in the smaller Canadian economy, then each Canadian branch plant may be a less efficient "miniature replica" of its American counterpart.

The Regional Impact of Canadian Commercial Policy

The costs and benefits of the tariff have not been shared equally by the various regions of Canada. The tariff structure since 1859 has been designed to protect the manufacturing sector concentrated in Ontario and Quebec. Since central Canada has consistently been the wealthiest part of the country, the sectoral bias of the tariff has adversely affected regional equity.

The major industry in the Maritimes—lumber—although deeply depressed in the 1880s, received no protection under the high tariff policy. It was expected that new protected industries would locate there to take advantage of proximity to Nova Scotian coal, but these hopes were not fulfilled. The coal could be shipped east during the summer and industrial entrepreneurs preferred the locational advantages of central Canada. The Nova Scotia coal industry itself had to face severe competition from U.S. coal in the Ontario market and had only intermittent tariff protection. The only clear Maritime beneficiaries of the tariff were the furniture and nail industries, which did not represent major sectors of the regional economy.

The main regional loser from the high tariff policy was the Prairies. Although they were hardly settled in 1859 or even in 1879, agrarian protest against Canadian commercial policy was soon heard, and the Prairies have remained opposed to a high tariff policy. The high ERP on manufactured goods means that Canadian farmers must pay more for their machinery and equipment than their U.S. competitors do. These higher production costs entail negative effective protection and put the Prairie farmers at a competitive disadvantage in export markets. The significance of the implement tariffs increased in the last two decades of the nineteenth century—just as Prairie settlement was accelerating. Until 1880 Canadian implement makers could outcompete U.S. producers. This changed in the 1880s, primarily because the increased efficiency of the U.S. iron and steel industry reduced input costs for U.S. manufacturers. Canadian firms remained competitive in Ontario, where the factories were located, but not in the Prairies. The deteriorating competitive position of Canadian producers was reflected in a series of increases in the tariff on agricultural machinery from 27 per cent in 1880 to 35 per cent in 1885 and 43 per cent in 1890. Although the tariff was cut back to 27 per cent in 1894 to appease agrarian discontent, it remained a high mark-up. Nevertheless, U.S. machines were still competitive in the Prairies, as revealed by the increase in farm machinery imports from $1.8 million in 1900 to $2.7 million in 1910, almost all of which went to the Prairie region. The implication is that machine prices in the Prairies would have been about one fifth lower in the absence of the tariff.

Three consequences of higher implement prices can be identified by comparing the actual situation in the Prairie economy with the situation which would have existed in the absence of the tariff. Firstly, the pace of settlement was slower. Marginal land which could have been profitably worked at lower input prices was not worth bringing into production. This illustrates the macroeconomic misallocation of resources; people stayed in the protected manufacturing sector of central Canada instead of moving west. Secondly, the higher costs of production imply a redistribution of income away from landowners and in favour of owners of other factors of production. Thirdly, techniques of production may have become more labour-intensive. The mechanization of agriculture was thus slower, because the real scarcity of capital was overstated, and labour productivity was reduced. Norrie (1974b) has estimated the magnitude of these effects under various assumptions about the production function and demand elasticity for Prairie wheat. He concludes that income redistribution within the Prairies was very important, but that there was not much loss of income to other regions. The final part of this conclusion seems implausible in view of the continued use of agricultural machinery, which involved either a transfer to Ontario producers or to government revenues in comparison with the no-tariff situation.

The regional bias of the tariff can be clarified in terms of Figure 5.1. Central Canada has been a net beneficiary because almost the entire gain in producer surplus has accrued to owners and workers there, while the loss in consumer surplus has been spread over the country. The Maritimes and British Columbia have received almost no benefits in increased producer surplus and hence little compensation for higher prices and loss of consumer surplus. The Prairies have actually lost some of their producer surplus because of the adverse effect of the tariff on the relative prices of inputs and outputs in wheat farming—and this in addition to their share of lost consumer surplus. A further regional bias, of unknown magnitude, arises from the unequal incidence of the consumption-side costs as a result of interregional trade diversion. In the absence of the tariff British Columbia would replace some of its imports from central Canada by imports from the Pacific states, and there would be similar trade reversion involving the Prairie provinces and the midwest states and the Atlantic provinces and New England. Canada's internal preferential trading arrangement leads to both trade creation and trade diversion; the burden of the latter is borne by western Canada and the Atlantic provinces, who purchase manufactured goods from a generally not least-cost supplier, whereas central Canada suffers little trade diversion as a result of the Canadian economic union. Thus, in the absence of heavy government redirection of its tariff revenues towards the disadvantaged regions, the net effect of Canadian commercial policy has been to exacerbate the economic disparities between central Canada and the less industrialized areas of the country.

This conclusion has been criticized on three points (Mackintosh, 1939, ch. 7A). Although the net benefits from the tariff may vary between regions in the short-run, interregional migration should ensure factor price equalization in the long-run. Secondly, since the tariff was imposed before the west was settled, the higher production costs due to the tariff would be accounted for in land prices and would not represent a redistribution from subsequent western settlers to other Canadians. Finally, the tariff revenues were primarily used to finance railways which benefitted western Canada and the Maritimes more than central Canada. The first two arguments assume idealized factor market conditions—perfectly mobile labour and a sophisticated efficient market for western land—while the third argument rests on an unsupported assertion. Mackintosh's arguments provide conditions under which the tariff may not have increased regional inequities in Canada, but the conditions do not appear applicable and the criticism of our conclusion is therefore not well-founded. The differential regional impact of a protectionist commercial policy today remains as true as ever, and the pressure for new trade restrictions in the 1970s and 1980s comes from Quebec and Ontario, while the western provinces favour free trade.

Commercial Policy and Foreign Investment

A salient feature of Canadian economic development since the mid-nineteenth century has been the large capital inflow. Table 4.8 showed the magnitude and timing of foreign investment in Canada, as well as its changing composition. The rapid inflow of foreign capital began during the high tariff regime of the late nineteenth century, and Canadian commercial policy was a causal factor, although not the only one.

The periods of rapid growth in foreign investment, e.g., the decades up to 1926 and the post-1945 years, are associated with economic booms in Canada rather than with variations in the tariff. It is especially true of portfolio investment that the level was strongly related to economic conditions in Canada and in the capital-exporting countries. For example, 1896 to 1913 were years of capital surplus in Britain, leading to low interest rates; while in Canada the high demand for financial capital, especially for railway construction, led to high interest rates. The floating of new Canadian issues in London and the willingness of British investors to purchase such issues depended on the interest rate differential (Meier, 1953, p. 7; Simon, 1970, p. 254). The Canadian tariff played little or no role in determining the flow of portfolio investment.

A noteworthy trend in the composition of foreign investment in Canada has been the declining importance of portfolio investment relative to direct investment. Moreover, it is the latter type of foreign capital which has recently been a cause of concern in Canada. Whereas the liabilities incurred by portfolio investment (bonds, debentures and non-controlling equity) involve no loss of sovereignty and can be liquidated by repayment, direct foreign investment creates a more permanent liability and implies loss of sovereignty insofar as decisions involving Canadian operations are taken elsewhere. With respect to the determination of direct foreign investment, the role of the tariff is not so clear as it was in the case of portfolio investment.

The level of direct foreign investment is related to the level of economic activity in Canada, as with portfolio investment, but the foreign producer faces a different decision than the purchaser of bonds, debentures, etc. Whereas the portfolio investor responds to improved Canadian economic conditions through the mechanism of higher interest rates, the foreign producer can respond either by increasing exports to Canada or by establishing production facilities in Canada (note that the decision may be more complicated if options such as licensing an existing Canadian producer exist). Thus, although a high tariff is not the sole or complete explanation of direct foreign investment, it may be important because it biasses foreign firms' choice of strategy in favour of branch-plant production in Canada rather than exporting to Canada. Exactly how important the tariff's effect on this decision has been is an empirical question which has not yet been adequately answered.

American corporations started to produce in Canada during the 1870s and 1880s, after Canada had adopted high ERPs. Among the early direct investors were Singer, Bell, Houston Electric (a forerunner of General Electric) and American Screw, and by 1890 there were some fifty U.S. branch operations in Canada. By 1912 the number had increased to two hundred and nine (Scheinberg, 1973). The phenomenon of U.S. direct investment in Canada had thus reached substantial proportions by the First World War, and in order to explain its genesis the preceding half century must be examined.

The specific reasons for U.S. direct investment in Canada varied from activity to activity, but the major incentives for U.S. firms to locate manufacturing establishments in Canada can be identified. (Investment in activities utilizing Canadian natural resources was less related to commercial policy and requires little explanation; for U.S. investment in mining and forest products see Wilkins (1970), pp. 137-9.) For a bulky product, requiring inputs available in Canada, it may make more sense to locate production near the Canadian markets rather than to produce solely in the United States and export to Canada. The "natural protection" provided by the transport costs of high bulk/value goods implies that, even without the tariff or other government policies, there would have been some direct foreign investment. A further stimulus to branch plant operations in Canada resulted from the Canadian Patent Acts of 1872 and 1903, which forced U.S. manufacturers either to produce in Canada or to allow a Canadian firm to produce their good under licence in order to qualify for patent protection. If a U.S. corporation followed neither of these paths, any new invention could be copied by Canadian producers— a situation which prevailed in the agricultural machinery industry until International Harvester established its Hamilton plant in 1903. A documented example of the significance of patent legislation concerns cream separators; the general manager of the leading U.S. producer (De Laval Separator Co.) testified before the U.S. Senate that the patent laws had driven De Laval to open a Canadian plant. All levels of Canadian government also offered direct incentives, in the form of tax concessions, free

land, etc., for U.S. firms to build Canadian branch plants; several munici-
palities were particularly vigorous in their attempts to lure branch plants,
leading to severe competition and bidding up the subsidies to the foreign
firm. In addition, Canadian commercial policy provided further reasons
for U.S. firms to establish Canadian operations. The tariff increased the
cost of foreign-produced goods, and where competing domestic producers
existed, foreign firms were placed at a disadvantage. An example of a
company which initially exported to Canada but finally established a
branch plant "because of the duty" is International Harvester; the quota-
tion is from the company's testimony before the U.S. Congress and is
interesting because, although International Harvester also had an incentive to produce in Canada in order to protect their patents, they specified
the Canadian tariff as the most important reason behind the decision.
The reintroduction of imperial preference just before the turn of the
century provided a further inducement for some U.S. firms to begin or
expand Canadian operations, because goods produced in Canada could
now sell at lower prices in the British Empire markets than could goods
produced in the United States. This is apparently the main reason why
Ford Motors established a Canadian branch in 1904.

The relative importance of the various incentives for U.S. firms to
undertake direct investment in Canada has not been established, but it
seems clear that Canadian commercial policy was a significant factor.
Some further evidence of the tariff's importance is provided by the reciprocity debate of 1911. When the U.S. government negotiated reciprocal
tariff cuts with the Laurier government, it was supported by the (U.S.)
National Association of Manufacturers, whose members wished to
increase their exports to Canada. The proposal was opposed by Canadian
manufacturers, and among the strongest opponents were the American
subsidiaries in Canada. The split between U.S. companies without
Canadian plants and those operating in Canada implies that the tariff was
significant to the foreign investment decision; the firms with Canadian
plants viewed reciprocity as a reduction in the advantage of producing in
Canada vis-à-vis exporting from the United States, and they wished to
prevent this change because they had already opted for the former
strategy. The defeat of reciprocity in the 1911 Canadian election was
followed by a rapid increase in the number of American companies establishing Canadian branches, especially during the years 1914 to 1919. The
behaviour of direct foreign investment between 1926 and 1939 also
suggests some significance for Canadian commercial policy. Although
the level of foreign investment was low during this period, a stimulus
was provided by the tariff increases of the early 1930s, and a response can
be observed in the annual foreign investment figures. In sum, Canadian
commercial policy appears to have been a reason for the establishment of
Canadian branches by U.S. corporations before 1939, but it was not the

only reason and we know neither the relative actual importance of the various reasons nor the course direct foreign investment would have taken under different commercial policies.

The Process of Tariff Determination

During the period when Canada has had an independent commercial policy, her government has adopted a restrictive trade regime. The main tool for restricting trade has been import duties, although non-tariff barriers have also existed (e.g., the provision in the Dominion Railway Act of 1900 that every railway receiving a national subsidy must use rails made in Canada) and have become increasingly significant as tariffs have been reduced since 1945. The high tariff policy has imposed costs on Canadians in the form of lower living standards and technical efficiency than would have existed under free trade. Further consequences of the government's commercial policy may include a higher turnover of population, increased regional inequality and greater direct foreign investment, as well as the establishment of infant industries and a larger economy than would have existed under free trade; whether these five effects were beneficial or not involves value judgements, although the Canadian consensus would probably be that the first two, and perhaps the third, were undesirable, while the last two effects were good. Assessment of the net benefit or cost of the high tariff, which involves weighing the importance of the various consequences, is also subjective. In fact, successive Canadian governments accepted the policy as desirable, and it is of interest to ask why they reached this decision.

There are two approaches to analyzing the process of tariff determination. One is to examine the motives of the government as it imposes the tariff. As was seen in the case of the Cayley–Galt tariff, it is unwise to rely on official policy statements, since they are often tailored for political ends. Thus, this approach requires deeper analysis, usually relying on private sources such as diaries, reminiscences, letters, etc. (which might also be written with a view towards currying public favour). The alternative approach is to work backwards and to deduce motivation from the tariff structure actually adopted. This approach was profitable with respect to the Cayley–Galt tariff because the tariff structure pointed so clearly to protection rather than revenue as the prime motive behind the tariff. It is also the approach which will be followed here. Since protection was the explicit aim of the 1879 tariff and the tariff structure remained fundamentally unchanged (although the tariff level rose), protection can be accepted as the major purpose of the tariff structure through the period from 1859 to 1939. The question to be answered, then, is why a protectionist policy was adopted.

Caves (1976) has analyzed the process of tariff determination in

Canada in terms of three models. According to the "National Policy" model the government, representing the will of the people or acting as leaders of the people, implemented a collective nationalist preference for extensive growth and industrialization. This accords with Sir John A. Macdonald's declared motive for the 1879 tariff: "No nation has arisen which had only agriculture as its industry. There must be a mixture of industries to bring out the national mind and national strength." A more cynical view of governments' motivation is that they act to maximize the probability of reelection. If consumers do not perceive the cost to them from tariffs (or the costs are too small to affect their voting behaviour) but owners and workers appreciate the gains to them from protection, then a government can attract votes from electors in various industries by granting protection to those industries. A third view of tariff formation is that the tariff structure does not represent any clear government plan; although there may be a general policy of high or low protection, individual tariff rates reflect the lobbying power of the various industrial pressure groups. Lower (1946, pp. 373-4) expressed this view in his description of the 1879 tariff as "a frank creation of vested manufacturing interests living on the bounty of government." Both the "Adding Machine" and "Interest Group" models have their foundations in the analysis accompanying Figure 5.1, which indicated that although trade restrictions incur a net static welfare loss this is accompanied by large welfare transfers between gainers and losers.

Caves tested the three models by examining the relationships between a number of industry characteristics and industries' effective rates of protection in 1963 (in the following assessment it is assumed that the tariff structure, but not its level, remained more or less constant during the century after 1859 so that the conclusions apply to the whole period of restrictive trade policy). Caves found that the most important variable in explaining the structure of effective protection was the existence of economies of scale, which were positively related to ERPs. There were also significant relationships between ERPs and value-added per worker, industrial concentration and transport costs, implying a tariff structure slanted in favour of industries with unskilled labour, little natural protection and no industrial concentration. Although the last point is ambiguous, Caves concludes that the results tend to fit the "Interest Group" model best and the "Adding Machine" model least.

The conclusion that the "Interest Group" model best describes the process of tariff determination in Canada is a rather strong interpretation of Caves' results. It is perhaps unnecessary to seek too strenuously for the best model, and in view of the bargaining and compromises involved in constructing a tariff schedule, elements of all three models may be reflected in the actual ERPs. A plausible argument might be that the government pursued a National Policy in the general outline of its commercial policy, but that many of the details were responses to lobbying or electoral considerations.

Commenting on Caves' article, Helleiner (1977) has argued that explanation of the historical tariff structure (as it existed by 1961) does not require a multivariate model, but that "unskilled-labour intensity is far and away the most significant variable in Canadian tariff structure" (p. 325). Using similar techniques to Caves and superior data (covering 87 manufacturing industries as opposed to the 29 to 35 industry observations employed by Caves), Helleiner found a significant negative relationship between wages per worker and ERPs and a significant positive relationship between market concentration and ERPs; the relationship between scale economies and ERPs was negative but not statistically significant. Helleiner's results imply that ERPs primarily reflect the degree of unskilled-labour intensity in an industry, with higher levels of protection where industry concentration enabled more effective lobbying. This conclusion appears more robust than that of Caves, but does not explain why Canadian governments have adopted protective tariffs favouring unskilled-labour-intensive industries. It may be that variants of the "National Policy" and "Adding Machine" models postulated by Caves are still relevant; if Canadian governments wished to promote broadly based industrialization, then unskilled-labour-intensive industries had to be protected or they would never have been established in Canada; and labour has the votes. A further point raised by Helleiner is that changes in Canadian rates of tariff protection since 1961 have not been significantly related to unskilled-labour intensity. This partly reflects an increased reliance on non-tariff barriers (e.g., "voluntary" export restraints and quotas for Canada's leading textile suppliers), but is also connected with an increased free-trade orientation of transnational corporations which are locating their unskilled-labour-intensive activities in low-wage countries. Thus, unlike the pre-1960 situation, where owners and workers were united in seeking protection for their industry, only in domestically owned industries (e.g., textiles and footwear) has this united protectionist front been retained into the 1970s.

Saunders (1980) has recently added weight to some of the conclusions reached by Caves and Helleiner. Using more recent data he found support for the negative relationship between foreign ownership and effective protection posited by Helleiner. He also found the expected negative relationships between ERPs and transport costs, the share of output exported and labour productivity relative to that in the United States. Saunders' most interesting finding is a significant positive relationship between seller concentration and ERPs when allowance is made for two-way causality. This is in contrast to Caves' results, which lump together both directions of causality, although it strengthens Caves' general conclusion about the "Interest Group" model best fitting the facts. A plausible explanation of the new finding is that a high ERP permits and induces less concentration as Eastman and Stykolt hypothesize, but more concentrated industries are better able to organize lobbying for protection.

Although recent research has shed some light on the previously unexplored question of tariff determination, the evidence remains inconclusive. It is clear, however, that the lobbying power of industrial interest groups was an important determining factor. Governments' claims to have acted purely in the public interest must be taken with a grain of salt, especially with respect to the determination of individual tariff rates. Nevertheless, whether the intent was to alter the general course of Canadian economic development or not, the commercial policy adopted by Canadian governments before World War II had a significant impact on that course.

2. Railway Policy

Because Canada is a large country, her transport network has always been extensive and important. For the fur trade the rivers were critical and, on the whole, adequate for transporting the low bulk/value staple. As wheat became the important staple export of the midwest and of Upper Canada, attempts were made to maintain the St. Lawrence's position as the main route to the Atlantic Ocean. In the face of competition from U.S. canals, the Canadian government invested in improving the St. Lawrence route by canal construction, which was completed in 1848. This was, however, far from the end of the government's financial involvement in subsidizing the construction of social overhead capital. With the coming of the railway, private enterprise was unable to construct a satisfactory rail network unaided. The government soon became involved, and railway subsidies were the major item of government expenditure during the second half of the nineteenth century. The analysis of government policy with respect to social overhead capital formation will be restricted to railway policy up to the 1920s, but the pattern then set was continued with later projects such as the creation of a national airline system, the TransCanada Highway and the St. Lawrence Seaway.

The Economic Issues

Before examining the Canadian government's railway policy we should identify the economic issues involved. In particular, it should be asked why the government felt a need to intervene directly in this sector of the economy at a time when the general government policy was one of nonintervention at the microeconomic level. The economic arguments in favour of government intervention are, firstly, that capital market imperfections made it difficult to raise finance privately for railway projects and, secondly, that the social benefits from railways exceeded the private benefits to their owners.

Transport projects are by their nature often indivisible (e.g., a railway line from Quebec City to Montreal has considerably greater economic value than one stopping ten miles short of Montreal). Their durability means that the revenue will accrue over a long period and may thus be miscalculated. Railway technology involved a large initial financial commitment with the prospect of long-term and perhaps risky future gains. These considerations were intensified in Canada by the long distances and the small size of the nineteenth-century economy. The capital required for railway construction was far in excess of domestic availability, and Canadian entrepreneurs were unable to raise foreign loans in sufficient amounts. If the railways were to be built, it was necessary for the government either to provide finance directly or to offer guarantees to foreign investors in Canadian railways.

The costs and benefits to society from a project frequently diverge from the net gains accruing to the private investors. Where social costs exceed private costs (e.g., when a factory exhales smoke into the clean air at zero cost to the factory owner) there is a case for government intervention in the form of taxation or other controls. Conversely, where social benefits exceed private benefits, there will be insufficient incentive for private entrepreneurs to operate at the socially desirable scale, and the potential net social benefits of a larger output will be unrealized. The nineteenth-century Canadian railways appear to be a case of net social benefits exceeding net private benefits, thereby justifying government subsidies. The economic arguments in support of this concern the direct effects and linkages of the railways.

Technical change is defined as a reduction in the inputs required to produce a given output. In the case of a transport innovation there is a shift in the production function for transport services, causing a reduction in the real cost of transport services. The resource-saving should be measured not just by the reduction in transport costs on existing traffic; the induced expansion of activities in which transport costs are significant should also be taken into account. The gain to society from the reduced transport costs can be measured by the increase in consumers' surplus, i.e., the difference between the consumers' surplus before and after the railway (area ABCD in Figure 5.3). The increased consumers' surplus could accrue to the railway company, if it could practise discriminatory pricing and charge each additional customer a different rate. If the company cannot discriminate and charges all rail-users a standard rate (P_2 in Figure 5.3), then the consumers' surplus accrues to the users and not to the owners, in which case the social benefit from the railway exceeds the private benefit. The divergence between the private and social benefits from reduced transport costs could be expected to have been large with respect to some railways, especially west of Lake Superior, because the reduction in price and the expansion of quantity (resulting from increased settlement in regions newly served by adequate transport facilities) were substantial.

Figure 5.3
The Increase in Consumers' Surplus
Due to Reduced Freight Rates

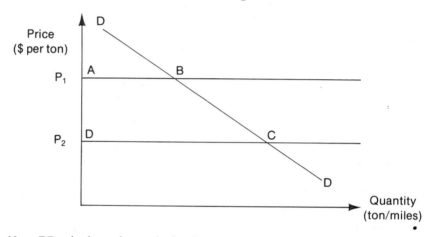

Note: DD = the demand curve for freight transportation, P_1 = the rate before the railway, P_2 = the rate charged by the railway.

The above analysis of the direct effects of railway construction is reminiscent of our earlier analysis of the welfare gains from tariff reduction (based on Figure 5.1), and transport improvements can be viewed as reducing the natural protection afforded to regions; the reduced natural protection encourages interregional specialization with gains in overall efficiency. In addition, transport improvements help to promote urbanization in order to realize gains from agglomeration. These effects, including the direct effects, could be grouped in the category of forward linkages, since they all result from the reduction in the price of transport services as an input. The railways also had backward linkages, for example, to the lumber, coal, iron and steel and engineering industries. In general, the stimulating effect of the railway's demand for inputs was not as great in Canada as in some countries (e.g., Britain and Germany), because at least before 1900 many inputs were imported; but it was still important for some industries. Additionally, the employment generated by railway construction had multiplier effects, which were felt in increased demand for the whole range of manufactured goods. The supply-side linkages are less definite than the increased demand for goods via forward, backward and final-demand linkages, but for the large railway projects the induced increase in labour, capital and entrepreneurship in Canada may have been significant. Capital and labour undoubtedly entered Canada to finance and to build railways, but in order to ascribe the increments as supply-side linkages of the railways we need to answer questions about the rate of factor growth without the railways (for example, was any Canadian capital crowded out by foreign capital? would Irish labourers still have emigrated to Canada in the absence of the railways?). Induced increases in the amount of entrepreneurship in Canada are even more difficult to measure. "Learning by doing" in railways may have improved management techniques and business organization methods, as well as providing a training ground for future industrial entrepreneurs; such gains in entrepreneurship may have been an important effect of railroads in the United States, but Canada had the alternative of borrowing new techniques and organizational forms from the United States instead of having to rediscover them.

Two noteworthy points about the linkage effects are that, in view of the size of railway projects, they were probably large and only a small proportion of them profited the railway owners directly. Given that economic growth, diversification and industrial development were government objectives, the linkages yielded social benefits in excess of the private benefits to the railway owners. In the absence of government intervention there was thus insufficient incentive for construction of the socially optimum mileage.

In addition to the economic benefits, the political benefits from some railways may also be important, even though they are difficult or even impossible to quantify. For example, an important argument for government support of the first transCanada railway was the political need to link the distant components of Canada after the accession of British Columbia in 1871. It is difficult for an economist to evaluate this argument; we can, however, try to estimate the economic cost to society of realizing the political benefits.

Even if the government is able to ensure that the socially optimum railway mileage is constructed, there remains a problem of price determination. A railway often forms a natural monopoly in that its users have no serious alternative. The profit-maximizing behaviour of the monopolist is to practise discriminatory pricing, charging each customer as much as they are prepared to pay so that the consumers' surplus accrues to the monopolist. If the monopolist cannot discriminate, he will maximize his profits by charging a higher price and selling a smaller output than would be the case in a competitive market. The higher price and lower output represent a welfare loss to society (similar to area IV in Figure 5.1). This is the background to the rate disputes between the Canadian Pacific Railway and the Prairie provinces, whose governments tried to force the company to charge lower rates and use its track more intensively.

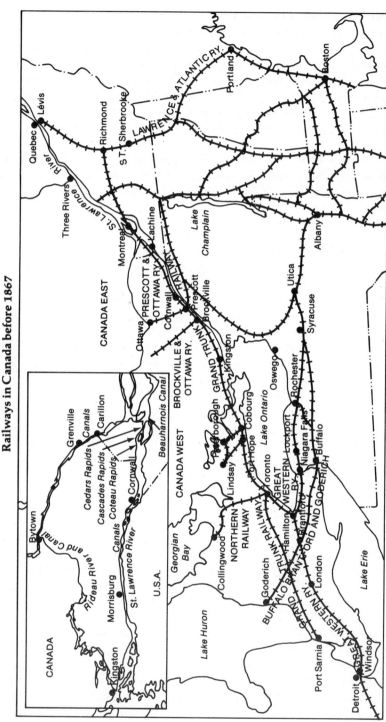

Map 6
Railways in Canada before 1867

Source: From J.M.S. Careless, *The Union of the Canadas, 1867*, p. xvi. Reprinted by permission of McClelland and Stewart Limited, Toronto.

Railways before Confederation

With the benefit of hindsight it can be seen that railways were important for Canadian economic development, but at the time when the new technology became available Canada was very slow to adopt it. Railway construction had taken place in Britain and parts of continental Europe during the 1830s and 1840s. Railway building was even more extensive in Canada's southern neighbour; U.S. railway mileage reached 3,000 in 1840 and 9,000 miles in 1850. British North America had 66 miles of track in 1850.

The slowness of Canadian railway construction was primarily due to the geography of the colonies. Since most of the population was scattered along the St. Lawrence–Great Lakes waterway, the presence of an alternative transport network reduced the advantages of railways. For example, even after Toronto and Montreal were connected by railway, freight rates between the two towns remained lower by water. Until 1848 the Canadian government's interest and construction activity were concentrated on canalization projects, and hence the government support necessary to make the major railways feasible was not forthcoming. Although several railway companies were chartered during the 1830s and 1840s, there was little important construction, and the lines which were built were of the "portage" type to overcome difficult sections of the waterways (e.g., the Montreal–Lachine line built in 1847).

Three major railway projects were planned during the 1840s: the St. Lawrence and Atlantic between Montreal and Portland, Maine (providing access to a winter port for exports using the St. Lawrence route); the Northern Railway between Toronto and the Georgian Bay; and the Great Western between Niagara and Windsor. All three railways had started construction by 1849 but were in serious financial difficulties. Their appeals to the government for assistance led to the first Canadian government participation in railway schemes. By the Guarantee Act of 1849 the government would under certain conditions guarantee the interest at 6 per cent on half of the bonds on any railway over seventy-five miles in length, provided that half the railway had already been built. The guarantee was important because investors were more willing to purchase government bonds (which, in effect, half of a railway's bonds now became) than bonds issued by a private company. The combination of government guarantees and good economic conditions led to rapid construction of railways in the early 1850s. Among the completed lines were the three above-mentioned projects, all of which had been eligible for assistance under the Guarantee Act. The new lines did not, however, represent any fundamental change in Canada's transport network. For the most part they were adjuncts to the waterway system acting as feeders to the Great Lakes or the St. Lawrence, or in the case of the St. Lawrence and Atlantic providing winter access to the ocean. The Great

Western was financed primarily by U.S. capital and was built to fit in with the United States, rather than the Canadian, rail network; for a time it was part of the only direct Chicago–New York route.

Although the canals of the 1830s and 1840s and the railways built in the early 1850s had improved the St. Lawrence route from the Great Lakes to the Atlantic, competition from the American railway system threatened to replace the St. Lawrence route by alternatives. Especially important was the Ogdensburg Railroad, completed in 1850, which linked Boston with the St. Lawrence just above Montreal. Just as the Erie Canal in the 1820s had diverted much of the midwest and Lake Erie traffic from Montreal to New York, the Ogdensburg Railroad now threatened to divert the Lake Ontario and Ottawa Valley traffic to Boston. This threat, combined with the old dream of directing midwest exports through Canada, led to plans for a trunk railway from the Detroit River to the Atlantic Ocean. The obvious solution was to link the Great Western to Montreal and then use the St. Lawrence and Atlantic line to Portland. The Maritime colonies, however, wanted the Atlantic terminus to be Halifax, and to that end they obtained British backing, in the form of interest guarantees, for the European and North American Railroad linking the Great Western and Halifax. The initial optimism raised by British support was short-lived, and when the British government tied its approval to a route which was unacceptable to the New Brunswick government, the project collapsed.

Although the Canadian government abandoned its part of the Quebec City–Halifax line when the European and North American negotiations broke down, it decided to go ahead with a Hamilton–Quebec City line and in 1853 granted the charter to the Grand Trunk Railway Company of Canada. With initial capital requirements set at £9.5 million, this was the largest single investment project yet undertaken in Canada. Since capital of this magnitude could not be raised domestically, the problem was how to attract British investors. The Canadian government guaranteed one quarter of the shares and bonds, but this support was insufficient. By 1855 the company could not meet its interest payments on bonds already sold, and its new issues were unmarketable. It turned to the Canadian government for financial assistance, which was granted continually. By 1867 the company's debt to the government was over $26 million, which was de facto the size of the government subsidy because there was no prospect of repayment.

Why was the Grand Trunk project a fiasco? The main reason was that costs were far higher than anticipated. The size of the project, relative to the size of the Canadian economy, itself affected factor market equilibria. This was not so important with respect to material inputs such as rails and rolling stock, which could be imported, but the increased demand for unskilled labour was a prime cause of the 40 per cent increase in wage rates between 1853 and 1854. External events led to an even tighter labour market in 1855 and 1856. The Crimean War pushed up world wheat prices, thus attracting more labour into the Ontario agricultural sector and increasing the opportunity cost of railway labourers. Further unanticipated costs arose from the decision to build the Grand Trunk to Sarnia rather than to Hamilton. The railway committee of the Canadian legislature advised against this plan, but it was overruled by the Minister of Finance, and the contract was awarded to a firm involving some prominent Canadians, who all made sizable fortunes from it. By 1860 the Sarnia–Portland line was in use, but the Grand Trunk's problems were not over. Running costs were higher than expected and revenues lower, because the company did not beat the competition; between Toronto and Montreal freight rates remained lowest by water ($2-3 per ton mile against $3.50 by rail), while farther west the Great Western had better connections to Detroit and Chicago and the U.S. lines took most of the midwest trade, leaving little traffic for the Grand Trunk.

The total financial aid granted by the government of the Province of Canada under the Guarantee Act and to the Grand Trunk was some $33 million. A further source of government aid was the municipalities, which were empowered in 1852 to raise money for railways with the backing of the provincial government. Many municipalities were energetic in this area because they were convinced of the importance of a railway for local prosperity. In consequence many feeder lines were constructed during the mid-1850s, but the municipalities were often excessively optimistic over the economic viability of the lines. The 1857 depression was accompanied by default on loans and the whole scheme eventually had to be taken over by the provincial government, adding a further $3 million to its debt.

Was government assistance to the railways money well spent? The answer of private investors was a resounding no. By 1865 Great Western shares stood at 65 per cent of their par value, while Grand Trunk shares were selling in London for 22 per cent of their par value. Evaluation of the social costs and benefits is more difficult. Government assistance helped to ensure that two thousand miles of railways were built during the 1850s, and undoubtedly the social returns from the pre-Confederation railways were greater than was indicated by private returns. In addition, the government had achieved its national objective of a trunk line from the Detroit River to the Atlantic. On the other side of the social balance sheet, the railways had incurred large costs to private investors and to the Canadian government, as well as unquantifiable costs such as the damage to Canada's London credit rating caused by the Grand Trunk affair. Although we can identify the major considerations, we do not have the information to determine whether the net social cost or benefit reinforces or reverses the private investors' view. An ideal study would evaluate the desirability of a subsidy for each part of the railway network, and also for potential but unbuilt rail links, in order to determine whether the government encouraged the optimum railway mileage. Abstracting from the optimum mileage issue, it is clear that the benefits from the pre-Confederation railway network could have been achieved at lower cost (e.g., by not building the Grand Trunk line to Sarnia) and therefore some of the government assistance was unjustified. In sum, it is difficult to assess whether the government railway policy encouraged the optimum mileage of track or yielded net social benefits on the track actually constructed, but it is certain that the policy was poorly implemented insofar as the subsidy was larger than that required to ensure the construction of the actual network.

Linking the New Nation

In the two decades following Confederation, government railway policy was dominated by two projects whose purpose was to bring together the separate colonies which had become Canada. The Maritimes–Quebec link was provided by the Intercolonial Railway, completed in 1876, and the railway from central Canada to the Pacific Ocean was finished in 1885. Both projects were politically motivated and there was no doubt that they would require government subsidies, but as with the earlier railways the questions of economic costs and benefits and of the appropriateness of the actual subsidies' size can still be asked.

By 1867 the Grand Trunk's eastern terminus was at Rivière du Loup, five hundred miles from the western end of Nova Scotia's Halifax–Truro railway, and there were no plans by private companies to bridge this gap. The British North America Act stated that a railway was to be built between Quebec and the Maritimes but did not specify the route. As in 1851–1852 the conflict was between military security, which implied an all-Canadian route following the St. Lawrence River, and commercial considerations, which pointed to a shorter route cutting across Maine. New Brunswick favoured the second alternative as the St. Lawrence route would pass far north of Saint John, but with British support the Canadian government decided upon the northern route. Construction began in December 1868 and was finished in July 1876, at a cost of over $34 million, financed by the federal government with British guarantees. Care was taken to build a railway which would last with low maintenance costs, and the result of ambitious construction standards was a large bill.

Choice of the northern route meant that the Intercolonial would never be an economic success. From the start it faced competition from water transport, which followed a similar route offering lower rates for bulky items, and from the Montreal–Portland railway (formerly the St. Lawrence and Atlantic, now owned by the Grand Trunk) which took goods to tidewater by a shorter route. Later railways, in particular the Canadian Pacific's short route from Montreal to Saint John through

Maine and the Quebec City–Moncton line built by the federal government for the Grand Trunk in the early twentieth century, attracted
further traffic away from the Intercolonial's circuitous route.

**Map 7
Montreal and Rail Routes to the Sea**

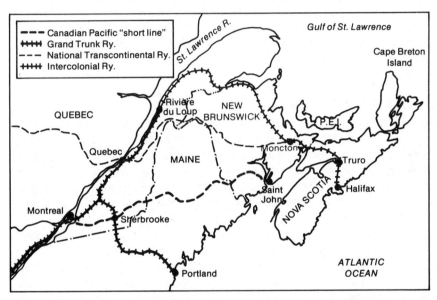

Source: From R.F. Legget, *Railways of Canada*, David and Charles, Newton Abbot, Devon,
England, 1973, p. 38.

The security considerations behind the choice of route were soon
proven to have been overrated as the possibility of open conflict between
Canada and the United States receded. Even the political gain appears to
have been overestimated. The Maritimes saw the railway link as a means
to improving their economic position by opening up coal and lumber
markets in central Canada, which would provide a sounder economic
basis for political union. This did not happen to any great extent, and if
anything, the railway may have contributed to wider economic disparities
by exposing Maritimes industries to competition from central Canada.
Still, it is difficult to deny that there was some gain in political unity from
the construction of an all-Canadian railway link between the Maritimes
and central Canada.

In British Columbia's accession treaty of 1871 the Canadian government undertook to have a railway from central Canada to the Pacific
Ocean started within two years and finished within ten years. The
Macdonald government determined that the railway should be built by a
private company, although it was clear that a subsidy would be offered. In

December 1871 Hugh Allan, a Quebec businessman, with the backing of the Northern Pacific Railroad submitted a proposal to build the railway. Allan's proposal was opposed by Ontario interests who wanted the eastern terminus to be Toronto. The government tried to conciliate the rival interests, and after the August 1872 election Macdonald granted a charter to the Canadian Pacific Railway Company, which included both Ontario and Quebec interests under Allan's presidency. The government offered a subsidy of $30 million plus a land grant of 50 million acres; after its experience with the Grand Trunk, the government now preferred a fixed sum grant of money and land to a long-term commitment in the form of interest guarantees. Macdonald's motive was to keep the project in Canadian hands, and the Ontarians were bought over, although Montreal remained the eastern terminus, while U.S. interests were excluded. Macdonald's plan failed, however, because when Allan agreed to it his American backers publicized letters from him concerning the provision of Conservative election expenses. The revelation that Allan had used funds from the Northern Pacific Railroad to help Macdonald's reelection led to a political scandal and the fall of the Conservative government in November 1873. Shortly afterwards, the CPR consortium gave up its charter.

Unable to find a private company to take over the charter, Mackenzie's Liberal government decided to build the railway itself. As with the Intercolonial Railway, public construction had become the only option if the government were to meet its political objectives, and in no way represented a philosophical shift in favour of public rather than private ownership (Glazebrook, 1964, p. 61). Progress was slow and cautious, as the government tried to avoid large expenses in any single year. It soon became clear that public construction would not meet the original deadline, and the terms of union with British Columbia were revised to postpone the completion date until 1890.

Upon returning to power in 1878, Macdonald restated his policy of private construction. For two years there were no bidders—presumably reflecting the difficulty of raising the capital and/or that anticipated profits were too low given the riskiness of the project. In 1880, however, a syndicate was put together which agreed to build the railway. The main terms of the CPR contract were: (1) the government gave a direct subsidy of $25 million cash and 25 million acres of land; (2) the sections already built by the government or under contract (which would be built at government expense) were donated free to the CPR; this involved over 700 miles of track costing some $38 million; (3) all materials required for construction or operation of the CPR were to be exempt from taxation; all imported construction materials would be duty-free, and CPR land would not be taxed for twenty years unless sold or occupied; (4) there would be no government regulation of freight rates until the CPR was making 10 per cent return on capital; (5) construction of any competing railway south of the CPR was prohibited for twenty years; (6) capitalization was set at $25 million and the CPR could offer bonds up to that amount on the security of the land grant; (7) the line from northern Ontario to the Pacific Ocean was to be completed by May 1891.

The contract succeeded in fulfilling the main government aim: the railway was built, and well ahead of schedule. The golden spike was hammered in on 7 November 1885. Although the CPR may have been politically indispensible for Canadian unity, there are two questions which economists should ask: (a) Was the government subsidy appropriate, in the sense of being just sufficient to encourage a private company to build the line? and (b) Can the subsidy be justified on economic grounds?

If the railway were to be built, the "appropriate" subsidy was clearly greater than zero. The events of the 1870s showed that there was no clamour of private companies seeking the charter, even when government support was promised. The two offers of 1872 and 1880 have been used as evidence that the terms of the 1880 contract were not unduly favourable to the CPR Company because the cash and land grant amounted to less than the 1872 offer (Easterbrook & Aitken, 1956, p. 429), implying that the actual subsidy was not excessive. This comparison is, however, invalid, because the 1880 contract contained far more than the cash and land grant. The relevant yardstick for measuring the "appropriate" subsidy is the difference between the private rate of return on capital invested in the CPR and the market rate of return on comparable projects. A subsidy which increased the private rate of return above the market rate would be excessive and an unjustified use of public funds.

The Company has consistently argued that the actual subsidy was necessary. In its submission to the 1949 Royal Commission on Transportation the CPR estimated the average annual rate of return on its assets to have been 3 per cent during its first decade of operation, 1886–1895. The CPR is not an unbiassed observer, and by calculating the return on the book value of its assets it understated the rate of return on the actual investment. George (1968) estimated the return on capital actually put into the project at over 3 per cent, but still well below the market rate of return for the period of 6 per cent to 10 per cent (depending on the degree of risk). George calculated that the subsidy required to bring the private rate of return up to 6 per cent would have been a lump sum in 1885 of $68 million, and to yield a 10 per cent return the required subsidy would have been $81 million.

In order to compare the actual subsidy to the required subsidy it is necessary to discount future benefits under the contract to express the subsidy as an 1885 lump sum. The calculated present value in 1885 will depend on the choice of discount rate, for which the appropriate range is the possible values of the opportunity cost of capital (i.e., 6 to 10 per cent). George estimated the 1885 value of the actual subsidy to lie between $121 million (at a 10 per cent discount rate) and $146 million (at a 6 per cent discount rate). The components of his calculated subsidy, in order of importance, are the gift of government-built track, the land grant, the cash grant (the order of these two items is reversed at the higher discount rate), the tax exemption and import duty remission. George's calculations omit terms of the contract which are difficult to quantify, e.g., the monopoly clause (item 5) and freedom from rate regulation (item 4), although these items were of pecuniary benefit to the CPR. Even with this downward bias George's estimates imply that the actual subsidy was higher than that required to guarantee a market rate of return on the private capital invested in the CPR. Moreover, the amount by which the actual subsidy exceeded the required subsidy was large (Table 5.3); at the normal rate of return of 6 per cent the actual subsidy was twice as large as was necessary, and even making a substantial allowance for risk the actual subsidy was 50 per cent too high. We should not place too much emphasis on the precise figures in Table 5.3, or on George's claim that these are lower bound estimates of the excess. Mercer (1975) has produced an alternative set of estimates suggesting a much smaller excess, although confirming that a subsidy was essential if the railway were to be made privately profitable. Thus, George's qualitative conclusion stands: even if the railway were indispensable on political grounds and a subsidy was necessary to ensure its completion, the government's actual subsidy to the CPR was unjustifiably large.

Table 5.3
"Required" and Actual Subsidy to the Canadian Pacific Railway
(1885 value in million dollars)

	Opportunity Cost of Capital	
	6%	10%
"Required" subsidy	68	81
Actual subsidy	146	121
Excess	77	40

Source: George (1968). Figures in column 1 do not add up because of rounding.

The question of whether an appropriate-sized subsidy to the CPR could be justified on economic grounds is more difficult to answer. The subsidy would be justified economically if the social return were greater than the social return on alternative uses of the government funds. It has generally been assumed that this was the case, because of the size of the reduction in transport costs from the Prairies and the increase in traffic (compare Figure 5.3). Although this assumption is plausible, it does not have very firm foundations and appears to derive largely from the staple theory's emphasis on the CPR as a prerequisite for the wheat boom (cf. chapter 3.1). In principle, alternative systems could have provided the transport services provided by the CPR (e.g., a water-cum-rail network or branch lines to U.S. railroads). Evaluation of the economic justifiability of subsidizing the CPR would have to compare the cost-effectiveness of these alternatives, in addition to estimating the impact of reduced transport costs on western settlement and the benefits therefrom. Such an evaluation has not yet been attempted, perhaps because the conceptual and data problems are large, but more likely because the question of economic justification is of little interest when the overriding raison d'être of the CPR was political.

Railway Policy, 1885–1923

The Canadian Pacific Railway affected the subsequent development of the rail network throughout Canada. Although the CPR charter concerned a line from northern Ontario to the Pacific coast, it also empowered the CPR to operate in central and eastern Canada. The 1880s saw a rapid expansion of CPR interests in central and eastern Canada both by acquisition and by construction. This expansion inevitably led to competition with the Grand Trunk. The two companies built new lines and absorbed smaller companies, until they controlled most of the railway mileage in the region. Honours in the competitive struggle were about even, with the Grand Trunk's established position and superior network offsetting the Canadian Pacific's greater political influence.

In the Prairies the CPR faced no competition from other railways but ran into conflict with the Manitoba government. The latter had welcomed the transcontinental railway, but not the monopoly clause. As early as 1880, and frequently thereafter, the Manitoba government chartered railways which would link with U.S. trunk lines, creating competition with the intention of forcing a reduction in CPR rates. The CPR opposed these plans and appealed to the federal government, which vetoed the charters. There was some justice in the Manitoba government's case insofar as rates were much higher in the Prairies than farther east (e.g., the CPR charged 34¢ per 100 lbs for the 398 miles from Moose Jaw to Winnipeg, while the rate between Brantford and Montreal, 403 miles, was 17½¢ per 100 lbs.), although the CPR argued that real costs were higher in the Prairies. Comparison was also made with rates in the western states, although Norrie (1978, pp. 16–22) argues that these do not support the Prairies' claim that their freight rates were artificially high.

In 1888 the CPR ran into financial difficulties and requested government assistance in raising money. The federal government agreed to guarantee the interest on a $15 million loan, on condition that the CPR accepted the repeal of the monopoly clause. The agreement meant that the federal government ceased to veto Manitoba railway charters, and this was an apparent victory for the Manitoba government. The Northern Pacific now built lines into Manitoba, but rates did not fall because the two companies preferred to fix rates rather than to have a price war. Only with the Crow's Nest Pass Agreement of 1897, when the CPR received further government assistance in return for a general rate reduction, did the Manitoba government succeed in achieving lower rates. The Crow's Nest Pass Agreement, with later amendments, has remained the basis of rail rates for grain traffic, although freight rates continued to be a bone of contention between the Prairie provinces and Ottawa during the twentieth century. The CPR, on the other hand, gained its objective in 1888, and despite its formal renunciation of the monopoly clause, it retained a practical monopoly on trunk traffic in the west until the 1900s.

The pressures on the CPR's western monopoly increased with the wheat boom. The considerations facing a potential transcontinental railway builder in 1900 were quite different from those in the 1870s. Much of the unwillingness of private entrepreneurs to undertake the project in the 1870s had stemmed from uncertainties about the Prairie environment, but the construction of the CPR had revealed that the risks and construction difficulties had been overestimated. In addition, the CPR's profitability by the late 1890s indicated the gains that could be made from Prairie rail traffic. The wheat boom led to a rapid increase in the demand for rail services in the Prairies during the early 1900s. Although the CPR widened its network, more track was needed, especially as the frontier of settlement moved northward. In this situation other railway companies became eager to tap this market by building trunk lines across the Prairies—in particular, the Grand Trunk, which wanted to extend its network westwards, and the Canadian Northern, which had been established by the amalgamation of two Manitoba railways in 1899 and had taken over the Northern Pacific's Manitoba network in 1901 to become Canada's third largest railway.

The Laurier government's initial policy was to try to bring the Canadian Northern and the Grand Trunk into a national plan, whereby the latter would remain in the east and the former in the west. Negotiations were held in 1902–1903, but they broke down. One reason for the failure of negotiations was that each railway company had its own ambitions, and both had autocratic managers. Nevertheless, the government was at fault in bringing insufficient pressure to bear on the companies and abandoning its plan too early. The consequence was a disastrous government policy under which two new transcontinental railways were built within twelve years, both with considerable assistance from public funds.

In 1903 the government entered into negotiations with the Grand Trunk over the construction of a second transcontinental railway. Agreement was soon reached on the route and terms. The western section from Winnipeg to Prince Rupert was to be built by the Grand Trunk Pacific Railway. The government guaranteed GTPR bonds up to $13,000 per mile across the Prairies and up to three quarters of the actual cost per mile of the remainder of the route, and agreed to pay the interest on these bonds for seven years. The eastern section from Winnipeg to Moncton was to be built by the government and then leased to the GTPR, rent free for three years and at 3 per cent of construction costs after that. The western section was completed in 1913 and the eastern section in the following year, but the GTPR refused to lease the latter because the construction costs came to $160 million instead of the estimated $60 million (partly because the government's standards were unnecessarily high).

The Canadian Northern put together a third transcontinental line during the wheat boom. In addition to its extensive Manitoba network, it had a Winnipeg–Edmonton trunk line and an Ottawa–Quebec City line in 1905. By 1915 the remaining sections of a Vancouver–Quebec City route had been completed. As with the GTPR, the construction of the Canadian Northern's transcontinental line received considerable government aid. The cash grants from the federal and various provincial governments amounted to just under $29 million. The Canadian Northern also received land grants of some 6½ million acres, because several of its charters had first been granted before the abolition of land grants in 1894. Finally, between 1903 and 1914 the federal government guaranteed $105 million in bonds, provincial governments guaranteed $130 million and Nova Scotia made a $5 million loan, all of which meant that the Canadian Northern had no problem raising funds before World War I.

By 1915 Canada thus had three transcontinental railways. Although conceivably there were grounds for a second line, there was no justification for a third. It was also clear which of the three was the most viable. The CPR had been making a large operating surplus for some years and derived further income from its land sales. Moreover, since it had been financed by grants and the sale of shares, the CPR had little fixed interest burden. In contrast, the GTPR and the Canadian Northern were both essentially incomplete; the former had few branch lines in the west to bring traffic to its trunk line, while the latter had low-grade track which already needed improvements. Both the GTPR and the Canadian Northern had financed their transcontinental lines by bond sales, which imposed fixed interest obligations.

With the outbreak of war in 1914, immigration ceased and the growth in demand for western rail services declined. The GTPR and Canadian Northern immediately experienced financial difficulties and requested government aid, which was granted. A further request in 1916 was met with temporary aid, and a commission was established to examine the situation. Since the government had decided that the two railways should not be allowed to go bankrupt (to protect small investors in the companies and Canada's credit rating abroad) and that lines already built should be kept in operation, the magnitude of the companies' financial straits implied such heavy government involvement that there was no serious alternative to nationalization. The Canadian Northern was taken over in 1917 and the GTPR in 1920, but the final consolidation of the Grand Trunk parent company into Canadian National Railways was delayed until January 1923 by long haggling over the price. The Canadian National was born of necessity, arising from misguided previous policies, rather than being part of any positive move towards public ownership.

Conclusions

Government railway policy follows a remarkably constant pattern between 1850 and 1914. Few railway projects in Canada would have been undertaken without government assistance. Although the government was rarely involved in direct construction activity (as it had been in the building of the St. Lawrence canals), it became financially involved in railway projects on a large scale after 1849, and this was by far the largest item of government expenditure until World War I. The railway policy was successful insofar as the major trunk routes were completed: the Grand Trunk in 1860, the Intercolonial linking Halifax to the Grand Trunk in 1876 and the Canadian Pacific in 1885. These projects were primarily supported for political reasons of national unity, and whether they were economically justified or not is uncertain. If they were beneficial to economic development, as at least the CPR probably was, then the government's willingness to subsidize social overhead capital formation in this way was a positive factor in Canadian economic development.

Evaluation of the appropriateness of the size of the subsidy is more firmly based and must be negative. The assistance granted by the government was consistently greater than was necessary to achieve its objectives. The older view that government assistance was only excessive during the 1850s and that politicians then "learned the lessons" (Easterbrook & Aitken, 1956, p. 319) is no longer tenable. The subsidy to the CPR was also excessive, and had the unfortunate consequence of encouraging further transcontinental lines, leading to the policy disaster of the early 1900s. Although some competition for the CPR may have been desirable, there was no justification for subsidizing two additional transcontinental lines—as was evidenced by their not being financially viable upon completion, leading the government to enter into public ownership. The reasons for government munificence towards railway companies are difficult to assess; uncertainty about costs and future revenues, incompetence and overconfidence, and corruption and the political ethics of the time all contributed to greater or lesser extent. When the government entered directly into railway construction (the Intercolonial and the eastern section of the GTPR), its high construction standards incurred large bills. In sum, although the government's railway policy contributed more to the country's economic development than a policy of non-assistance would have done, similar results could have been achieved at less cost and the excess used in better ways.

3. Land Policy

In its "golden age" after 1821 the Hudson's Bay Company enjoyed a fur-trading monopoly west of the Great Lakes. Apart from the Red River colony and the semi-nomadic Métis, settlement was virtually nonexistent. There were, however, destabilizing forces at work. The gold rush of 1858 and the subsequent creation of British Columbia ended the Hudson's Bay Company's rule west of the Rockies. The westward movement of the U.S. frontier of settlement and the rise of expansionist sentiment in the United States led to increased British and Canadian concern over the Company's role in the remainder of the west. The consequence was that in 1870 the title to this territory was passed to the new Dominion. The power to dispose of the public lands was assumed by the federal government (in Manitoba as well as in the future provinces of Saskatchewan and Alberta) until the "purposes of the Dominion" were achieved—the prime "purposes" being the construction of a transcontinental railway and westward settlement. By the 1920s both of these objectives had been met, and in 1930 the remaining public lands were transferred to provincial control. Although the land policy achieved its aims eventually, it has been questioned whether the pace of settlement was adversely affected by this policy and whether land grants were a suitable method of subsidizing railway construction.

Land Policy and Western Settlement

When the Hudson's Bay Company surrendered its rights in 1870, it received £300,000, certain land around its trading posts and one-twentieth of the fertile Prairie land. The federal government also preempted one-eighteenth of the land for schools, and a third preemption was the railway land grants, which amounted to 31.8 million acres by 1908. The remainder of the land could be homesteaded by any settler over eighteen years of age, who could obtain the title to 160 acres after three years of residence, subject to a minimum use of the land and payment of a $10 fee. The basis of the public lands policy was the alternation of railway and homestead sections (Figure 5.4).

Figure 5.4
Plan of a Prairie Township

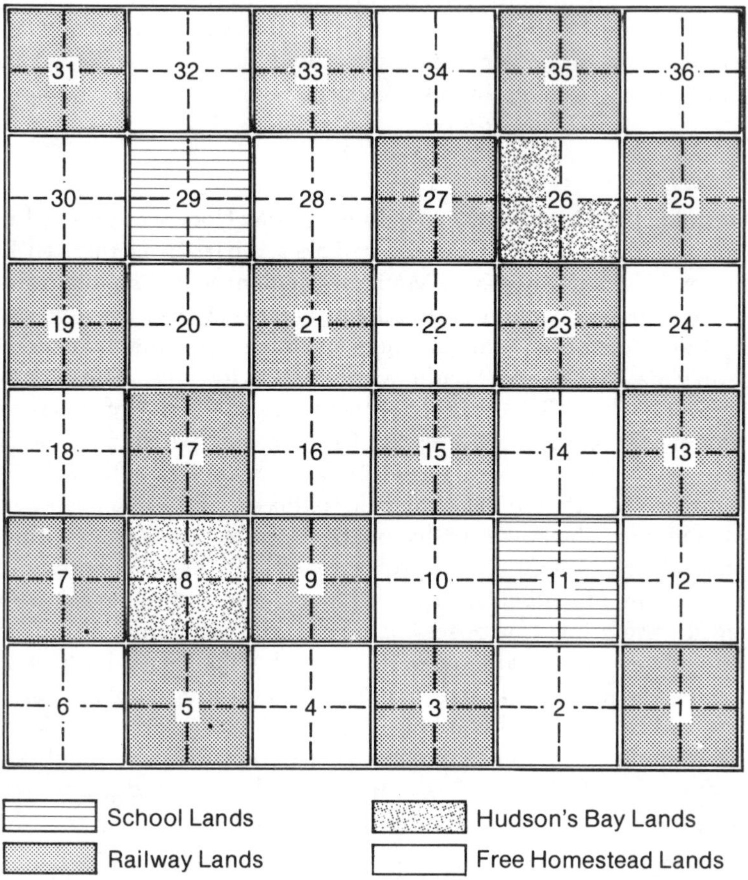

| School Lands | Hudson's Bay Lands |
| Railway Lands | Free Homestead Lands |

Plan of township showing: (a) School lands (Sections 11 and 29), (b) Hudson's Bay lands (Sections 8 and three-quarters of 26; the whole of 26 in every fifth township), (c) Free Homestead lands (even-numbered sections, except 8 and 26), (d) Railway lands (odd-numbered sections reserved for selection as railway land grants). Each section is bounded on three sides by road allowance (66 feet). A section was 640 acres, so that the standard township was one mile square.

Source: Martin, 1938.

In his extensive study of "Dominion Lands" policy, Martin (1938) concluded that the policy was a wise one. The homestead lands helped overcome the initial inertia toward land settlement, but their low cost led many settlers to select land unwisely and encouraged speculators. The railway land, on the other hand, was more carefully considered before purchase and had the beneficial consequence of allowing a homesteader to expand his holdings to take advantage of scale economies (whereas unrestricted homesteads would have led to all the better lands being settled immediately in contiguous quarter-sections). Fundamental to Martin's favourable verdict was the assumption that western settlement was inelastic with respect to the price of land.

The most glaring question mark against this verdict is the land policy's failure to achieve its goal of promoting western settlement for over twenty years. By 1900 only a fifth of the eventual net homestead entries had been recorded, while the proportion was almost 90 per cent by 1914. One view of events, outlined in chapter 3.1, is that the frontier moved westward south of the Great Lakes because the Canadian Shield blocked settlement north of the Lakes, and only reached Canadian territory in the late 1890s. From this viewpoint the availability of the railway and a wisely administered land policy helped and may even have been necessary for rapid western settlement, but they were not sufficient conditions. This geographical determinism is, however, a simplistic approach, because homesteaders were already settling in Manitoba during the 1870s. Although Manitoba was a feasible alternative, the majority of Canadian immigrants chose U.S. destinations at that time, and not until the 1890s was a clear majority of Canadian migrants settling in the Canadian west (Table 5.4). External events, such as rising world wheat prices and falling ocean freight rates, are insufficient to explain the slow pace of Canadian settlement after 1870; although world

Table 5.4
Estimated Number of Native-Born Canadian Migrants to the West

Destination	1870–1880	1880–1890	1890–1900
North Dakota	6,600	18,400	9,000
South Dakota & Minnesota	20,000	25,600	11,400
Iowa, Nebraska & Kansas	21,000	6,200	500
Total for the 6 U.S. states	47,600	50,200	20,900
Manitoba	24,100	38,700	32,600
Northwest Territories	900	17,100	21,700
Total for Canadian west	25,000	55,800	54,300

Source: Studness (1964).

wheat prices rose more or less continuously from the mid-1890s to 1913 while ocean freight rates were falling, the average level of wheat prices at Chicago was lower between 1896 and 1913 than between 1879 and 1895. The important determinant of the pace of Prairie settlement was the choice between U.S. and Canadian land. Research on this choice has focussed on differences in railway building, land policy and natural endowments between the American and Canadian west.

An important factor in the distribution of western settlement was the railway network. Without good transport services a region was less accessible to settlers, and production of a bulky item such as grain was less likely to be profitable. In 1870 Manitoba and North Dakota had no railways, but Iowa, Nebraska, Kansas and southern Minnesota did. Farming was thus more profitable in the latter regions; additionally, most Canadian migrants to the west journeyed via Chicago, and many stopped off in the United States "en route." Thus Canadian frontier migration during the 1870s was channelled to these four states. The first railways in the Dakotas were built in the early 1870s, and the first line to Winnipeg was completed in 1878. The effect was an increase in the number of migrants settling in the Dakotas and Manitoba during the 1880s. Still, however, almost half of the Canadian migrants of that decade chose to settle in the American frontier rather than the Canadian frontier, despite the completion of the Canadian Pacific Railway. Studness (1964) concluded that although railway developments can explain broader settlement patterns, they are insufficient to explain settlers' choice between the Dakotas and Manitoba. This conclusion may be too strong, insofar as feeder lines were of greater economic importance than the CPR main line, and when these branches were built they had a larger impact on settlement; Marr and Percy's (1978) finding that the elasticity of homestead response to new railway mileage was greater between 1887 and 1896 than between 1879 and 1885 is consistent with this hypothesis. Still, the impression is that the CPR, even when its feeder network had been built, was a necessary rather than sufficient condition for western settlement.

A migrant leaving a relatively unattractive life in the east for the golden west might be expected to settle in the area where his standard of living would be highest. Studness (1964) has tried to capture this element of the migrant's decision by comparing the profitability of wheat farming in Manitoba and North Dakota. Although soils and precipitation are similar near the border, yields are generally higher in Manitoba as a result of the cooler summers. Studness estimates that through most of the 1880s and 1890s the farmgate price at Brandon, Manitoba, was about 3½¢ per bushel higher than at the comparable North Dakota location of Devil's Lake. The combination of higher yields and higher prices gave the Manitoba farmer an estimated revenue per acre between $2 and $2¼ greater than his North Dakota counterpart. As a result of the tariff on agricultural implements and the shorter agricultural season, costs per acre were about 75¢ to $1.25 higher in Manitoba than in North Dakota. In sum, the economic advantage lay with Manitoba over North Dakota— and even more so vis-à-vis other U.S. states which were inferior to North Dakota in the 1880s and 1890s. Studness concluded that Canadian emigration to the U.S. frontier was not in response to economic incentives, and he identified as the crucial variable the difference in land policies.

The homesteading law in the United States was similar to that of Canada, apart from a minimum age of twenty-one and residence requirement of five years. An important difference between the two countries' policies in the 1880s was that the last land grant to a U.S. railroad had been in 1874. In the northern half of North Dakota all land was available to homesteaders except school lands and two Indian reservations. Studness considered the contrast with southern Manitoba, where less than half the land was homestead land, to be crucial to late-nineteenth-century settlement patterns. By 1890 two thirds of the homestead land was settled in Manitoba, including all the land in regions serviced by railways, while only one sixth of the homestead land in North Dakota was settled. The railway land in Manitoba was scarcely settled before 1900, despite the not very onerous terms (the CPR sold to bona fide settlers at $2.50 per acre with credit terms available and a 50 per cent rebate per acre of sod broken). Since the profitability of wheat farming was not so much higher in Manitoba than in North Dakota, even fairly cheap railway land in Manitoba was less attractive than free land in North Dakota. Studness believed that settlers went first to homestead land close to railways in Manitoba and second to homestead land in North Dakota; when the demand for homestead land outpaced railway construction in Manitoba during the 1880s, many Canadians emigrated to North Dakota where free land was still abundant. In this view, the Canadian government's land policy was suboptimal insofar as emigration could have been reduced by greater availability of homestead land and by more rapid railway construction.

The conclusion that land policy was an important determinant of western settlement has been criticized by Norrie (1974a). He argues that Studness's profitability estimates are only applicable after the CPR reached Winnipeg in 1883 and grain elevators were built at the lakehead in 1884, whereas most of the North Dakota settlement occurred in the first half of the 1880s. Furthermore, the greater risk attached to wheat farming in Manitoba, because the low rainfall and possibility of early frost increase the probability of crop failure, reduced the attraction of Manitoba. These criticisms are not altogether convincing; Norrie himself argued elsewhere that the difference in transport costs from Winnipeg before and after 1883-1884 was not very substantial (Norrie, 1975, p. 424), and the risk argument does not explain the changing settlement patterns. A variation of the latter argument, based on the crucial point that western land is not homogeneous, has been developed further (Norrie, 1976). During the nineteenth century most settlement was in the sub-humid plains (areas with twenty to thirty inches annual rainfall), i.e., most of the land east of the 100th meridian in the United States and in the Red River Valley and southern Alberta in Canada. In the remaining areas, where rainfall was below twenty inches, farming was much riskier, so that in Canada only the Red River Valley could be satisfactorily settled given the state of technology and the railway network. By 1886 most of the sub-humid lands in the United States and Canada were occupied. The following decade saw the development of new techniques of dry-farming, and the westward settlement which increased with world wheat demand after 1896 went to the semi-arid areas. It is for this period, Norrie argues, that Studness's profitability estimates are valid, which explains the U.S. emigration to the Canadian west. In Norrie's view technical factors and market conditions explain the pace of Prairie settlement, while government policy plays no explicit role.

The verdict on whether the government's land policy retarded western settlement by limiting the availability of homestead land remains unclear. Martin's assumption that the price of land had no impact on the pace of settlement is probably too extreme, but Studness's opposing conclusion that with more homestead lands and cash subsidies for railways substantial settlement would have occurred sooner is unproven. Norrie's description of the evolution and impact of dry-farming techniques casts doubt on Studness's conclusion, but the strength of Norrie's (1975) original econometric support for his hypothesis has been questioned by Grant (1978) and by Marr and Percy (1978), although the evidence of all three studies is consistent with the dry-farming hypothesis. Marr and Percy also show that government policy and the need to develop dry-farming techniques are not mutually exclusive explanations of the delay in Prairie settlement; they found that changes in the federal government's promotional expenditures, which increased from just over $200,000 per annum 1878-1896 to $¾ million per annum 1897-1911, had a significant positive impact on the pace of settlement.

Recently the land policy has been criticized from a different angle— indeed an opposite direction from the above debate. Southey (1978, pp. 553-7) argues that the institutional arrangements of homesteading encouraged a misallocation of resources in the form of premature western settlement. From society's point of view the optimum time to bring land into use is when the difference between the present value of future returns and clearance costs is maximized. Theoretically, this timing could have been assured by competitive auctions of western land, where price paid per acre would equal the anticipated economic rent and the purchaser would earn a normal return. Giving away homestead land converts the auction from a cash to a time basis; in order to appropriate future rents it is necessary to cultivate a quarter-section before anybody else. If homesteads are competitively distributed each quarter-section will be taken up at the date when the opportunity costs of early settlement exactly equal the value of expected economic rents; in other words, all future rents are dissipated by premature settlement. Thus, by undervaluing property rights and encouraging individuals to devote their resources to assuring these rights before the socially optimal moment, the land policy incurred resource misallocation. The quantitative significance of Southey's argument is, however, unclear if the actual and optimal cultivation dates were close together and accompanied by uncertainty about future rents or shifts in anticipated rents. Moreover, from a Canadian viewpoint, the argument is weakened because some of the costs of the global resource misallocation were borne by other countries from which Prairie settlers emigrated with their capital. Finally, Southey's argument should be construed not as a case against the land policy but as illustration of a possible cost of achieving the political goal of rapid western settlement.

The effects of the settlement pattern induced by the land policy have been analyzed even less than the pace of settlement. The chequerboard system of Figure 5.4 affected income distribution through the monopoly or monopsony position enjoyed by seller or buyer of adjacent lots, but it is not clear whether this situation enabled the CPR, the Hudson's Bay Company or the federal government to sell their 160 acre lots at the full price which a settler would be prepared to pay for 320 acres or whether the farmer ended up paying half the price per acre normally charged by land companies. Martin's hypotheses about the wisdom with which land was chosen and the role of speculators remain untested, and perhaps untestable, but his hypothesis about scale economies is supported by Norrie's research on dry-farming; the new techniques raised the minimum efficient size of Prairie farms, and the transition from 160 to 320 acre farms would have been more difficult if there had been no preemptions.

Railway Land Grants

The second major objective of land policy was the construction of a railway network across the Canadian west. There was a need to subsidize western railway construction and one of the tools at hand was the land grant. The system of railway land grants was abandoned after 1894 and officially ended in 1908, by which time over thirty million acres of Prairie land "fairly fit for settlement" had been alienated to railway companies. The system ceased under a wave of criticism, primarily because of the inroads made into homestead land. We have also seen that the subsidy granted to the greatest land grant railway, the CPR, was excessive, and may still have been so without the land grant. Southey's argument about premature enterprise could also be applied to land grant railways, although in the CPR's case timing reflected political expediency rather than any necessity for the CPR to establish prior claim to land grants. On the other hand, land grants may have been a particularly efficient way to encourage construction of the socially optimum railway mileage.

From Figure 5.3 we can recall that a uniform rate policy implies that the railway generates additional consumers' surplus, which will be reflected in the real rental value of land whose output can be transported by the railway. The beneficiary of the increased surplus is determined by the method of land alienation:

(a) on homestead land the settler captures the surplus;
(b) on land auctioned by the government after railway construction the surplus goes to public funds;
(c) on land sold by the railway company the company gains the surplus.

Land policy therefore affects railway rate policy. Under options (a) or (b) the railway will adopt a monopoly pricing policy reducing railway use below the social optimum. Under (c) the railway will maximize profits by providing the socially optimum level of transport services, because what it loses vis-à-vis monopoly pricing in freight revenue will be more than offset by the gain in income from land sales. Thus, although the railway land grants may have been harmful to the pace of Prairie settlement by reducing the acreage of homestead land, they may have helped quicken the pace by increasing railway mileage and countering the railways' tendencies toward monopoly pricing.

Whether the net effect of the railway land grants on Prairie settlement was positive or negative is uncertain. The actual implementation of the policy tended, however, to emphasize the negative aspects. The Canadian land grant system followed its American predecessor in the principle of granting alternate sections in a railway belt on either side of the track, but contained the proviso that land grant acreage must be "fairly fit for settlement." The possibility of exchanging unfit land for superior land elsewhere in the Prairies led, in Martin's words, to "an unseemly scramble for desirable reserves which resulted in railway land grants 'fairly fit for settlement' in almost every eligible area of Western Canada." The result was that the geographical distribution of the land subsidies bore little relation to the location of the land grant railways (Table 5.5). In consequence, much of the best land in Saskatchewan and Alberta was preempted by railway companies before potential home-steaders arrived. Where the land was not a potential source of freight traffic to the railway concerned, these parts of the land grant had little effect on railway construction or use. They thus raised the price of land and probably slowed the pace of settlement, without any compensatory beneficial effect on the provision of railway services.

Table 5.5
Land Grant Railways' Mileage and Land Subsidies by Province

	Mileage	Land Subsidy (million acres)
Manitoba	1251	3.6
Saskatchewan	886	15.2
Alberta	805	13.1

Source: Martin (1938), Table IV.
Note: Although over 650 miles of the CPR main line ran through northern Ontario, no land subsidy came from that province.

Full evaluation of the railway land grant system would also require comparison with other methods of financing the railways. George's research on the CPR suggests that the required subsidy could have been paid without the land grant, but the other components of the subsidy may also have had social costs (cf. section 5.4). In a study of the U.S. transcontinental line of the Union Pacific, Fogel (1960) concluded that construction by the government would have been the least cost approach. In Canada, government construction was not very successful during the 1870s, but this may reflect the lack of firm commitment rather than any deficiency inherent to the approach.

4. The Government's Development Strategy: An Overview

After 1848 the newly "responsible" Canadian government vigorously pursued policies with consequences for economic development. A tariff structure establishing high effective rates of protection for the manufacturing sector was introduced in 1858–1859 and retained until the post-1945 era. Private construction of railways was encouraged by substantial public subsidies, until the final most extravagant projects faced financial ruin during World War I and had to be saved from bankruptcy by nationalization. Finally, the federal government administered the Prairie lands between 1870 and 1930 in order to promote western settlement and railway construction. In this overview of the government's development strategy, three questions will be posed:

- why was the strategy adopted?
- were its components mutually consistent?
- were the individual policies optimal?

In his analysis of tariff determination Caves concluded that the best explanatory hypotheses were the influence of vested interests and the government's attempt to promote a national policy. These two hypotheses have also been the most favoured explanations of the government's development strategy as a whole. Traditional historians tend to stress the second hypothesis, accepting Macdonald's characterization of the package as a unified "National Policy" aimed at extensive growth and economic diversification. The adoption of the "National Policy" has been further elaborated in a theory of defensive expansion (Aitken, 1959), whereby the policies are seen, not as visionary steps in the building of a new country, but rather as a defensive reaction to the threat of the United States achieving its "Manifest Destiny" of occupying the entire continent. Other writers have emphasized the role of vested interests in Canadian policy formation. The protective tariff benefitted manufacturing interests in central Canada who were politically influential, but even more clearly the building of the railways served some private interests immensely. The fortunes made by individuals from railways subsidized out of the public purse are most graphically described in Gustavus Myers' *History of Canadian Wealth*. Rather than trying to arbitrate between the two hypotheses, it appears more reasonable to emphasize that they are not mutually exclusive. The government in Ottawa may have attempted to pursue a "National Policy" aimed at thwarting potential U.S. encirclement, but in implementing the policies it served the interests of specific groups and individuals (who were not uncommonly Cabinet ministers themselves).

The Canadian government saw its commercial, railway and land policies as forming a coherent strategy for extensive growth and economic diversification. The protective tariff directly encouraged the growth of the manufacturing sector and (if Dales' hypothesis is correct) extensive growth, and helped railway construction by providing east-west traffic and by raising government revenue which could be used to subsidize railways. Railway construction and western settlement were complementary to each other and to the promotion of extensive growth. The internal consistency of the railways and western settlement was, however, slightly soured by the particular policy tool of railway land grants, which may have had an adverse effect on the pace of Prairie settlement. More substantial inconsistencies surround the tariff policy. The new tariff structure adopted in 1858–1859 and confirmed in 1879 did not in fact increase government revenue, so the previous non-progressive tariff could equally well have supplied the government revenue for railway subsidies. Moreover, the need for revenue for this purpose is over-stated by the actual subsidies which were consistently larger than was necessary. The greatest internal conflict is between the protective tariff and the goal of rapid western settlement. The tariff raised the Prairie farmers' production costs, reducing their profits and the incentive for potential settlers to move to the Canadian west.

Viewed in the light of its internal inconsistencies the "National Policy" appears distinctly less than national. The transcontinental railway was built, the Prairies settled and American Manifest Destiny withstood, but the rewards from the policies were not equally distributed across

Canada. The Maritimes were almost ignored, although they bore their share of the costs from the protective tariff while little of the tariff revenue was spent there. The Prairies gained their railways, but suffered from the protective tariff and perhaps from the land policy; they would have been better off under free trade and, perhaps, with more free land. The only region to benefit unconditionally was central Canada, and in particular the manufacturing interests and potential railway operators from Montreal and southern Ontario. This helps to explain why commercial and railway policies were so consistent between the pre-1867 Province of Canada and the post-1867 Dominion of Canada, as well as the retention of western lands under Dominion rather than provincial control.

The final question concerning the optimality of individual policies has been discussed in detail in the preceding sections of this chapter, and the conclusions need only be summarized here. The protective tariff had positive and negative effects, and an evaluation would depend on whether some of the consequences are viewed as good or bad (e.g., the encouragement of direct foreign investment) and on the weight given to the different consequences. One of the benefits, the encouragement of infant industries, could theoretically have been achieved more efficiently by subsidies than by protective tariffs, but this alternative may have been administratively infeasible at least until the late nineteenth century. The government can be credited for following an active railway policy. Without government aid the trunk lines would have been built much later, if at all, probably to the detriment of Canadian economic development. The size of the railway subsidies was, however, excessive, and the resulting income redistribution or income losses were scarcely desirable. The nature of the subsidies varied, as interest guarantees, cash grants and land grants were adopted, discarded and revived without any conclusion about their relative merits being reached; the indecisive verdict remains to this day. The land policy is the prong of the "National Policy" upon which least research has been done. Although arguments for and against the federal government's methods of Prairie land alienation have been rehearsed, no conclusion has been universally accepted. If all of the land had been homestead land, then Prairie settlement may have been faster; but, if wheat market and technical conditions were crucial and the demand for western land were thus price inelastic, then the increase in the pace of settlement would have been minimal. Acceptance of the latter argument and hence of the unimportance of government land policy may explain the relative lack of interest in this aspect of the "National Policy."

Chapter 6

The Industrialization
of Central Canada, 1850–1914

There is a widely held misconception that Canada, although a "developed" country, is not an industrialized nation, but owes her wealth solely to abundant natural resources. The wheatfields of the Prairies, her mineral and timber wealth, and the hydroelectric schemes in the north should not distract from the significance of the geographically concentrated manufacturing sector. Two-fifths of Canadian GNP consists of industrial output, and even if mining, construction and energy are omitted, manufacturing still accounts for over a quarter of total output and almost a quarter of total employment. These proportions are among the highest in the world; by the end of the Second World War Canada ranked second only to the United States on the basis of manufacturing output per head (Maizels, 1963, p. 31). The present chapter examines how Canada set out on the path to becoming an industrial nation, and the story is taken up to World War II in chapter 9.3.

1. The Beginnings of Modern Industry

The first step in analyzing Canadian industrial growth is to identify when the process began. Manufacturing activity existed in the earliest European settlements. The brewing industry, for example, dates from the seventeenth century, and by 1850 the Montreal brewers alone had sales of £750,000 per year. By the 1830s there were an estimated 500 industrial establishments in Montreal, but their labour force of 1,300 workers reveals the small-scale nature of industry at that time. There were some larger enterprises, in particular in the Quebec shipbuilding industry, and a few "modern" enterprises using techniques adopted from the British industrial revolution (e.g., maritime engine construction). Nevertheless, the premodern characteristics of small-scale, artisan-based activities using muscle power as their energy source were still dominant in Canadian industry during the first half of the nineteenth century. The key question of when the industrial sector lost its premodern characteristics is clearly a matter of degree; we could equally well reword it to ask when the modern industrial sector became a significant part of the Canadian economy.

The predominance of the staple approach in interpreting Canada's economic past led to a relative lack of interest in industrial development and a downgrading of its importance; industrial growth was seen as essentially derivative, following staple expansion via spread effects and only producing a substantial manufacturing sector during the wheat boom. Some historians suggested earlier beginnings; Ryerson, for example, pointed to the opening of the Lachine Canal in 1846. The rapid expansion of manufacturing establishments utilizing hydraulic power from the Lachine Canal has been documented by Tulchinsky (1977), who describes some of the thirty enterprises which lined the Canal banks by 1854. This type of anecdotal evidence, however, is inadequate to answer the question raised at the end of the previous paragraph, because it gives no indication of the relative importance of these establishments in the industrial sector or in the economy as a whole.

A fuller picture of the size and nature of the manufacturing sector is given by the decennial censuses. The census-based estimates of manufacturing output discussed in chapter 4.5 all revealed the existence of a substantial and growing manufacturing sector. Firestone's estimates (Table 6.1), for example, show that value-added in manufacturing already accounted for 18 per cent of GNP in 1851 and point to the 1860s and the 1880s as decades of rapid growth in manufacturing. By 1890 the share of manufacturing in GNP was almost as high as it is today. Meanwhile the structure of industry was changing. In 1851 the average labour force and capital stock per establishment were small, indicating the predominance of specialized workshops (usually attached to the owner's residence) with operations done by hand. The flour and log mills used water and wind power, but steam power was rare. The only large-scale industry was the Quebec shipyards. Other industries supplied essentially local needs on a custom or repair basis. The relative unimportance of consumer goods industries implies that households were largely self-sufficient, producing their own food, clothing and housing. Large plant, with increased machinery and equipment per worker, became more common during the 1860s. Firestone concludes that Canada's industrial revolution began with the development of the factory system during this decade, although it spread slowly (Firestone, 1960, p. 230). By 1900 the 430 largest plants in Canada produced 36 per cent of manufacturing output, and the thirty largest produced a third of this. The adoption of modern methods by large-scale industrial units was accompanied by a near doubling of productivity (annual real output per worker) in the manufacturing sector

Table 6.1
Value-added in Manufacturing as a Percentage of GNP, 1851–1900

	1851	1860	1870	1880	1890	1900
(A) GNP ($million)	169	319	459	581	803	1057
(B) Value-added in manufacturing ($million)	31	48	87	110	189	223
(B) as a percentage of (A)	18%	15%	19%	19%	24%	21%

Source: Firestone (1960), p. 225.

between 1850 and 1900, although working hours fell substantially. The changes in size structure were accompanied by changes in the composition of manufactured output (Table 6.2). The manufacturing sector became more diversified, with the four leading branches accounting for 29 per cent of total output in 1900 as compared to 60 per cent in 1851. There was also a movement away from resource-based industries producing largely for export and toward consumer goods industries. Meat-packaging, butter and cheese, bread and refined sugar were among the ten leading sectors in 1900, reflecting the interaction between industrial growth, urbanization and diminishing self-sufficiency.

Table 6.2
The Share of the Four Leading Branches in Total Manufacturing Output
(by Gross Value of Production), 1851 and 1900

1851		1900	
Flour & grist mills	31%	Log products	10%
Log products	13%	Flour & grist mills	9%
Shipbuilding	9%	Meat packaging	5%
Boots & Shoes	7%	Butter & Cheese	5%

Source: Firestone (1960).

The early history of the trade union movement in Canada also provides indications of the pace of industrial mechanization. The picture of trade union development during the 1840s and early 1850s is one of small unions confined to particular cities and trades (Langdon, 1973). In Montreal stonecutters and printers formed unions during the 1840s, and shoemakers, bakers and engineers during the 1850s; in Toronto stonemasons, printers and shoemakers during the 1840s, and tailors in the early 1850s; and in Hamilton, printers during the 1840s and tailors and shoemakers during the 1850s. These first unions were formed in response to the threat of mechanization rendering skilled labour redundant. The printers' union, the Toronto Typographical Society, was founded in 1844, the same year that the *Globe* introduced the first cylinder press in Upper Canada. Similarly, the formation of the early tailors' unions was stimulated by the introduction of the steam-run sewing machine. In 1851–1852 the Toronto tailors combined to wreck the first of these machines brought to the city and to prevent the introduction of others. The Journeyman Tailors' Protective Society in Hamilton reacted in the same way in 1854, but the ability of skilled workers to prevent mechanization was limited, and the Society's executive was arrested for conspiracy. Such protoindustrialization of artisan activities is a typical precursor of the factory system, and the craft unions were unable to stop its progress.

Larger unions of unskilled labour did not develop until the late 1850s and the 1860s, and they were formed in the sectors where technological change was accompanied by increased establishment size. The cigar-making and boot and shoe industries both mechanized production rapidly in the early 1860s, as new techniques were borrowed from the United States and developed behind the 1858–1859 tariff and the natural protection offered by the U.S. Civil War. The Journeyman Cigarmakers Union was formed in Ontario in 1865 and the Boot and Shoemakers Union of the Province of Ontario in 1867. The machinery industry also grew quickly in the 1860s as the pace of agricultural mechanization accelerated. The Amalgamated Society of Engineers grew from one local with 21 members (in Montreal) in 1853 to include four locals and 207 members (in Montreal, Hamilton, Toronto and Brantford) by 1867. In the metal-working sector, the International Molders Union, founded in 1859, had 270 members in Canada (mostly in Toronto and Montreal) by 1867, and the formation of the employers' Canadian Iron Founders Association in 1865 in order to unite action against the International Molders Union indicated the employers' determination to enforce mechanization and to prevent increased labour costs. The key to union expansion after the mid-1850s was industrialization, which brought workers together in factories but also exposed them to the insecurity of industrial capitalist change.

What light can early trade union history shed on Canadian industrialization? The trade union evidence suggests a picture of modern techniques being introduced in several industrial branches by the late 1840s and the factory system becoming a significant feature of the economy by the 1860s. This is consistent with the characterization (by Ryerson, and by Kilbourn, 1960) of the Lachine Canal in 1846 as the birthplace of Canadian industry and (by Firestone) of the 1860s as the decade of Canada's industrial revolution. Further support for this time pattern is provided by the emergence of the business cycle during the late 1860s (chapter 9.1), demand shifts in the financial sector (chapter 8.3) and the rapid urbanization of southern Ontario between 1860 and 1890 (chapter 10.3).

2. Two Manufacturing Industries of the 1860s

Although support for the existence of an industrial revolution during the 1860s can be provided and some of the manufacturing branches involved can be identified, so little research has been done on the subject that we cannot say why the industrial revolution occurred. Possible causes are numerous. Commercial policy may have been important either indirectly through the stimulus offered by reciprocity trade in natural goods or more directly through the protection offered by the Cayley–Galt tariff on manufactured goods. Also in this decade fortuitous protection from

U.S. exports was provided by the Civil War, which disrupted American exports as well as increasing the demand for many goods which Canadian producers could export. Within the Canadian economy, there were the various linkage effects emanating from the railway construction of the 1850s. Rising wage rates during the 1850s and 1860s may have contributed to the introduction of labour-saving machinery. Such a listing of possible causes is, however, of little value without knowledge of their relative importance, and this can only be guessed at in all but a few cases. Two of the best documented cases will be analyzed here.

The Agricultural Implements Industry

By the 1860s the major product of the agricultural implements industry was the mechanical reaper. Although commercially produced in the United States during the 1830s and sold in Canada during the 1840s, use of the reaper only became significant in Canada at the end of the 1840s. The demand for reapers was increasingly met by the establishment of Canadian producers, who succeeded in driving American made reapers almost completely out of the Canadian market by the early 1860s. The strong competitive position of domestic producers depended principally upon: (1) natural protection—the early reapers were bulky, weighing half a ton, and hence expensive to transport; (2) lower labour and material input costs than in the United States—the latter resulted from Canadian duties on iron being less than those of the United States at a time when the cheapest and best iron came from a third country (the United Kingdom); (3) lack of protection for U.S. patents—many early Canadian firms were founded by U.S. émigrés who made models which were patent-protected in the United States.

The ease of entry into the industry and high transport costs meant that production was small-scale and local. The localization was reinforced by the unreliability of the early machines, which required producers to offer on-the-spot repair facilities. Hence the industry in the 1850s consisted of little more than blacksmith shops supplying a range of implements.

After the railway construction of the 1850s reduced transport costs, firms started to specialize and to sell outside their immediate neighbourhood. During the 1860s this coincided with a huge increase in demand for reapers. The industry's sales grew from $413,000 in 1861 to $2,685,000 in 1871, and the number of establishments increased from 46 to 252.

In order to explain the increased demand for mechanical reapers, we must look at the farmers' decision to mechanize. He would purchase a machine if his costs during a harvest season would then be less than the cost of doing the work by hand. Thus the decision depended upon the annual cost of a reaper (c), the number of man-days of labour saved per acre (Ls), the daily wage rate (w) and the number of acres under small grains (S). Before 1860, c exceeded the annual saving in labour costs for all but the very largest Canadian farms, which explains why few farmers had mechanical reapers. During the 1860s, although the capital cost did not change, the other three variables did:

(1) improved reaper design reduced the number of operators from two to one (i.e., increasing Ls);
(2) wage rates rose;
(3) rising world wheat prices and U.S. barley prices induced farmers to put more acreage under small grains.

The significant point about these changes was that many farms were now pushed over the threshold farm size where a mechanical reaper became a profitable investment. The largest contributor to increased reaper demand was the reduced labour requirement of the self-rake reaper, which indicates the continuing importance of free access to American technology, and the second-largest contributor was the increased scale of operations (Pomfret, 1976). The latter points to some relevance for external demand for staple exports, although staple theorists have generally ignored the role of Ontario grain exports in Canadian economic development during the 1850s and 1860s. Agricultural mechanization was concentrated in Ontario (36,874 machines in 1871, compared to 5,149 in Quebec and insignificant numbers elsewhere in Canada, reflecting the lower wage rates and smaller farms outside Ontario), and in consequence the agricultural machinery industry was located there.

Two features of the growth of the agricultural machinery industry during the 1860s were the competitive structure of the industry and the lack of any direct role of government policy. During the 1870s the movement towards larger plant and greater specialization began to accelerate, and for the remainder of the nineteenth century continued output growth was accompanied by decline in the number of firms (Table 6.3). Economies of scale were one element of competitiveness in the industry, but good product lines and marketing were at least as important. All three elements were forces leading to increased seller concentration in the industry.

Table 6.3
Output and Number of Establishments in the Agricultural Implements
Industry, 1861–1906

	1861	1871	1881	1891	1901	1906
Output ($million)	0.4	2.7	4.4	7.5	9.6	12.8
Number of Establishments	46	252	234	221	114	88

Source: census data.

The early leaders in the industry were those entrepreneurs who established Canadian patents on good machines. Among these firms, Massey and Harris were the two most successful because they also mastered the art of selling, with displays at county fairs, field contests, "delivery day" parades, catalogues, newspaper advertising, competitive price-cutting and easy credit terms. After the first generation of machines, when Massey and Harris often failed to get the best patents on new machines, they used their hegemony to take over competitors who had superior patents. For example, Massey's solution to the problem of obtaining a successful binder was to take over in 1881 a local rival which had a light twine binder. Unfortunately for Massey, however, the binder was technically inferior to that of their largest competitor, Harris. The 1880s were a decade of fierce competition between Massey and Harris for the protected Canadian markets opened up by the CPR, and although Massey was the larger company with greater resources, Harris was more successful because of its superior binder. Both companies, however, suffered from the price-cutting and high selling costs involved in the competitive struggle, and the final solution was their 1891 merger. Despite having over half of Canadian sales, Massey-Harris continued through the 1890s and early 1900s the policy of acquisitions to broaden its product range and to remove competition from superior products (Phillips, 1956).

The consequence of the mergers and take-overs was the realization of economies of scale in both production and distribution. As competing lines were taken over the inferior product was dropped and production runs became longer. Also, production increasingly became geographically concentrated in Toronto, Brantford and Woodstock. Amalgamation led to rationalization of selling services, e.g., by removing duplicate dealerships. Transport costs were reduced because larger firms could ship by carload lots rather than by individual items. Finally, after-sales services were improved by superior spare parts availability.

Upon its formation in 1891 Massey-Harris, with the long experience of its constituent firms and its economies of scale, was already an efficient producer by world standards. Its efficiency was reflected by its success at exporting and its success in withstanding U.S. competition in the Canadian market. Both Massey and Harris started to produce for export in the late 1880s. Massey-Harris increased exports from $376,198 in 1891 to $1,692,155 in 1901. This immediate success reflected three factors. There had been little mechanization of grain harvesting in Europe before the 1880s, because wages were lower and farms were smaller or more irregular than in North America. Thus, Massey-Harris faced European competitors which were smaller and less efficient than itself. Secondly, the Canadian tariff schedule encouraged exports because import duty paid on inputs into exported goods was refunded. Finally, ocean freight rates had fallen rapidly during the 1800s. Massey-Harris was able to establish a substantial market share in Europe, Australia and South Africa during the 1890s. When tariffs on agricultural machinery were increased in these export markets during the twentieth century, Massey-Harris was able to move into overseas production with already established markets.

The advantages over U.S. competitors, which had permitted the establishment of an independent Canadian agricultural machinery industry during the 1850s and 1860s, disappeared during the following decades. American iron and steel became superior to any other, and natural protection for Ontario producers was small, or even negative, in the Prairies. The Canadian producers, for whom tariff protection had been unnecessary in the 1860s, began lobbying for protection, and the tariff on agricultural machinery increased substantially after 1879. International Harvester opened a plant at Hamilton in 1903 in order to circumvent the Canadian tariff. Despite this competition and despite tariff reductions in response to farmers' protests, Massey-Harris and another Canadian manufacturer (Cockshutt) survived. When U.S. agricultural machinery tariffs began to fall after 1913, Massey-Harris was even able to compete successfully with American corporations in the U.S. market, and today the company's sales in that market are some three times as large as their Canadian sales.

The history of the agricultural implements industry can now be briefly summarized. Domestic production of agricultural machinery was initially due to natural protection, favourable factor prices and easy access to foreign technology. Demand for mechanical reapers was a derived demand, and the rapid growth of the industry during the 1860s was a result of increased grain production, as well as the borrowing of an important technological improvement. The importance of product differentiation and of scale economies led to rapid concentration in the industry during the remainder of the nineteenth century. Because the Canadian industry enjoyed a period free from serious foreign competition, during which its efficiency increased, it was in a position to export when demand for agricultural machinery outside North America expanded and also to withstand U.S. competition when the initial advantages were eroded. Finally, the relative unimportance of the Canadian tariff in the early development of the industry may be noted, although the tariff did help later in securing the Prairie market for Canadian producers.

The Cheese Industry

The 1860s saw the beginning of rapid expansion in the cheese industry. Output growth was even more rapid than in the agricultural implements industry, and by 1900 cheese was second only to wheat among Canada's exports. An important similarity to the agricultural implements industry was the easy access to U.S. technology, but there were also significant differences between the two industries' economic characteristics. For the cheese industry, natural protection was less important than tariff protection. Cheese factories exhibited more or less constant returns to scale during the nineteenth century. The growth of cheese factories was a direct result of agricultural change, and the linkage from the cheese industry to agriculture was backward in contrast to the forward linkage from the agricultural implements industry to agriculture. Much of the continued expansion of the cheese industry was induced by the general process of industrialization rather than being an autonomous component of the process.

Cheese had been made in Canada long before the nineteenth century. If a farmer had a surplus he would sell it to the local storekeeper, and there is evidence of longer distance trade by boat along the St. Lawrence as early as 1801. In most years of the first half of the nineteenth century, however, Canadian demand exceeded domestic production, and cheese was imported from the United States. The overall picture at that time is of dairy farming as a sideline; most farmers had four or less cows, to which they paid little attention, leaving that side of the farmwork to the womenfolk.

The stagnation of the Canadian cheese industry was due to two principal considerations. The domestically manufactured cheese was of highly variable quality, which made it difficult to sell for a good price, and in most areas of Canada wheat offered a higher return to farmers for lower investment than did dairy farming. The technology for overcoming the first obstacle became available during the 1840s with the development of "cheese factories" which could produce cheese of fairly even quality. The first cheese factory began operations in New York in 1851, and they spread rapidly in that state; but none came to Canada during the 1850s. At current prices Canadians were not prepared to enter into competition with U.S. producers.

In the early 1860s the relative profitability of cheese production improved. The midge, rust and soil exhaustion made wheat farming increasingly risky in some areas of Ontario, even though total wheat acreage continued to expand during the 1860s. Meanwhile, the American Civil War reduced the supply of U.S. cheese, leading to higher cheese prices. The result was that the first cheese factory in Canada opened in the spring of 1864, and five had been constructed by the end of the following year.

The most important stimulus to the cheese industry was the end of reciprocity in 1866. With the end of North American free trade in cheese, Canadian cheese prices rose by a third. The result was a phenomenon labelled "cheese mania" by contemporaries—by the end of 1867 there were 235 cheese factories in Canada. Cheese mania led to overproduction and frequent low quality, and some early enterprises soon collapsed. Attempts by the Dairymen's Association to control quality were successful during the 1870s. At the same time the emergence of specialized cheese merchants who introduced innovations such as a weekly refrigerated train service from Stratford to Montreal (Jones, 1946, p. 259) helped to ensure that the cheese would reach overseas destinations in good condition. As Canadian cheese gained acceptance abroad, in particular in the British market, cheese exports grew from 8.3 million pounds in 1871, to 49.2 million in 1881, 106.2 million in 1891 and 189.8 million in 1899, by which time cheese was Canada's second largest export by value. The industry's prowess was illustrated by a Canadian contribution to the 1892 World's Fair at Chicago; the "Canadian Mite" was the largest cheese ever made, weighing 22,000 pounds and measuring 28 feet in circumference by 6 feet in height (Ruddick, 1937, p. 67), and a special train was provided to carry the giant across Ontario.

The above account suggests that cheese provides a perfect example of a successful infant industry. Tariff protection was the cue for the establishment of a cheese industry in Canada. For a decade or so after that, the new industry would have experienced difficulties in competing with imports in the absence of tariff protection. Once good and consistent quality had been established during that period of "learning by doing," Canadian cheese could compete on world markets and became a major export.

The infant industry parable is, however, an incomplete explanation of the cheese industry's development. Although the cheese industry was one of the expanding sectors during the industrial revolution of the 1860s, its further growth was in part a consequence of the general growth of the manufacturing sector—an example of the way in which linkage effects can make industrial development self-sustaining once it reaches a certain level. The major link was the association between the growth of the manufacturing sector and urbanization, which led to an urban market for fresh milk (especially after the adoption of refrigerated railcars during the 1870s). Cheese mania plus the increased demand for milk encouraged changes in dairy farming, including greater specialization and the introduction of new breeds. Jerseys, whose milk had high butterfat content, were introduced to Canada in 1868 and Holsteins, the most prolific milk-producers, in 1882–1883. Despite their advantages, these breeds were not introduced earlier because of the high capital cost of establishing a thoroughbred herd (one farmer paid $1,500 for a Holstein bull and $1,200 for three heifers in 1884). Such an outlay could only be recouped by a large-scale dairy farm, and such farms only existed after cheese mania and the growth of urban demand for milk. These changes benefitted the cheese industry by improving its input supply, with respect to both price and reliability, and this helped to improve the Canadian industry's competitive position. Perhaps the demand from cheese factories could alone have stimulated increased productivity in dairy farming, but the concurrent urbanization certainly strengthened the stimulus.

Unlike agricultural machinery factories, cheese factories remained small, and their number grew in the remainder of the nineteenth century. In 1901 the average number of employees per factory was two. Production was at first geographically concentrated. Of the 353 cheese factories reported in the 1871 census, 323 were in Ontario, and of these 150 were in Oxford County with most of the rest near Brockville or Belleville. During the 1880s and especially the 1890s the Quebec dairy industry grew rapidly and overtook the Ontario industry in number of butter and cheese factories (1,992 against 1,886), although not in output ($13 million against $15 million). Factory production of butter had to await the introduction of cream separators in the 1880s. The spread of butter factories contributed to the dairy industry's continued growth, although in the nineteenth century the profitability of cheese production tended to discourage commercial butter production. Butter never became a major Canadian export item, and the big expansion of factory production took place during the early twentieth century in response to growing domestic demand.

3. The 1879 Tariff and Industrial Development

The Canadian industrial revolution of the 1860s took place in the wider environment of a rapidly expanding "world" economy. Although the relative importance of causal factors varied from industry to industry, the growth of world demand and increase in world prices (accentuated in North America by the U.S. Civil War) and the accelerated innovating activity during the 1850s and 1860s were an important general stimulus to the Canadian manufacturing sector. The second phase of rapid industrial growth in nineteenth-century Canada, the 1880s or more specifically 1879–1884, coincided with a period of less spectacular growth in the world economy. The year 1879 did, however, see a substantial increase in the Canadian tariff, which was the immediate cause of several industries' expansion during the following five years.

During the 1870s there was little pressure from the manufacturing sector for tariff increases. Firms which had grown during the 1860s were sufficiently firmly established to withstand foreign competition, and some were already exporting. These firms, in industries such as agricultural implements, woollen goods, boots and shoes and secondary iron products, were calling for renewed reciprocity in order to gain cheaper materials or access to U.S. markets. The firms which did want higher tariffs were mainly in two types of industries: (1) some primary producers, e.g., oil, coal and iron; (2) some consumer goods industries facing heavy competition from imports, e.g., sugar refining and cotton textiles.

The pro-tariff industries were usually characterized by a small number of firms (in the absence of foreign competition they would be able to adopt monopoly or oligopoly pricing) and by political influence in the Conservative Party (Naylor, 1975, vol. I, pp. 35-55). The position of the pro-tariff forces was strengthened by high levels of unemployment before the 1878 election, which the Conservatives won. Now that increased tariffs were firmly on the agenda, almost all industries lobbied for protection, but among the beneficiaries of protection the pro-tariff industries stood out.

The primary producers with monopoly positions in domestic production benefitted from tariff protection through being able to charge higher prices. The oil industry of southwestern Ontario almost entirely met Canadian demand, but the threat of imports regulated prices; the 1879 tariff permitted Canadian oil producers to raise the price from 50¢ a barrel to $1.50 a barrel. Nova Scotian coal interests had hoped to benefit from Confederation by preferential access to Canadian markets, but when customs duties were imposed on coal in 1870 opposition in central Canada led to their early removal. Between 1873 and 1879 Nova Scotian coal output declined by 35 per cent while Canadian coal imports from the United States were increasing, and by 1879 no Nova Scotian coal was being used in Ontario because the price per ton of anthracite was 80¢ for U.S. imports but $1.50 from Nova Scotia. The National Policy tariff on coal was 50¢ per ton, which was not enough to generate sales of Nova Scotian coal in Ontario but did increase sales in Quebec. The single important iron producer in Canada, located in Londonderry, Nova Scotia, had expanded during the 1870s with the help of an 1874 tariff increase, but by the late 1870s it was experiencing trouble in meeting foreign competition. The industry claimed increased protection to prevent further market loss, but the principal effect of the 1879 tariff increase was higher Canadian prices and greater profit margins for the Londonderry company (from 17¢ per 100 lbs. in 1879 to 30¢ in 1881), rather than a larger domestic market share due to increased price competitiveness (Donald, 1915, pp. 94-5).

The common characteristic of the oil, coal and iron industries was that in the absence of domestic competition Canadian prices were set by the price of competing imports. The 1879 tariff raised the prices of imports and permitted domestic producers to increase either their market share (coal) or their profit margins (oil and iron). In each case the value of Canadian output increased and was a component of Canadian industrial growth during the early 1880s.

The simple fact of an increased output by value is no proof of the desirability of this type of industrial growth. These were not infant industries; all were established before 1879, and none of them gained in efficiency or competitiveness on world markets as a result of the tariff. There was a welfare transfer from consumers to producers and to the government, plus a deadweight loss to Canada (cf. Figure 5.1). For example, in central Canada coal cost 50¢ per ton more, and in Ontario the 50¢ accrued to the federal government while farther east it accrued to the Nova Scotia coal-owners (many of whom lived in England). The costs of fostering these industries went deeper because their consumers were often secondary producers, who now faced higher prices for crucial inputs. The tariff on iron and steel especially brought protests from all branches of machine-making and engineering. When the iron tariff was raised again in 1887 it led directly to the closure of some secondary producers. An indicator of the economic cost of the policy is that the bankrupt firms may have been basically more efficient than the iron and steel industry, but the latter enjoyed a high effective rate of protection (ERP) while the former had a lower (or even negative) ERP as a result of the iron tariff.

Among the pro-tariff consumer goods industries, sugar and cotton stand out. In the early 1870s the two Canadian sugar refineries supplied only part of the domestic market. One refinery closed in 1876, and two years later the other threatened to close if a tariff of 1¢ per lb. were not levied on imported refined sugar. The 8 per cent dividend paid by the Redpath refinery in 1878 suggested that the situation was not desperate, and the demanded tariff was described in the House of Commons as a $1,000,000 subsidy of Redpath by Canadian consumers. Nevertheless, a 1¢ per lb. duty plus a 35 per cent ad valorem tariff was imposed on imported refined sugar. Not surprisingly, the Canadian industry boomed. Five new refineries were opened between 1879 and 1882. Prices and output both increased, and huge profits were made. By the mid-1880s excess capacity existed, prices fell by 40 per cent in 1884 and the boom turned to bust for some firms. The experience of the cotton industry was remarkably similar. During the 1870s Canadian producers supplied about a quarter of domestic consumption of cotton goods. The 1879 tariff imposed low duties on raw cotton and on cotton machinery but high duties on cotton textiles. The high ERP on cotton textiles induced a rapid expansion of domestic output and of profits; despite high rates of reinvestment, dividends exceeded 10 per cent in the years 1880–1882. The incentives to new entrants, however, soon led to overcapacity, and despite a further tariff increase in 1884, failures occurred.

Both the sugar and cotton industries provided a boost to Canadian manufactured output during the early 1880s as domestic producers cornered the Canadian market with the help of tariff protection. In the long run, however, neither industry contributed positively to Canadian economic welfare. Neither was an infant industry, and Canada had no basis for developing a comparative advantage in either product. Long-term stability was only achieved after monopolization enabled the Canadian industry to reap maximum profits behind its tariff wall. The fundamental problem of lack of competitiveness at world prices continues to this day, as Canadian textiles producers demand greater protection against increasingly competitive foreign producers and receive it from a government afraid of creating unemployment by deserting the industry. The cost has been higher Canadian prices than would have ruled under free trade—a century of lost surplus for Canada's consumers.

Most other existing industries would have preferred reciprocity to protection, but once it became clear that this would not happen each industry lobbied for and accepted tariff protection on its particular output. There is, however, little evidence that they gained much from protection, and as pointed out above, many suffered from increased input prices as a result of the 1879 tariff. It is also difficult to find examples of new industries developing as a result of the tariff.

The boom of the early 1880s was in large part a consequence of the 1879 tariff, but the industrial development was not of a healthy nature. Growth in the value of output was fastest in concentrated industries where price or domestic firms' market shares were limited by competing imports. The tariff increases gave Canadian firms an artificial edge over foreign firms, which permitted realization of greater monopoly profits by domestic firms (perhaps after the replacement of the now high-priced imports). None of these industries established a subsequent international competitiveness, and they required continued protection and an absence of competition in order to survive. The economic cost was severe in the case of coal and iron because increased prices of these goods resulted in higher (and distorted) costs throughout the manufacturing sector. In the long run, however, the welfare loss to consumers from higher prices for the necessities of food, clothing, lighting and fuel may have been still higher, since the first two have persisted to this day.

In contrasting the experiences of the 1860s and 1880s we must beware of reaching oversimplistic conclusions regarding the desirability of high tariffs. All of the cases examined in the present section imply a negative verdict on high tariffs, but the earlier account of the successful cheese industry provides a counterexample. On the basis of Canadian history, high tariffs cannot be categorized as bad per se; whether they are better or worse than no tariffs depends on the specific case. In the absence of more case studies, the assessment of the infant industry benefits from the high tariff policy must be left in abeyance.

4. Industrial Concentration and Combines Policy

By the turn of the century several branches of manufacturing industry were characterized by large production units. In addition to internal growth by firms trying to realize the advantages of large scale production, industrial concentration was being increased by a movement towards consolidation, which reached its first peak in the merger boom of 1909–1912. This movement has, of course, continued, and today there are many Canadian industries where a few producers account for a large share of the total output. The phenomenon is not unique to Canada, but it does appear to have been stronger than in other countries, such as the United States (Rosenbluth, 1957).

Most Canadian industries during the 1860s and 1870s were composed of small firms, and markets were fairly competitive. The deflationary period 1883–1896 brought pressure on firms' profit margins and led to fierce competition by price-cutting, easy credit terms, etc. The solution adopted in many industries was the formation of cartels, which aimed first to restrict credit terms and then to prevent price cuts. There is evidence for the formation of over one hundred cartels before 1900, and as many agreements were not documented, this is an understatement of their true number.

Competitive pressures were felt most keenly in industries which had expanded too rapidly after 1879 and had excess capacity by 1883. The leading example was cotton textiles. A "Cotton Congress" was held in 1883 to bring the producers together, and further attempts to form a cartel were made between 1883 and 1886. The agreements involved price and credit terms, prohibition of false invoicing or use of gifts, and restrictions on output. All, however, failed to last because of the "free rider" problem. Although restricting output in order to keep up the prices may increase the industry's total profits, any individual firm can benefit by producing its maximum output, instead of its allocated share of total output. In the cotton textile industry there were too many firms during the 1880s to be regulated effectively, and free riders soon broke up the cartels. In the early 1890s the two leading Montreal cotton manufacturers began a process of amalgamation by merging fourteen firms into two companies controlling 70 per cent of Canadian capacity. These mergers helped to stabilize output and prices during the 1890s. In the early 1900s the construction of new mills brought a threat of renewed instability, and the final solution was the effective monopolization of the industry by a merger creating the Dominion Textile Company.

The pattern of intermittent, unenforceable cartels was a common one; salt, twine, flour, canning and packing, tobacco, nails, paper and many other industries fell into this category. Successful cartels were formed by barbed wire, oil and some other industries, but they were a minority. In a period of falling prices and costs there were continuous incentives for undercutting rivals. The problem was exacerbated by the unmanageably large number of firms in most industries, which meant that a free rider could hope to evade detection for a while at least.

After 1896 the situation changed as an inflationary period provided little incentive for firms to break cartels by price-cutting. Moreover the process of failures and the effecting of mergers was making more industries easy to regulate. The passing of combines legislation in 1889 and its strengthening in 1900 had no direct effect, although it may have encouraged some colluders to be more discreet. Between 1900 and 1905 some eighty new cartel agreements were made, and presumably there were many further cases of tacit collusion.

Cartel agreements are not ideal long-term arrangements. The existence or threat of free riders is a constant source of instability, particularly when there are more than a handful of producers. There is thus an incentive for formal mergers to enable closer coordination and to reduce the free rider problem. This process had already occurred during the 1890s in industries where the incentives to merge were particularly strong or the finance for mergers was readily available (e.g., agricultural machinery and cotton textiles). On the west coast the salmon canning industry was converted into a concentrated industry by mergers between 1885 and 1902, although in this case the motivation was to control factor markets by providing a united bargaining front against the fishers rather than to control the product market (Reid, 1975). Apart from these examples, however, merger activity was limited before 1909.

The constraint on merger activity was the need for large financial resources. This appears true of Canada as well as of the better documented cases of the United States and Britain. Early merger booms occurred in the United States, in 1888–1892 and 1898–1902, and the development of the modern corporation and the modern capital market appears to have been an important precondition. The expansion of U.S. securities markets and the amendment of state laws on limited liability both occurred in the last quarter of the nineteenth century. The institutional changes occurred more slowly in Canada, where railway activity had less impact on the domestic securities market, and there was no corresponding merger boom. However, some of the new corporate giants in Canadian resource-based industries were limited liability companies registered in New Jersey, the state with the most liberal corporate legislation. Although banks played a role in financing some early Canadian mergers (e.g., the Bank of Montreal was involved in the consolidation of the cotton industry), in general the banks were slow to become entangled in the manufacturing sector (cf. chapter 8.3).

Canada's first merger boom occurred between 1909 and 1912. Merger activity in these four years greatly exceeded that of the previous nine years, although estimates of the boom's absolute size differ (Weldon, 1966; Naylor, 1975, vol. II, p. 190). The merger boom of 1909–1912 was managed primarily by professional merger promoters. Capital market conditions favoured this activity after 1907, and especially after 1909, when interest rates and share prices were low and portfolio investment was flowing to Canada from Britain. The promoters provided the finance to take over the constituent companies of a merger and then capitalized the new company at a larger amount. The shares in the new company included, in addition to those sold on the open market, stock issued to the promoters themselves ostensibly for services rendered. The part of the new stock issue which did not represent any real investment is called "water." The motive for the 1909-1912 mergers appears to have been rarely industrial, in the sense of improving technical efficiency, but rather to exploit market power in order to pay high dividends even on the watered stock (Naylor, 1975, ch. 14).

Merger activity has continued in Canada throughout the twentieth century. The boom of the 1920s saw a peak in activity even higher than that of 1909-1912, and the postwar period has seen still larger mergers. The most detailed historical study of Canadian mergers (Weldon, 1966) covers the period 1900-1948 and reveals two characteristics of the mergers. Firstly, the overwhelming proportion (71 per cent) of mergers were "horizontal," i.e., involving firms producing for the same product market. Secondly, the mergers could more aptly be described as take-overs since the absorbing enterprise was on average ten times larger than the absorbed enterprise; Weldon (p. 269) concludes that "apparently equals rarely enter into consolidation. Rather, the large enterprise absorbs the small." These characteristics suggest a continuing motivation of increasing market power. Horizontal mergers cannot yield economies of integrated production runs, and the size disparities imply that any increases in scale economies were minimal for the absorbing firms.

Whether increased concentration in an industry benefits society or not depends upon the shape of the industry's long run average cost curve. In a constant cost industry a competitive market structure would ensure that price was equal to unit costs (which include the opportunity cost of producers). At any price above P_c in Figure 6.1, new firms will be encouraged to enter the industry, increasing output and pushing the price back down to P_c. The industry's profits are, however, maximized at the price-quantity combination P_m, Q_m, where marginal cost is equal to marginal revenue and earnings exceed opportunity costs by the shaded area. This situation can only be maintained if the industry can restrict output to Q_m and represents a social welfare loss because output is lower and price higher than would obtain under perfect competition; the loss in consumer surplus exceeds the gain in producer surplus by the triangle DWL (cf. Figure 5.1). If monopoly power were being exercised in the industry to hold prices above P_c, then it would be in the public interest to regulate this behaviour, perhaps by changing the industrial structure; a reduction in the size of firms would not entail any loss in efficiency because there are no economies of scale. This conclusion would, however, not be true in a

Figure 6.1

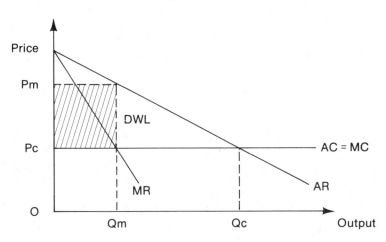

where AC = average cost, MC = marginal cost, AR = average revenue, MR = marginal revenue

declining cost industry, where many small producers could have higher costs and prices and lower total output than a monopolist, even though the latter earned monopoly profits. Where economies of scale are large relative to the size of the market, a reduction in concentration may involve a social loss as a result of higher average costs. Thus the growth of industrial concentration in Canada may have yielded costs or benefits. If the government wishes to intervene in the process it is faced with the problem that, whether the industry has economies of scale or not, firms will conspire to increase their market power, and they will always claim that this was done to realize scale economies.

The government has two principal instruments for regulating monopoly power: combines legislation and commercial policy. Canada has had legislation against conspiracy or mergers among domestic producers since 1889, but it has been largely ineffective. Two principles of the legislation were that restrictive practices and mergers were not illegal per se, but only if they "unduly" restrained competition, and that publicity should be the main regulatory device. The word "unduly" made it difficult to obtain convictions, and the envisaged punishment served as no great deterrent. Hardly any cartels were charged under the act, and during the 1909–1912 merger boom the combines legislation was never enforced. This pattern has continued, and despite some publicized cases the impact of the combines legislation on industrial structure or market behaviour has been minimal. The Canadian government has also foresworn the use of commercial policy as a means of reducing market power. The protective tariff has had the opposite effect, sheltering Canadian producers from international competition and, in the case of the 1879 tariff (cf. chapter 6.3) and the 1907 tariff increases, providing an incentive for further abuse of monopoly power or increased consolidation.

The importance of large industrial enterprises in Canada has been growing since the 1870s, and today Canadian industry is characterized by high levels of concentration. Although internal growth has been important in many firms, mergers appear to have been the major route to large Canadian-owned firms (foreign-owned subsidiaries are another matter). The mergers seem to have been aimed at increasing market power rather than realizing economies of scale, but the latter may have been among the consequences of some mergers. In retrospect, it might be expected that the government would have taken steps to impede this flight from competition, but in practice the government only passed ineffective legislation. The role of the government was essentially not to prevent cartels or mergers which were occurring, and to give an additional boost to the gains from domestic monopoly power by imposing protective tariffs.

5. Direct Foreign Investment

Canadian industry is characterized by a degree of foreign ownership unmatched among major economic powers. The time path and nature of foreign investment have been described in chapter 4.5, and the effect of commercial policy on foreign investment has been examined in chapter 5.1. A broader view of the phenomenon of direct foreign investment (DFI) will now be presented.

The first U.S. branch plant in Canada appears to have been the agricultural implements plant of Hall Bros., established in Oshawa in 1860. Although this soon went out of business, other small branch plants were established, particularly in border towns. The most substantial direct foreign investment during the 1870s and 1880s was, however, in resource industries. In these decades, the firms which would merge in 1902 to form International Nickel were incorporated in the United States and were mining Canadian copper and nickel for smelting and refining in New Jersey. The 1880s also witnessed American investment in Quebec asbestos mines. These and other mining investments were part of a more general U.S. search for raw materials (DFI in mining in Mexico was approximately double that in Canada). Somewhat similar was American DFI in Canadian timber, as U.S. supplies of timber were becoming depleted. Much of this occurred piecemeal, but the total holdings were substantial by the end of the century; for example, the International Paper Company revealed in 1899 that it owned some 1.6 million acres of timber land in Canada. In the case of timber there was public concern about the location of processing activities outside Canada, and from 1886 a series of measures restricting unprocessed timber exports led to an increased number of pulp and paper mills in Canada, many of which were American-owned. Other natural resources also attracted foreign investment, especially the cheap and abundant hydroelectric power which was critical for the establishment of the aluminum industry and various electrochemical activities.

The turn of the century saw a change in the pattern of direct foreign investment. Branch plants of U.S. manufacturing industry started to become more important than resource-based DFI, and the rapid expansion of DFI during the first two decades of the twentieth century occurred mainly in the manufacturing sector. Incentives for the establishment of branch plants in Canada were provided by the protective tariff, bonuses and the patent legislation (cf. chapter 5.1), but these dated from the 1850s, 1860s and 1870s and cannot explain the surge of branch plant establishment after 1900. It would therefore appear that Canadian policies were not basic causal factors, and the invasion of American branch plants after 1900 was largely a matter of proximity ("spillover" is the term used by Wilkins, 1970) during the geographical expansion of the U.S. manufacturing sector (Aitken, 1961, p. 14). Industries located in the northeastern United States and the industrial midwest began to expand in all directions after 1900, opening branch plants especially in the western states, Canada and Mexico (American DFI in Mexico in 1900 and 1914 was almost exactly the same as in Canada at those dates). Further evidence in support of this geographical explanation is the relative unimportance of British direct investment. British direct investment was concentrated west of Ontario (Paterson, 1976), an area of relative neglect by American firms which located their branch plants closer to the industrial heartland of the United States.

In the absence of any barriers to DFI in Canada, the fact that U.S. corporate expansion included Canada should not be surprising. What is surprising to later Canadians is the government's lack of concern over the loss of economic sovereignty. The government's attitude can perhaps best be explained by the novelty of transnational corporations and the definition of Canadian production as production in Canada. The latter was clearly revealed in the attempt to encourage "Canadian" steel production by stipulating in 1900 that every railway receiving federal subsidies must use rails "made in Canada" if they could be bought "upon terms as favourable as other rails can be obtained"—the principal lobbyist for this clause was an American promoter who intended to build a steel rail plant in Canada! In this instance, and in many others, the Canadian government's attitude to direct foreign investment was not neutral, but distinctly positive. Municipal bonus schemes were angled directly at U.S. corporations considering a Canadian branch plant. Canadian combines and fiscal legislation provided further attractions to U.S. corporations; Canadian affiliates could enter into cartel negotiations with European producers whereas U.S. antitrust legislation banned such behaviour by the parent, and the absence of corporate income tax in Canada before 1917 encouraged American corporations to register foreign stock holdings under their Canadian affiliate in order to avoid taxation. These were scarcely basic causes of DFI, but they did provide added incentive for the establishment of a Canadian branch.

Foreign corporations were also active in the financial sector. American insurance companies, acting in the context of their domestic expansion programs, crossed the border to market policies and had to invest funds in Canada to cover deposit requirements there. The value of these investments was some $68 million by 1913. Commercial banking, however, provided a striking exception to American "spillover." This was partly due to differences in banking practices in the two countries, but also to the statutory requirement that a majority of the directors of every Canadian bank must be British subjects domiciled in Canada.

The significance which foreign investment has assumed in the Canadian economy stems from the nature of that investment. Other countries industrializing during the nineteenth century borrowed heavily, but without great lasting effect. British investment in Canadian railways and later in the Canadian west fell into this pattern, too. But the most significant part of foreign investment in Canada was that by American industrial corporations, which established non-liquifiable branch plants. These branch plants have persisted and grown in number and size to become a prominent characteristic of the Canadian economy and a major political issue. Initially, however, there was little antipathy towards the branch plants, and government policy was not discouraging. Whether the government was right not to legislate against the "spillover" in manufacturing, as it did with respect to unprocessed timber and banks, depends on one's assessment of the desirability of direct foreign investment. The branch plants were not responsible for the establishment of modern industry in Canada, but they did bring capital into Canada and provide competition for Canadian firms. These may not have been net benefits if U.S. branch plants crowded out rather than augmented domestic investment, and if they put domestic firms out of business, but we do not know the answers to these empirical questions. A clearer cost, at the heart of the present debate over foreign ownership, is the loss of domestic control over the economy and the reduced efficacy of government economic policies when decisions affecting large parts of Canadian industries are taken south of the border.

6. The Naylor Thesis

An ambitious attempt to formulate a theory of Canadian industrialization is that of Naylor. His starting point is a view of industrial development which divides industrialized countries into two groups on the basis of the path which they followed to industrialization. In the first group, modern manufacturing evolved "naturally" by a process of capital accumulation in small-scale units of production, which were usually extensions of pre-industrial cottage industries or artisanal modes of production. Profits were reinvested to finance future growth, and in time the units of production became larger. This was approximately the path followed by the early European industrializers and in New England. The second group of countries, latecomers trying to cut corners in industrializing, moved directly to large-scale enterprises. This path requires some external financing, by the government or financial intermediaries or by foreigners.

According to Naylor, in Canada during the second half of the nineteenth century "both paths were available and both were being utilized" (Naylor, 1975, I, p. 38). The first path could be seen in the progress of the agricultural machinery and cheese industries in Ontario and of the boot and shoe and woollen industries in Quebec, while the cotton and sugar industries provided evidence of the second path. The outside capital for the latter industries came primarily from merchants. In the colonial systems of France and England, the merchants had been the dominant class, and they now had the capital and contacts with other sources of capital through their political influence and links with international finance.

Naylor sees the crucial issue in the late nineteenth century as being the struggle over which path Canada would follow. The industrialization of the 1860s consisted primarily of "natural" development along New England lines. The 1870s witnessed the merchants' reaction to this new development; as they saw their economic domination slipping they tried to set Canada on the second path with themselves at the helm. The 1879 tariff was a victory for the merchants, the result of their political dominance and the beginning of their industrial preeminence. Only behind tariff barriers could the merchants build up the industries which they controlled.

An implication of the strategy of rapid industrialization with large-scale enterprises was that innovations and capital from abroad should have easy access into Canada. The 1872 Patent Law encouraged rapid diffusion of foreign inventions and, together with the high tariff and bonuses, stimulated foreign investment. The government, at various levels, also provided finance for industry and infrastructure. The merchants themselves were unwilling to meet the capital requirements (even had they been able) because they had neither the expertise nor experience of large investments in manufacturing. Their capital flowed more easily into staple investment abroad than into manufacturing at home, so that once they had established trade-related industries like sugar and cotton they faded in importance relative to the American multinationals, especially after 1900. Although losing control of the manufacturing sector, the merchants retained control over the financial institutions, servicing commerce and big business, and reinforcing the problems of small Canadian enterprises starved of access to capital. Thus Naylor explains not only the nature of industrial development in late-nineteenth-century Canada, but also the ubiquity of U.S. branch plants in twentieth-century Canadian industry.

Although Naylor's thesis has aroused widespread interest and has been accepted in toto by some Canadian economic historians (e.g., Watkins, 1976), there are problems with respect to his definitions, chronology and locational analysis. The distinction between industrial and mercantile capital is not as clear in reality as in Naylor's theory. Although there are cases of opposition between merchants and manufacturers, especially in preindustrial economies, they do not necessarily have to be in conflict. In western Europe and New England, many early manufacturers were men who had made their initial wealth as merchants, and manufacturing enterprises which were partnerships between inventors with ideas and merchants with capital were not uncommon. Cases of cooperation between industrialists and merchants also existed in Canada, especially with respect to railways. Canadian railways were industrial projects run by merchants and manufacturing interests and were also by far the largest industrial investments in the second half of the nineteenth century (Macdonald, 1975). In practice, members of the two groups were so closely linked in Canada that merchants and manufacturers are frequently inseparable at both high and low levels; George Stephen, for example, was in the cotton, wool and steel industries, as well as railways, but is frequently referred to by Naylor as a leader of the merchants.

Chronologically, Naylor emphasizes the 1879 tariff as the signal of the merchant's victory. Canada's high tariff policy dates, however, from 1858–1859, that is, before the "natural" industrial development of the 1860s. More importantly, Naylor emphasizes Canadian government policy, especially the 1872 Patent Act, the 1879 tariff and the multifarious bonus schemes, in explaining American direct investment. Government policy was favourable from the viewpoint of the American corporations, but was not the fundamental reason for their establishing Canadian branch plants in the twentieth century.

The location of manufacturing activity in Canada also appears to argue against Naylor's thesis. He presents the 1879 tariff as the victory of Montreal mercantile interests over manufacturing interests, which were primarily located in southern Ontario. Montreal did, in fact, have one major victory over southern Ontario (concerning the CPR terminus), but otherwise the battle went the other way and it was between 1850 and 1900 that Toronto made rapid progress towards overtaking Montreal (cf., chapter 10).

Finally, it may be noted that although Naylor's thesis is closely related to that of Gerschenkron, it is Naylor's additions—especially the merchant-manufacturer dichotomy and the explanation of American branch plant activity—which are the weak part of his thesis. The basic relationships between industrial development and economic backwardness observed by Gerschenkron appear to hold for late-nineteenth-century Canada. Agriculture played some role in Ontario, but not as great a role as in England. Modern industry grew rapidly, with the help of foreign technology and capital, and was soon characterized by large production units. Canadian governments played a more substantial part in industrial development than those of western Europe or the United States, but did not intervene directly in industrial production in the manner of Japanese and Russian governments. In sum, the characteristics of Canadian industrialization correspond to her condition as a more backward economy than that of England, the United States, etc., but less backward than that of Japan or Russia at the beginning of the growth of modern industry.

7. Conclusions

This chapter has attempted to date the growth of modern industry in Canada and to explain two of the salient characteristics of Canadian industry. The peculiarities of Canada's manufacturing sector have led to several attempts to construct specific theories of Canadian industrialization, explaining its "dependence" on foreign capital. Naylor's thesis is the best-developed of these theories, but it has serious weaknesses.

The root of the problem with Naylor's approach and other specific theories of Canadian industrialization is their view of Canada's industrial development being radically different from that of other countries. Every industrialization process is unique, but only up to a point. Gerschenkron's theory of industrial growth is rather vague, but the consistency of Canada's experience with this theory suggests that Canadian industrialization is not independent of patterns drawn from international comparisons. The behaviour of Canada's investment-output ratio, which rose significantly between 1900 and 1910 some four decades after her "industrial revolution," is also consistent with the pattern found in other industrialized countries (Kuznets, 1966). The high levels of direct foreign investment in Canadian manufacturing since 1900 can be explained in terms of North American trends. In sum, if cognizance is taken of Canada's degree of economic backwardness in 1850 and of her geographic location, no specific theory is needed to account for the nature of her industrial development.

This conclusion is not intended to force the industrial development of diverse countries into a single pattern. The uniqueness of the Canadian case stemmed from her location and intermediate degree of backwardness, and also from her specific culture, resource base and opportunities. Thus, although Canada's industrial structure followed a common path from an initial emphasis on consumer goods (e.g., clothing, footwear, food and tobacco products) to an increased share of producer goods, the particular structure at any point in time was uniquely Canadian. For example, whereas agricultural machinery has retained a continuing importance, textiles and iron and steel products never assumed the significance they possessed in other cases of industrialization. Differences in industrial structure do not, however, necessarily imply a need for alternative theories of industrial development.

Finally, mention should be made of the major industrial development of the 1896–1914 period—the growth of the primary iron and steel industry. This industry had played a central role in other countries industrializing in the mid- and late-nineteenth century through its focal position as a producer good industry, and especially because of backward linkages from railway construction. In Canada, however, railway construction had not stimulated the industry, because rails had been imported; in the 1850s tariffs were not protective, and later the CPR had been exempted from import duties. The primary iron and steel industry was still not large by 1896. The volume of Canada's domestic demand could have been met by two or three blast furnaces using 1890s technology, but such a small number of plants could not have produced the variety of grades demanded. After 1896 primary iron and steel production increased rapidly. Pig iron output grew from 104,882 tons in 1896–1898 to 1,937,144 tons in 1909–1911, and over a million tons were produced in the single year 1913. Steel output grew even faster, from 23,945 tons in 1900 to 880,278 tons in 1911 (Donald, 1915). Demand conditions were favourable during the wheat boom era, and so was government policy. The tariff on iron and steel was raised in 1897, non-tariff barriers to imports were imposed (especially through municipal aid and railway legislation) and bounties paid to primary iron and steel producers increased from $610,607 over 1883–1895 to $16,785,827 over 1895–1913. The 1900 Railway Subsidy Act, forcing federally subsidized railways to purchase rails domestically, was especially important on the eve of the second and third transcontinental projects. It would be interesting to know the relative impact of the various government measures, particularly as the subsidies provide a rare example of the first-best method of encouraging an infant industry. The industry was established in Canada by 1914, and the subsidies were then terminated, but it is unclear whether they were a significant cause of the industry's establishment.

Chapter 7

The Prairie Wheat Economy

A dramatic feature of Canada's history since Confederation has been the transformation of an unlikely agglomeration of unconnected colonies into a transcontinental nation. The key to this transformation was the peopling of the Prairies after the expropriation of the Hudson's Bay Company in 1870. Sixty years later a quarter of Canada's population lived in the Prairie provinces, and the economy of the region was almost totally dependent on wheat. Although emphasis on the wheat boom as the prime mover in Canada's economic development is no longer accepted, the growth of the Prairie wheat economy must still be recognized as an important feature. Moreover, the particular problems of the wheat economy and the distrust which these raised are the root of many of the east–west tensions in present-day Canada. In this chapter we will first describe the growth of the wheat economy, and then examine the economic problems associated with the operation of the Prairie wheat economy. The appendix discusses a controversial attempt to assess the contribution of the wheat boom to Canadian economic growth.

1. Chronology

Settlement of the Prairies was fairly slow during the 1870s and 1880s, when Canadian land policy and climatic conditions combined to make the Canadian west less attractive than competing American frontier areas. By the 1890s the U.S. agricultural frontier on the sub-humid plains was practically closed and techniques of dry-farming had been developed, so that when rising wheat prices induced renewed westward migration the settlers gravitated to the Prairies (cf. chapter 5.3). Of 675,000 homestead entries between 1870 and 1930, 440,000 were made during the period 1900–1914, the years of greatest activity being 1909–1912. Prairie population tripled between the 1901 and 1911 censuses, and the acreage under fieldcrops increased fivefold. The Prairie economy was geared to rapid growth; railway mileage in the region increased from 4,100 miles in 1901 to 11,600 miles in 1914, and an investment boom occurred, financed to a substantial extent from abroad (primarily British portfolio investment in companies providing farm mortgages).

An increase in British interest rates in 1912 was the first warning of trouble for the Prairie wheat economy. Reduced capital outflows from Britain led to a tightening of farm credit in Canada in 1913. Wheat prices fell in 1913, and a serious depression threatened farmers who were deeply in debt. The Prairie farmers' problems were emphasized by a poor 1914 crop and the disruption of international trade by war.

The war soon turned out to be a boon to Canadian farmers, and recession was averted by increased wheat purchases by Canada's allies. The British government, in particular, believed that bread was "the only diet which sufficed in isolation and was therefore indispensable" (Fowke, 1957, p. 166) and turned to Canada for their wheat purchases. Wheat prices rose and the boom continued in the immediate postwar years; the average price of No. 1 Northern wheat at Fort William (now Thunder Bay) increased from $1.07 per bushel for 1910–1916 to $2.31 for 1917–1920. Although averting recession, the war boom increased the wheat-growers' vulnerability as they responded to high prices and government exhortations by raising production; to this end, Prairie farmers bought land and equipment at inflated prices and went deeper into debt. Such optimism was, however, scarcely justified, since the boom rested on the temporary disruption of European, and in particular Russian, agriculture.

The 1920s were a decade of mixed fortunes for the wheat economy. Wheat prices fell rapidly between 1920 and 1924, but then turned up again in 1925. In the following years the Prairies enjoyed a combination of high wheat prices and good harvests, reaching a peak harvest in 1928 which was not repeated until 1952. Canadian wheat exports doubled between 1925 and 1929 to reach almost $500 million, which accounted for about half of the total world wheat exports. This was the high point of the Prairie wheat economy.

During the 1930s, depression in the United States and Europe reduced the demand for wheat, and at the same time most governments reacted to the depression by protecting domestic producers. The reduced demand for wheat by the importing countries caused a steep fall in the world price. Drought conditions in the Prairies exacerbated the region's difficulties, and the combination of lower prices and lower output led to a disastrous fall in Prairie farmers' net income (estimated by Fowke at $218 million in 1928, $42 million in 1933 and $18 million in 1937). The costs of overextension, which had threatened in 1913–1914 and 1920–1924, had to be met after 1929 when no revival of world wheat prices came to bring relief. Net emigration from the Prairies during the 1930s was about a quarter of a million people. For those who remained, living standards fell drastically; in Saskatchewan, the worst hit province, per capita income fell by 72 per cent between 1928–1929 and 1933.

The growth of the Prairie wheat economy was accompanied by instability. In this respect it is similar to some earlier staples (e.g., fur), but instability was more harmful in the wheat economy in terms of the human cost. Also, the cause of instability differed. As with fur, external demand was inelastic, but in the case of wheat world supply was highly variable since it depended on climatic conditions. Large fluctuations in supply coupled with an inelastic demand curve led to great variations in price. Although the Canadian harvest was a major component of world supply, it was not the sole component, and in some years Prairie farmers could enjoy high prices and a good harvest yet in other years face low prices and a poor harvest; when this happened in the late 1920s and early 1930s, it accentuated the boom-bust pattern. A further destabilizing factor was the over-optimism and unjustifiably high investment during the boom periods. For example, 1927–1930 was a period when tractors, combines and trucks were introduced on a substantial scale. The succeeding bust periods were thus accompanied by severe debt repayment problems.

By the late 1930s it was widely recognized that the principal cause of instability was monoculture and that parts of the Prairies were more suited to other uses than wheat growing. Therefore, when World War II ushered in a new boom and there was a large wheat crop in 1940, the government stepped in to forestall overexpansion. This was accomplished more easily than during World War I because of the German Atlantic blockade. The government also encouraged diversification, so that whereas two thirds of Prairie income derived from wheat in 1939, less than a third came from wheat by 1942. In particular, livestock farming supplanted wheat in much of Alberta. The trend towards diversification has continued since the war as oil and other natural resources have brought renewed prosperity. Although wheat retains its leading position, the Prairies are no longer as dependent on this single crop.

2. The Farmers versus Monopoly Power

Monopoly power characterized the Prairie wheat economy, just as it had the fur trade before; there were many producers but few purchasers of the product. In the fur trade this had led to little conflict between producers and traders because the former were not in a position to protest effectively. The wheat farmer, on the other hand, was acutely aware of the inequality of bargaining power, and he could make his protests heard in Ottawa and, especially, in the capitals of the Prairie provinces.

The first conflict over monopoly power concerned the "monopoly clause" in the CPR charter (chapter 5.2). The Manitoba government's attempts to bypass the clause by chartering new railway lines were vetoed by the federal government. In 1888 the CPR was induced by the federal government to renounce the monopoly clause, but the company was still able to prevent effective railway competition in the Prairies until further transcontinental lines were constructed in the twentieth century. Prairie protest did, however, have some effect in reducing freight rates on grain under the 1897 Crow's Nest Pass Agreement, and rates were reduced again in 1903. Although the rate structure remained a source of discontent, it was no longer in the front line after that time.

The CPR also used its monopoly position to standardize grain loading procedures. The earliest practices had been to use loading platforms or to load the grain from flat warehouses. Loading platforms erected by a siding enabled farmers to load grain direct from their wagons into a boxcar, but they had the drawback of requiring coordination of the arrival of the farmer and the boxcar. The flat warehouses, which were easy to build and provided shelter from the elements, were the simplest means of overcoming this drawback. Grain elevators had two major advantages over these procedures: they provided superior storage facilities, and they required less labour to load the grain into boxcars. The extensive construction of elevators during the 1890s was supported by the CPR, which pressured flat warehouse proprietors to close down or build elevators, although for the Railway's own convenience it discouraged construction of more than one elevator at any point along its track.

The CPR's policy granted a local monopoly to each elevator, and the degree of monopoly power possessed by elevator owners was enhanced by the concentration of ownership. Five companies owned 301 of the 447 elevators existing in 1900, and only 26 were owned by farmers. In the 1897 season the non-farmer-owned elevator companies formed a cartel which was soon formalized, taking the name North West Grain Dealers' Association, in 1903. The power of the elevator companies derived largely from their fulfilling several functions in addition to the provision of storage facilities; in particular, they usually acted as purchasers of wheat. Although storage charges and practices were a source of dispute, they were relatively easy to regulate, and this was done by the government, particularly after 1912. The main use of monopoly power lay in setting the purchase price of wheat. The cartel agreed upon a price at each location, which was the terminal price minus appropriate costs and profits; by setting their own allowance for profits, which was not subject to competitive pressures or to government regulation, the elevator companies were able to benefit from their local monopolies.

The first attempt by the farmers to reduce the elevator companies' monopoly power was to break the CPR's support of the elevators' local monopolies. In 1900 the federal Parliament passed legislation requiring the railway to provide boxcars without discrimination for loading from flat warehouses, loading platforms or elevators, and to construct (upon written application from ten farmers) loading platforms which were to be available free of charge. The law was upheld in the courts in a 1902 test case, when a CPR agent was found guilty of discrimination. After that, the law was observed by the CPR, but it had little effect in providing competition for the elevators because the greater labour requirements, inconvenience and uncertainty of the loading platforms damaged their popularity vis-à-vis the elevators.

The second approach of the farmers was to press charges against the North West Grain Dealers' Association under the combines legislation.

In this they were encouraged by a 1906 Royal Commission, which had reported that "the main object of the association evidently is the regulating of the buying of grain in the country" and had described the method of open pricing by which a daily telegram listing purchase prices was sent to all buying points. When the case came before the courts in 1907, however, the judge ruled that there was no "undue" restraint of competition and found that "the very acts complained of, taken in connection with their surrounding conditions, made on the whole for a more stable market at the fullest values and so for the public good." Since the price being set was that to farmers and the export price was determined outside Canada, the effects of the cartel's operations were solely to redistribute income in Canada from the farmers to the elevator companies. The judge's view of the "public good" was thus highly selective. Nevertheless, this strange verdict was upheld even after appeal.

The failure to provide competition for elevators and to prosecute the cartel led some farmers to cooperate in raising capital to build their own elevators. The number of farmer-owned elevators increased from 26 to 60 between 1900 and 1910, but this increase was rather modest in a decade when the total number of non-terminal elevators grew from 447 to 1,830. The farmer-owned elevators were generally characterized by lack of success. This was apparently due to bad management in many cases, but was also a result of predatory behaviour by the cartel.

The growing pressure for government intervention had its first success in Manitoba, where the government invested over a million dollars in buying 164 elevators from private owners and in constructing ten new elevators. The experiment was an unqualified fiasco; huge financial losses were made, and the scheme was abandoned after two crop years (1910 and 1911), after which the elevators were leased and later sold to a farmers' association. The disaster stemmed partly from the lack of commitment by a government which was not pro farming interests but which tried to buy farmers' support, and partly from incompetence. The government purchased badly located elevators, which farmers saw no reason to patronize, and provided only warehousing services, which did not meet all farmers' requirements.

The schemes introduced in Saskatchewan in 1911 and Alberta in 1913 were more successful. These provincial governments were unwilling to manage elevators directly, but they did set up cooperative companies consisting of individual locally owned and run elevators underwritten by the government. The cooperative ventures led to elevators being located where required, provided effective competition to non-farmer-owned elevators, and were profitable. In 1917 the Alberta Farmers' Cooperative Elevator Company amalgamated with a Manitoba farmers' association to form the United Grain Growers Limited, and by 1920 the UGG and the Saskatchewan Cooperative Elevator Company were operating 650 elevators successfully. The two cooperative companies provided alternatives to private elevators at almost half the local shipment points, and handled about a quarter of Prairie grain. This market share seems to have been sufficient to curb the private companies' use of the spread between local and Winnipeg prices in order to reap monopoly profits.

The successful establishment of the cooperative elevator companies marked the limit of farmers' ability to significantly improve marketing conditions at the local level. Future improvements in the farmers' economic position had to come through higher prices received at the grain market. It should be noted, however, that Prairie farmers continued to suffer indirectly from a situation where they sold in competitive markets but had to purchase consumer goods and inputs in Canadian markets which were frequently not competitive. The Prairies have consistently been on the side of free trade and tougher combines legislation, but with little effect. The result has been that farmers not only face unfavourably distorted relative prices, but have also been less capable of withstanding fluctuations than other sectors. For example, between 1929 and 1933 agricultural prices fell by 50 per cent while output rose by 4 per cent, but agricultural machinery prices fell by only 7 per cent as production was cut back; the monopolistic industry had a choice between lower prices or lower output or some combination of the two, but farmers were price-takers.

3. The Marketing of Wheat

Before 1920 Prairie protest was primarily aimed at the unequal bargaining power of the farmers vis-à-vis the elevator companies. After the proven success of the cooperative elevators the protest shifted against the free market system itself. On this issue, however, the farmers' calls for government intervention met stronger opposition. Governments could sympathize with complaints based on the view that the free market would be fine if purged of monopoly interests; after all, the federal government was committed to western settlement and was prepared to provide some support for the farmers. The new protest viewed the free market itself as detrimental to farmers' interests; it struck at the heart of the free enterprise system and was thus unacceptable to the government. The changed attitude of the federal government is revealed in the composition of Royal Commissions examining the wheat economy; before World War I they were filled with farming interests, but after the war farming interests were excluded from membership and reduced to just presenting evidence.

Before World War I the free market was the exclusive outlet for grain, and Prairie wheat was increasingly channelled through the Winnipeg Grain Exchange as the main trading place. In 1917 the government intervened in the grain trade, closing the Winnipeg exchange and marketing grain itself. The intervention was born of necessity in the face of commitments to Canada's war allies rather than to any change in economic philosophy, and as soon as possible the government restored the free market. The Winnipeg Grain Exchange reopened in August 1920. Psychologically, this was a bad time to reopen, for although the falling wheat prices of the next four years were determined in the world market, the Winnipeg Grain Exchange became associated with low prices and the government-administered market of 1917–1920 with high prices.

The wheat market was characterized by a year-round demand for wheat and by farmers' sales being concentrated in the autumn. The Prairie farmers did not have adequate storage facilities to hold grain over the winter, and they needed the cash to pay off debts accumulated during the year. The Winnipeg Grain Exchange was therefore heavily involved in future trading, as merchants bought wheat in the autumn for future delivery to the terminal. In its basic form this is legitimate trading, but the futures market also provided an arena for speculation as purchasers gambled on buying cheap and selling dear. Speculators would trade contracts for future delivery without any grain changing hands, and it was this type of activity which particularly drew farmers' opposition; farmers believed that speculators were making large profits by contributing nothing and that it was at the farmers' expense.

After the reopening of the Winnipeg Grain Exchange, the farmers realized that their preferred solution of a government monopoly in wheat marketing would not be implemented. Their second best solution was the organization of wheat pools in Alberta in 1923 and Saskatchewan and Manitoba in 1924. The producer-owned-and-controlled pools collected the wheat under contract from member farmers and sold it through a jointly run Central Selling Agency. The farmer was paid an initial price after the harvest plus an increment when all the wheat had been sold, such that the total price per bushel was the average price received for that quality of wheat minus the pool's costs. The pools financed the autumn advances through a loan arrangement with the commercial banks. The Central Selling Agency bypassed the Winnipeg Grain Exchange by establishing agencies for direct selling in Europe, China, etc. The aim of the pools was to reduce the spread between local and overseas prices and the seasonal price spread, rather than to affect world prices which were accepted as given. The significant point about the pools was that after 1923 the free market never provided the sole outlet for Prairie farmers' crops.

Despite its apparent superiority, the pool system was responsible for marketing only half of the wheat harvested in the Prairies from 1924 to 1928. It is not clear whether individual farmers received higher prices through the pools or on the free market, nor is it known what the free market prices would have been in the absence of the pools. The most plausible explanation, however, is that by providing competition to the Winnipeg Grain Exchange, the pools increased the prices received by farmers, but given their existence free-rider farmers could benefit by selling to private grain-dealers and thus avoiding contributing to the pools' running costs. The pool system also had its internal problems. Every year there were differing opinions on when to sell the pools' wheat and when to hold it off the market, and there was often conflict between the agents abroad and the Central Selling Agency management in Canada.

The 1929 and 1930 crop seasons saw the collapse of the pool marketing system. Unpredicted drops in wheat prices meant that the pools' initial payments to farmers were too high. The banks pressed for repayment of their loans, and the pools turned to the federal government for aid, which was granted subject to the appointment of a new Central Selling Agency manager who was acceptable to the banks. The appointee, J.I. McFarland, was an outstanding figure in the private grain trade. He immediately closed the Central Selling Agency's foreign branches, and direct selling was essentially finished by the end of 1930. Although the Central Selling Agency continued to exist, the amount of wheat sold through it fell drastically and the pools became little more than cooperative elevator companies.

As Prairie farm incomes dropped during the early 1930s, there was growing pressure for the reestablishment of the Wheat Board. The government resisted at first but eventually relented in 1935 on the eve of a general election. The new Wheat Board did not go all the way toward meeting farmers' demands since it was established on a voluntary basis, i.e., as an alternative to the free market rather than as a government monopoly. The payment procedures were similar to those of the pools' Central Selling Agency, except that there was no contractual arrangement between farmers and the Wheat Board. Thus, a farmer could wait until the Wheat Board's initial payment was announced and then decide on his marketing channel. In 1935 the Wheat Board's initial payment was higher than the current free market price so farmers sold to the Wheat Board, but in 1936 and 1937 the initial payment was less than the free market price and the Wheat Board was not used. In 1938 world prices were lower than expected and the initial payment exceeded market prices throughout the selling year, so that farmers sold to the Wheat Board which made substantial losses. In sum, farmers saw the 1935-1938 Wheat Board as a provider of minimum price support, which had not been the government's intention. After the 1938 crop year losses the government moved to abolish the Wheat Board, but western pressure led to its retention into World War II.

A major reorganization of the Wheat Board occurred in 1943. The government was worried about meeting its wheat commitments under Mutual Aid, but did not want soaring wheat prices to encourage over-expansion of the wheat economy as had happened during World War I. To these ends, the Wheat Board was made into the compulsory market-ing agency for all Prairie wheat. Although the measure was announced as a temporary one, the Wheat Board's monopoly has remained until today.

One force for the retention of the Wheat Board has been the dimin-ishing importance of the free world market for wheat since the 1930s. Many importing countries have placed restrictions on wheat imports and their governments have acted as single purchasers, so that exporting countries' governments have been induced to act as sole agents for their wheatgrowers in order to wield countervailing market power. Bargain-ing power has, however, continued to revolve more on demand and supply conditions than on the number of bargainers. In the 1960s an excess supply of wheat led exporters to try to cut back their production, while during the 1970s it was a sellers' market.

Prairie farmers have benefitted from the government monopoly in wheat marketing. The profiteering middlemen (of unknown quantitative importance) have been cut out, farmers are guaranteed a minimum price, and Canadian wheat producers have a stronger say in an oligopsonistic world market. On the other hand, government marketing cannot solve the fundamental problem—that widely fluctuating world supply and inelastic world demand combine to produce large variations in world wheat prices.

4. Farm Credit

Prairie farmers were not only discontented with the working of goods markets, they were also dissatisfied with the operation of Canadian financial markets. The problems arose from farmers' high demand for both long-term and short-term credit; the former for the establishment of a farm and purchase of equipment, and the latter to finance seed and other expenditures which many farmers could only pay for after the year's crop had been harvested and sold. The Canadian banking system was oriented towards commercial, rather than agricultural, loans, and in particular the chartered banks were sceptical about accepting land as collateral for a loan. The role of the government was largely passive before World War I. Governments aided farmers in coordinated projects (e.g., larger drainage and irrigation ventures) and sometimes offered minor credit aid to encourage settlement of sparsely populated areas, but in general there was little government intervention in providing farm credit or in improving the attractiveness of agricultural loans for private lenders (e.g., by offering guarantees).

The same problem of farm credit had arisen in central Canada, especially during the Ontario grain boom of the 1850s and 1860s. One solution had been the emergence of agricultural loan companies, which raised money from the sale of debentures in Britain and then used the proceeds to lend to farmers. These companies were important in Ontario until the end of the century, by which time the spread between London borrowing rates and Ontario lending rates had narrowed and indigenous Ontario institutions were undercutting the agricultural loan companies. Interest rates on the Prairies were higher, and the agricultural loan companies moved west. Up to 1914 the main source of Prairie credit was institutions using foreign capital, and by 1914 over $200 million of foreign capital was outstanding on farm mortgages. The farmers' complaints centred on the high interest rates and the lack of flexibility in lending practices.

During World War I the provincial governments in the Prairies passed moratorium legislation preventing foreclosure for failure to meet loan repayments. This and other measures restricting the powers of institutional lenders to press for repayment on time were particularly important during the 1915 drought, when many borrowers fell behind in their payments to the loan companies. The governments' actions were a temporary wartime measure to ensure that Canada's wheat contribution to the war effort was unharmed by farm failures, but the institutional lenders were frightened by the precedent of annulling the sanctity of contracts. In consequence farm credit became more difficult to obtain, particularly in less-settled riskier areas, and pressure for government intervention increased.

Direct government loans were instituted with the establishment of the Manitoba Farm Loans Association and the Manitoba Rural Credits Act in 1917; the former provided loans upon farm mortgage security, while the latter supplied short-term credit. Similar developments occurred in Saskatchewan, but in both provinces the schemes were only really successful for five years or so, after which they ran into financial difficulties. The Alberta administration was more successful because it followed more conservative lending policies, and its farm credit scheme incurred fewer losses. The general lack of success of the provincial bodies led to growing pressure for federal action. In 1929 the Canadian Farm Loans Board was established, and provision for short-term farm credit was made under the Farm Improvements Loans Acts of 1944.

Thus the two problems of marketing and credit, where governments tried to maintain the operation of free markets but farmers pressed for government intervention, had both been settled in the farmers' favour by the end of World War II. The monopoly question, ·which had been raised even earlier by Prairie farmers and on which they received some government support, has been less satisfactorily resolved from the farmers' point of view; abuse of railway and elevator monopolies has been limited, but other inputs (and consumption goods) are still purchased from companies with monopoly power. Finally, the basic cause of Prairie farmers' economic problems remains the instability of world wheat prices which make this sector subject to major economic fluctuations.

Appendix:
The Wheat Boom's Contribution to Economic Growth

Having examined the growth and internal workings of the Prairie wheat economy, we now turn to the broader question of its importance for Canadian economic growth. Earlier Canadian economic historians ascribed a major contribution to the wheat boom, beginning with the upturn in world wheat prices of 1896. In an attempt to quantify this contribution, Chambers & Gordon (1966) developed a stylized model of the Canadian economy and concluded that the wheat boom was not an important source of intensive economic growth in Canada. Their iconoclastic conclusion engendered a heated controversy in which the criticisms centred on whether their model provided a satisfactory representation of the Canadian economy and whether they accurately measured what they claimed to measure.

Before reviewing the debate, it is necessary to identify just when the wheat boom occurred. Although wheat prices rose from 1896, there is no upward trend in wheat production until after 1901. The economic boom of 1896–1901 was more closely related to minerals, whose exports increased by 500 per cent during those five years, and most of all to Klondike gold. The growth of the Prairie wheat economy was fastest in the twelve years up to 1913: wheat output rose from just under 56 million bushels in 1901 to 224 million bushels in 1913; grain exports increased by 600 per cent and their share of total Canadian exports went from 14 per cent to 42 per cent. After 1913 problems of overexpansion constantly threatened, even though good spells broke up the bad ones until 1929. The key period is thus 1901–1913, but because the latter year was not a census year the availability of data has led to the empirical debate being focussed on the period 1901–1911.

In order to consider the appropriateness and empirical application of the Chambers & Gordon model it is first necessary to understand how it works. Their "simplest" model divides the economy into two sectors: in agriculture "wheat" is produced with labour and land, while in manufacturing "gadgets" are produced with labour alone. Commodity prices are set outside Canada and are not affected by changes in Canadian output (the price of "gadgets" is set by competing imports). The marginal physical product of labour (MPP_L) in wheat declines as less favourable land is brought into use, but the MPP_L in gadgets is constant. The size of each sector is determined by the interaction of the demand for and supply of labour (Figure 7.1).

Figure 7.1
Chambers & Gordon "Simplest Model"

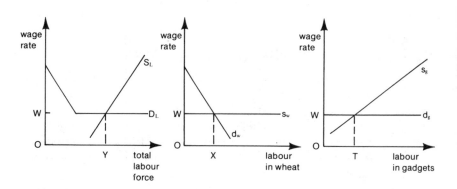

S_L is upward-sloping because net immigration is directly related to the Canadian wage rate.

D_L is the horizontal sum of d_w and d_g.

d_w is the marginal value product curve of agricultural labour and is downward sloping because of diminishing returns ($MVP_L = MPP_L \times P_W$).

d_g is horizontal because constant marginal productivity is assumed in the gadget sector.

s_w is perfectly elastic because the wheat sector can attract labour from the gadget sector at the wage rate W but not at any lower wage rate.

s_g is a residual, i.e., all willing to work at the wage rate W whose labour is not demanded in the wheat sector, and is the horizontal difference between S_L and d_w.

Whether the wheat boom was due to technical change in wheat production or to increased wheat prices, it can be represented in the model by a rightward shift in the d_w curve (to d_w' in Figure 7.2) increasing employment in the wheat sector. Since the gadget labour force contracts by the same amount as the wheat labour force grows ($s_g' = S_L - d_w'$), wage income does not change, but there is a gain in total income equal to the increased rents from land (area ABEF in Figure 7.2). Concurrently with the wheat boom, however, technical change was taking place in the gadgets sector, shifting d_g upwards to d_g' (and therefore shifting s_w to s_w') and increasing the population and total wage income. In this situation the appropriate measure of the wheat boom's contribution to total income is the difference between the actual post wheat boom rents from land and the value of these rents if the d_w curve had not shifted (i.e., area ABGH in Figure 7.2). Chambers & Gordon estimated the area ABGH for the period 1901–1911 to be $40.4 million, or 1.94 per cent of Canada's national income in 1911; without the wheat boom per capita income would have been 1.94 per cent lower in 1911 and intensive growth in the decade

Figure 7.2
The Contribution of the Wheat Boom
to Increased National Income

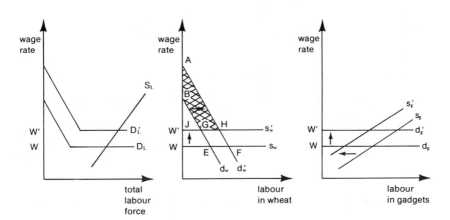

total
labour
force

labour
in wheat

labour
in gadgets

The demand curve for labour in wheat shifts to the right (from d_w to d_w') as a result of the wheat boom. The demand curve for labour in gadgets shifts upward (from d_g to d_g') as a result of technical change. Each labour supply curve shifts in consequence of the shift in the demand curves of the other sector.

The actual rents in the wheat sector after the wheat boom are equal to the area AJH. In the absence of the wheat boom the rents would have been BJG. Therefore the contribution of the wheat boom is measured by the area ABGH.

1901–1911 would have been reduced from 23.6 per cent to 21.5 per cent. Thus, Chambers & Gordon concluded that the contribution of the wheat boom to intensive growth between 1901 and 1911 was just under one twelfth (8.4 per cent).

In the remainder of their 1966 article, Chambers & Gordon argue that expanding the model or adjusting the empirical estimates does not alter their conclusion as to the unimportance of the wheat boom. The simple two sector-two factor model can be made to appear more realistic by adding more factors or more sectors. The presence of additional factors of production has no effect on the measurement of the wheat boom's contribution to growth as long as their supply is perfectly elastic; d_g and s_w must be redefined to include payments to factors other than labour, but the additional factors earn no economic rent. The presence of additional sectors affects the composition of the labour force after the wheat boom but not the contribution of the wheat boom to growth; e.g., a purely domestic sector ("haircuts") would respond to the wheat boom-induced higher income by charging higher prices and thus earning quasi-rents, but in the long run labour will move from the gadget sector into the haircuts sector and push prices down again.

Chambers & Gordon claimed to have made their estimates as favourable as possible towards the staple thesis and state that reasonable adjustments to the estimates would only reduce the wheat boom's contribution to economic growth still further. The wheat boom may have affected immigration because the homestead system meant that immigrants may have been attracted not only by higher wages, but also by the possibility of capturing some of the increased rental value of land. Chambers & Gordon assume that 200,000 immigrants came for this reason, which reduces the wheat boom's contribution to intensive growth from 8.4 per cent to 5.2 per cent. Even the revised estimate is too high since some Prairie land was owned by non-Canadians, in which cases the wheat boom's contribution was to other countries' national income. Finally, Chambers & Gordon argue that their actual choice of data was guided by the desire to avoid underestimates (1966, Appendix A). The only counteracting factor is the possibility of economics of scale, but they dismiss this as unimportant.

Chambers & Gordon's article challenged a basic belief of the staple theory, which at that time was still the dominant approach to Canadian economic history. The staple theorists' response came in a paper by Dales, McManus & Watkins, which was essentially a gut reaction, throwing all the adverse comments which came to mind and in a very bitter tone for an academic paper; Chambers & Gordon replied in kind. This debate does not greatly increase our understanding of the model or of the wheat boom because it mainly consists of irrelevancies and misconceptions by the avenging trio. For example, Dales, McManus & Watkins argue that extensive rather than intensive growth is the central interest of Canadian economic historians and support their case by judicious selection of quotations against which Chambers & Gordon supply a set of counter-quotations; neither set is necessarily a guide to what is important, but more significantly the Chambers & Gordon estimates could be applied equally easily to extensive growth as to intensive growth so that the whole quoting exercise is rather beside the point. Dales, McManus & Watkins do, however, make two valid points. Firstly, in the Chambers & Gordon model the wheat boom causes a transfer of labour from gadget production to the wheat sector, leading to lower domestic production and higher imports of gadgets. The income gain to Canada comes not only from the higher output per head in wheat, but also in the form of tariff revenue on the increased imports. This is accepted by Chambers & Gordon, who calculate it to increase the wheat boom's contribution to intensive growth by a sixth, which leaves intact their conclusion about the relative smallness of this contribution. Secondly, Chambers & Gordon try to prove the existence of a gadget sector by listing manufacturing industries which were subject to competing imports in 1911, but this is no proof that these industries had all the characteristics of gadget producers. The non-existence of a gadget sector would be a fatal blow to the model's applicability, but Dales, McManus & Watkins provide no evidence to support their case.

A more thorough attempt to revise Chambers & Gordon's calculations was undertaken by Caves (1971). He makes allowance for higher tariff revenues and economics of scale, and also introduces two further contributions of the wheat boom to intensive growth. Firstly, Caves argues that immigration is responsive not only to high wages and the possibility of capturing rent on cheap land, but also to job availability and expectations about future wages. Potential immigrants' conception of what Canada had to offer in these respects was raised by the wheat boom. By ignoring this, Chambers & Gordon underestimate the population increase due to the wheat boom, which Caves assesses at 392,000. Moreover, within the induced population increment Chambers & Gordon assume participation rates similar to those for the Canadian population as a whole, which Caves considers unlikely because immigrants contained a disproportionate number of working-age males. Secondly, Chambers & Gordon ignore the increase in the capital stock from the savings brought in by the induced immigrants and from the savings out of the wheat boom's contribution to national income. Caves estimates the total contribution is $193.6 million (Table 7.1), and combining this figure with the induced population increase he arrives at a contribution to 1901-1911 intensive growth of 21.4 per cent. Caves concludes that, although technical change moving costlessly into non-wheat sectors accounted for most of Canada's 1901-1911 intensive growth, it is rare that a single other source accounts for as much as 21 per cent of a country's intensive growth. Thus Caves not only arrives at a higher estimate than Chambers & Gordon, but he also interprets it more positively than they would have done, raising the question of just how large a "contribution" would make the wheat boom an important source of growth.

Table 7.1
Caves' Estimate of the Wheat Boom's Contribution to 1911
National Income ($ million)

Original Chambers-Gordon rent estimate	40.4
Increased tariff revenue	13.0
Extra immigrants' wages	118.5
Induced scale economics	9.9
Interest on additional capital	11.8
Total	193.6

Source: Caves (1971).

Caves' estimates are, however, not completely convincing. Quantitatively they rest heavily on the induced population growth, which is assumed rather than rigorously linked to the wheat boom; by making the link psychological he takes it out of the realm of testability. The higher participation rate among immigrants, which is crucial for making the induced population growth's contribution to intensive growth positive rather than negative, is also assumed rather than proven; an alternative assumption would be that, although total immigration had a working-age male bias, it may have been those with families who went farming, while single males stayed in the eastern cities. Thus, Caves shows that alternative assumptions about population would substantially alter Chambers & Gordon's estimate, but he does not provide a convincing case in favour of his assumptions.

Further criticisms of Chambers & Gordon's empirical work have come from Bertram (1973) and Grant (1974). Bertram argues that Chambers & Gordon's rent estimate, based on census data, is too low for 1911. He derives alternative estimates by decapitalizing farm land values, which yields similar rent figures to those derived from the censuses for 1901 and 1921 but not for 1911. Substituting Bertram's 1911 rent estimates into Chambers & Gordon's original calculations raises the wheat boom's contribution from 8.4 per cent to 19.5 per cent. Bertram explains the divergence in terms of the prevalency of share tenancy, which was ignored by Chambers & Gordon, and by the disequilibrium situation in 1911. Disequilibrium is, however, a more serious problem for Bertram's method. Farm land values represent not only capitalization of actual rental value, but also include an allowance for expected appreciation. In 1911 expectations were optimistic and decapitalization of farm values would overstate the current rental value of Prairie land. Thus Bertram's rent estimates are upward biassed, and his higher estimated contribution of the wheat boom to intensive growth is illusory. Grant (1974) criticizes Chambers & Gordon for omitting the return to entrepreneurial expertise and risk-bearing by Prairie farmers. As empirical support for this position he shows that the other factor returns (to labour and to land) alone do not sum up to Prairie grain output, but his calculations are unconvincing. Bertram also argued, without empirical support, that farm inputs were not in perfectly elastic supply. Such criticisms based on omitted inputs are, however, only valid if the input's supply elasticity can be shown to be significantly less than infinite. Finally, Bertram criticizes Chambers & Gordon for relying on Firestone's GNP estimates for their intensive growth rate. Use of Buckley's estimates, which have a lower 1911 GNP, would give lower intensive growth for 1901–1911, and hence the calculated wheat boom contribution would be a higher percentage. This however, does not challenge the conclusion that the wheat boom was relatively unimportant for intensive growth because, although the wheat boom's

1901–1911 contribution is higher using Buckley's GNP estimates, those estimates reduce the importance of that decade as a period of rapid intensive growth.

The most recent contribution to the debate (Lewis, 1975) has returned to the question of whether a "gadget" sector existed—or, at least, whether it was large enough to play the wage-setting role required in the Chambers & Gordon model. Lewis estimates that Canada's 1911 gadget imports could have been produced domestically by 80,000 workers. The labour force in wheat production, however, had increased by 200,000 since 1901. If the wheat boom had not occurred the gadget sector would have absorbed these extra workers, ceasing to face competing imports and suffering from reduced prices and wages. Without the wheat boom both Prairie rents *and* wage income would have been lower. Allowing for both of these and for the different tariff revenue (but ignoring population changes) leads to at least a doubling of the wheat boom's contribution to intensive growth. Lewis's revised model had, however, two major omissions. Some gadgets could be, and were, exported by Canada, which shifts the kink in the gadget sector's marginal value product curve. For the non-tradeable gadgets, prices may have been lower in the absence of the wheat boom, but this should have been included as a gain as well as a loss. Lewis estimates changes in money income, but ignores the effect of lower prices on real income. In fact, in Lewis's model national money income will fall by exactly the same amount as the price level, leaving real income unchanged as a result of the lower prices.

In the face of many attempted refutations the analysis and conclusion of Chambers & Gordon's 1966 article have proved remarkably robust. The only certain omission from their original calculations is the tariff revenue accruing from shifting labour out of the protected gadget sector into wheat which can be traded for imported gadgets, and this omission is quantitatively small. Caves' estimates of the gains in the form of scale economics and increased savings are more contentious, but are also small. The attempts by Bertram and Grant to revise or augment the rent estimates are conceptually unsound. It could even be argued that the original rent estimates are too high because homestead laws gave an incentive to stake a claim even before a piece of land yielded positive rents in order to have property rights on future rents; such premature farm enterprises represent a social loss from the wheat boom insofar as the labour could have been better used elsewhere, and the negative economic rent should be subtracted from the rent estimates (Southey, 1978). Similarly the excess railway construction which resulted from overoptimism about the wheat boom is a cost which is omitted. The wheat boom's effect on Canada's population is more difficult to resolve. The induced population figures given by Chambers & Gordon and by Caves both leave the impression of rabbits from a conjurer's hat rather than well-reasoned estimates. Population certainly grew substantially between 1901 and 1911, but the relative importance of potential Prairie rents, Canadian wage rates and push factors in the countries of origin has not been thoroughly analyzed. The answer may not be so important for the wheat boom's contribution to intensive growth because increased population will raise both the numerator and the denominator of per capita income, but it would be more important to an analysis of the wheat boom's contribution to extensive growth.

The literature surveyed in this appendix is important because Chambers & Gordon appear to have completed the refutation of the hypothesis that the wheat boom played a major role in modern economic growth in Canada. Firestone's GNP estimates and various estimates of manufacturing output had already suggested an earlier industrial revolution; Chambers & Gordon show that even at its height the wheat boom contributed little to national intensive growth. Their conclusion should not be surprising. By 1900 Canada already had a diversified economy, and the previous chapter showed that plenty was happening in the manufacturing sector between 1901 and 1911 which could explain that decade's intensive growth.

Chapter 8
The Financial System

The importance of financial development in economic development stems primarily from two functions of money: it is a medium of exchange and a store of wealth. The use of money as a medium of exchange removes the need for a double coincidence of wants, which is the prerequisite for barter, and permits greater specialization and division of labour. Money's store of wealth property eases the investment process by removing the necessity for a potential investor to control the physical surplus (either of labour time or in commodity form); money permits the possessors of surplus (savers) to lend to people wishing to make physical investment in plant, machinery and equipment, etc. The financial system is contributing to economic development if forms of money are available which fulfil both functions satisfactorily, and also if financial intermediaries exist to reduce any obstacles to the flow of funds from savers to investors.

This chapter examines how the Canadian financial system has developed in response to changing demands for financial services. Section 1 analyzes the problem of finding a satisfactory means of exchange, which was eventually solved by notes issued by chartered banks. The relative unimportance of demand for financial intermediary services before the mid-nineteenth century was reflected in the Canadian reaction to the U.S. Bank War of the 1830s, which led to the victory of free banking in the United States but left the Canadian banking system in its original European pattern of a small number of multi-branch banks (section 2). The rising demand for financial intermediaries in the second half of the century posed a more serious challenge to the Canadian chartered banks, which is examined in section 3. The role of the government in the financial sector has, on the whole, been restricted to providing the legal framework, and only since the depression of the 1930s has the government accepted responsibility for controlling the money supply; this development is dealt with in the final section. The first two sections of this chapter will focus on central Canada because, although there were minor regional differences in the issue of paper currency and in banking practice before 1867, when the Dominion government assumed responsibility for banking and currency matters the policies adopted were essentially continuous from the financial policies of the Province of Canada.

1. Early Financial Problems

The nature of the currency shortage problem was already clear under the French regime. Although barter worked well enough in the fur trade because of the narrow range of wants on both sides, it was less satisfactory for transactions within the colony. In order to overcome the disadvantages of barter trade a number of media or exchange were widely used in New France, but all had serious flaws. Commodities such as skins and wheat were used and even became legal tender for a time, but because of fluctuations in price they were poor standards of value. The Indians used wampum (cylinders of seashells about three quarters of an inch long), and it was legal tender in New France until 1670. The colonists continued to accept wampum as payment until after 1700 and the Indians used it until c. 1800, but its value was destroyed by imported cheap glass from Europe which was a good facsimile of wampum. In retrospect, these early media of exchange might appear bizarre because of their obvious weaknesses, but the colonists' willingness to accept them is a clear indicator of the cost of barter even in seventeenth-century Canada.

In Europe the problem of finding a stable medium of exchange which was easy to carry and difficult to counterfeit had been solved by the use of precious metals, the most convenient form being preweighed gold and silver coins. These coins, or their precious metal equivalent (specie), were acceptable means of exchange in the colonies, but in North America there was insufficient specie to meet the demand for means of exchange. No gold and silver was mined in New France, and a brief experiment in copper coins was unsuccessful. The colony therefore had to rely on gold and silver imported from France in payment for fur exports, for government expenditure or as funds transferred by religious orders. Foreign currency also entered New France from illicit trade with the British colonies to the south. On the other hand, however, New France's trade deficit led to an outflow of specie, which resulted in the search for second-best media of exchange described above.

A major financial innovation was the introduction of card money in 1685. When the boat from France failed to arrive before the ice, the government paid its bills with playing cards which were signed by the intendant with a personal pledge of payment. The cards were accepted without question until the first boat came after the thaw and they were redeemed. The experiment was repeated in succeeding winters, and the cards became so acceptable that in 1690 not all cards were returned for redemption. This development was not unappealing to the colonial government since the outstanding card money left specie in their hands to cover additional expenditures, and after 1690 the supply of card money increased. After 1700, however, holders of card money experienced difficulties in redeeming cards for specie because the French government needed finance for its European war. The value of card money declined, until in 1717 the French government, no longer requiring war finance, redeemed all card money at half its face value, which was approximately its circulating value by that time.

Between 1719 and 1729 specie was the sole circulating medium of exchange in New France. The continued specie outflow, however, meant that the earlier shortage persisted. Personal notes were increasingly used as a localized means of payment, but there was a widespread belief that they should be under government control. In consequence, card money was reintroduced in 1729. The new issue of card money was intended as a permanent paper currency with no eventual convertibility into specie. The system worked well between 1729 and 1749 because convertibility into bills on the French government was sufficient to establish confidence in the colony's paper money. After 1749 the financial demands of the colonial government increased, and particularly when assistance from France declined after 1755, the colonial government resorted to printing money to finance its expenditures. The amount of paper money in New France rose from one million livres in 1749 to forty-one million livres in 1760, most of which was irredeemable and practically worthless after the Conquest. Eventually, after the end of hostilities, the French government agreed to redeem the paper money at a quarter of its face value. The episode caused serious losses to many French-Canadians, who had parted with their paper money holdings at even less than 25 per cent of their face value when the occupation administration had declared them valueless.

Card money was a solution to the currency shortage which worked well during peacetime but not as well during wartime. When government expenditures increased rapidly there was too great a temptation for the colonial government to print money. In consequence, the paper currency lost value between 1710 and 1717 and collapsed in the late 1750s. The disastrous loss of value in 1755–1760 seriously affected confidence in paper money in Quebec. Similar experiences with paper money had occurred in the British North American colonies, and in 1764 all further colonial issues of paper money were banned. Although the measure appeared sound in the light of recent experience, the seriousness of the currency shortage was reflected in widespread discontent with the ban, particularly in the middle colonies.

After 1763 specie became more common, but remained inadequate and mixed. The legal standard and unit of account was sterling, but British currency was rare. The most common means of exchange was the Spanish dollar whose sterling equivalent was standardized by legislation in 1764 and 1767, but a wide variety of other coins circulated whose ratings varied from town to town. The confusion became worse after American independence when the establishment of a uniform U.S. currency led to an outflow of foreign specie north to Canada.

At the end of the eighteenth century most large domestic and foreign financial transactions were conducted by mercantile houses, mainly located in Montreal and involved in the fur trade. Because of the shortage of means of payment, these houses issued to their customers notes or "bons" (so called from their wording: "Bon pour . . ."), redeemable in goods. The bons started to circulate, and although technically illegal, the colonial administration recognized the value of the practice and turned a blind eye. A similar practice emerged on a smaller scale in Upper Canada, where the key figure was the village merchant. The lack of currency particularly complicated government purchasing of provisions for garrisons and civilian establishments. Payment was made in bills on Quebec or London, which Upper Canadian farmers did not redeem in person but sold to middlemen at a considerable discount. In an attempt to improve the situation John McGill, who was appointed Agent of Purchases in 1794, bought direct from farmers with transferable certificates which were redeemable in Upper Canada for British treasury bills. Although they had no status of legal tender, the certificates circulated widely as a means of exchange. The success of the certificates as paper currency was limited, however, by their only being issued for actual government purchases, and the less reliable "bons" continued to provide most of the circulating medium of exchange. The continuing currency shortage caused paper money to be readily accepted if the backing was at all reasonable. Even so, barter and commodity "money" remained widespread; for example, whiskey was a common medium of exchange in Upper Canada, indicating to one economist that "the pioneer country was by no means devoid of all liquid assets" (McIvor, 1958, p. 17).

The obvious solution to the currency shortage was the issue of reliable paper money. In Nova Scotia provincial treasury notes circulated after 1812, but this type of paper money was probably illegal, and a provincial note issue was considered undesirable in Upper and Lower Canada until the eve of Confederation. The alternative to a government note issue was commercial banks of issue, which would be regulated by the government. The first serious attempt to establish a commercial bank came in 1792 when an English firm and two of the Montreal mercantile houses issued a prospectus and began business, but the bank lapsed almost immediately, perhaps as a result of the outbreak of war in Europe. Subsequent attempts to start banks in Montreal, Quebec, Kingston and Halifax during the early 1800s all failed to gain government approval. The early moves toward commercial banking may have been premature, insofar as public confidence in paper money had not yet been sufficiently restored after the experience of 1755–1760, but this thesis is belied by the general acceptance of government certificates and the fairly wide acceptance of merchants' "bons." Perhaps a more important cause of failure was the political situation in both Upper and Lower Canada, where oligarchic governments were more closely associated with land and clergy than with commerce and were suspicious of new financial practices. Some rejections of petitions to form banks were politically motivated because they came from opposition groups, but all the rejections may have reflected a more general distrust of limited liability among the ruling oligarchies.

The climate of opinion towards commercial banks of issue was improved by the experience with Army Bills during the War of 1812. As in previous North American wars the colonial government's financial needs outran its available specie and were met by issuing paper currency. The Army Bills bore 6 per cent interest and were redeemable in specie after five years or in British government bills on demand. They were declared legal tender and were eagerly accepted, but their use as a means of exchange was limited by the initial absence of small denominations. This deficiency was met by the issue of bills with face values between $1 and $20, which bore no interest but were automatically transferable into interest bearing larger denominations. By the end of the war £1¼ million (or $5 million) in Army Bills were outstanding. The entire issue was recalled in 1815 for cash redemption, but the Army Bills were so securely valued that redemption proceeded slowly. The success of the Army Bills increased confidence in paper money; the psychological effect was aided by the general prosperity of the years 1812–1815, which was associated with the Army Bills. The withdrawal of the Army Bills, indicating the imperial government's unwillingness to provide a permanent paper currency, revealed both a need and an opportunity for alternative note-issuing institutions.

In 1817 nine Montreal merchants signed the Articles of Association forming the Bank of Montreal, and their charter was granted in 1818, although royal assent was delayed until 1822 (thus British North America's first officially chartered bank was the Bank of New Brunswick, which obtained royal assent in 1820; but the Bank of Montreal had already been operating for several years by then). The Bank of Montreal was authorized to issue notes, which were intended to circulate as money and which were redeemable on demand in gold or silver coin. The issue was limited to the bank's paid-in capital plus bullion holdings plus securities issued or guaranteed by the provincial government. Agencies were soon established in Quebec, Kingston and Toronto, but the last two were closed in 1823 when the Upper Canadian government required notes to be redeemed in Upper Canada. Two other banks were established in Lower Canada in 1818, the Bank of Canada (in Montreal, and not to be confused with the central bank which was established in 1935 under that name) and the Quebec Bank. Also in 1818 the Bank of Upper Canada was opened in Kingston, but this bank encountered delays in obtaining a charter because of political opposition from the Family Compact in Toronto. Intense competition from branches of the Montreal banks and poor management caused the early collapse of the Kingston bank. When the Bank of Upper Canada's charter finally received royal assent, it was usurped by Toronto interests who established the bank there with assistance from the provincial government. The paper currency issues of the chartered banks were by far the most satisfactory means of exchange of the time and encountered immediate acceptance, to the extent that already by 1825 the circulating media are estimated at £105,000 in bank notes and £30,000 in specie.

The Bank of Montreal, which took over the Bank of Canada in 1831, and the Bank of Upper Canada were jealous of their dominant positions and enjoyed political influence with their respective provincial governments. The British government also played a conservative role in delaying or refusing applications for bank charters during the prosperity of the late 1820s and the 1830s. A beneficial consequence was that the 1837 depression was not accompanied by widespread bank failures, in contrast to the U.S. experience. A more important consequence was the small number of chartered banks existing in British North America by 1841. Canada East and Canada West each had three chartered banks, and the former also had two unchartered banks while the latter had one. In addition, the Bank of British North America, based in London (England) and operating under royal charter, had branches in both Canada and the Maritimes. The number of banks in New Brunswick and Nova Scotia was also small—four and two respectively.

2. Free Banking versus Chartered Banks

Economic conditions in Canada have been strongly affected by events in the United States, and the American influence has also been felt in the evolution of institutions. In the political sphere this influence has been limited because British institutions were often transplanted into British North America; but in the economic sphere the American influence was stronger because economic institutions are more frequently shaped by local economic conditions and these were similar in the United States and Canada. The banking system is an interesting case in that American institutional influence was strong, but the end result has been a Canadian banking system quite dissimilar from that of the United States and closer to the European pattern.

The first chartered banks were established in the United States during the late eighteenth century. These banks, located in the eastern commercial centres, were successful in providing acceptable media of exchange and in financing mercantile activity, and the early Canadian charters were modelled after U.S. prototypes. The behaviour of the U.S. chartered banks up to the 1830s was similar to that of the Canadian banks during the 1820s and 1830s, in that the established banks succeeded in restraining the growth of new banks. The American banking situation was, however, much less stable than its Canadian counterpart. On the demand side, banking services were in greater demand in the United States, not just for the provision of means of exchange but also for financial intermediaries which could direct funds to dynamic sectors of the economy (note that in the 1820s the New England textile industry was growing and the Erie Canal had opened up the west). On the supply side, it was difficult to prevent new entrants into banking because of competition between the states. These pressures culminated in the "Bank War" of the 1830s and the Jacksonian government's decision to allow states to charter banks more or less at will. Some states then adopted the principle of free banking, whereby anybody could start a bank under certain general conditions without requiring a specific charter. Despite a major crisis in 1837 the number of banks grew rapidly (to over 700 by 1840), reflecting the latent demand for their service and the ease of opening a bank. The state banking system had two major disadvantages, the opportunities for fraud and its susceptibility to panics and non-redemption of bank notes. On the other hand, the U.S. banking system helped to channel funds to regions where potential borrowers exceeded savers; in particular purchases by the west were paid for by notes on western banks which continued to circulate in the east. Current evaluations of the U.S. banking system after the 1830s are that the "system clearly encouraged American economic growth" and that the costs to society from frauds and panics were not high (Temin, 1975, p. 52).

The early Canadian banking system followed U.S. practice, but in the 1830s there was far less pressure for change in Canada. The demand for financial intermediaries in the saving-investment process was still negligible, and the dominant banks exerted considerable and secure monopoly power in their respective provinces. After 1837 the chartered banks' position was strengthened by legislation reserving for them the sole right to issue bills of $20 or less. In the 1840s, however, demand for a more flexible banking system grew, especially in Canada West where commercial agriculture and industry were expanding.

The growing pressure for the introduction of free banking was met by the Free Banking Act of 1850, which permitted any individual or joint stock company to open a bank with paid-up capital of £25,000, and these banks could issue notes against government securities. The influence of the established banks on this legislation can be seen in the restrictive conditions and in the idea of having unchartered banks operating side by side with chartered banks rather than repealing charters. In principle the Free Banking Act might have led to the emergence of unit banks on the U.S. pattern, but in practice it had little effect. Only six banks took advantage of the Free Banking Act, one of which was the Bank of British North America, whose imperial charter did not permit it to issue notes of less than $20. Of the five free banks, two soon collapsed and the other three took out charters. Why was the free banking experiment so unsuccessful in Canada? The capital requirement of £25,000 was a significant barrier to entry, in contrast to the generally easy entry requirements in the United States. More importantly, the Canadian legislation offered no advantages to forming a free bank. The requirement of using government securities as backing for note issues was good for the provincial government, giving it a ready source of buyers of securities, but it was an expensive method of note issue for the banks. The Free Banking Act was partially repealed in 1866 and not renewed after Confederation.

The most obvious difference between Canadian and American commercial banking was thus established by the time of Confederation. In 1867 there were nineteen chartered banks in the Province of Canada and four each in New Brunswick and Nova Scotia, compared to over a thousand in the United States. At that time propaganda on behalf of the Canadian banking community emphasized the fewer opportunities for fraud and fewer bank collapses than in the United States before the mid-1860s. This emphasis reflected the continuing preoccupation with the means of exchange function of the financial system and relative lack of demand for intermédiaries to channel funds to expanding sectors. The latter function only became important in Canada in the immediate pre-Confederation period, when several large banks failed as a result of injudicious lending (notably the Bank of Upper Canada in 1866 and the Commercial Bank in 1867). The currency shortage problem had been satisfactorily solved by the growth of the chartered banks, whose banknotes provided a reliable paper currency; the critical issue after the 1860s was whether these chartered banks would prove adequate in channelling funds from potential savers to potential investors.

3. The Decline and Rise of the Chartered Banks

At Confederation the Canadian financial system was dominated by the chartered banks, which had a virtual monopoly over the provision of media of exchange in the form of banknotes and, after 1850, chequing accounts. Other institutions, providing other financial services, had developed before 1867 but were relatively unimportant. Savings banks had been established soon after the first chartered banks and aimed to promote thrift among the lower classes, but the atmosphere of charity was not conducive to efficient management. An 1855 act increasing their capital requirements further limited the savings banks' expansion, and they came under heavy competition from building societies. Although building societies had begun operations in the 1840s, their growth was retarded because they were not authorized to take deposits (until 1859) or to issue debentures (until 1874). Contractual savings agreements were also introduced by life insurance companies, first via agents of British and American companies during the 1830s and after 1847 by a sole Canadian company. Government savings banks in New Brunswick and Nova Scotia and thirty fire insurance companies completed the list of asset-owning financial institutions in 1867 (Table 8.1). A final development worth mention was the emergence of brokers' houses which formed stock exchanges in Montreal (1842) and Toronto (1852), although neither exchange was publicly incorporated before Confederation and the number of issues listed was small.

Table 8.1
Relative Size of Canadian Assets of Canadian Financial Intermediaries,
1867–1968

	1867	1896	1910	1968
Chartered banks	78%	48%	60%	29%
Private savings banks	3%	3%	2%	1%
Government & post office savings banks	3%	8%	3%	0%
Building societies and mortgage loan cos.	9%	22%	11%	3%
Life insurance cos.	1%	13%	12%	14%
Fire & casualty insurance cos.	3%	3%	3%	3%
Other	4%	3%	9%	50%

Source: Neufeld, 1972, Appendix.
Note: Percentages may not add to 100 because of rounding.

The two major features of the Canadian financial sector since Confederation have been the emergence of new institutions and the rapid growth of financial intermediaries' assets. Although the financial sector has consistently grown faster than GNP, the growth has not been even. The most rapid total growth has been since 1950, but in terms of constant dollar assets per capita the period of fastest growth was 1870–1910 (Neufeld, 1972, p. 59). The 1870–1910 growth is not difficult to explain in view of the intensive and extensive growth of those decades, but this period is also interesting because of the changes in composition of the financial sector. In particular the chartered banks declined in importance relative to other established institutions between 1870 and 1896, but this trend was reversed between 1896 and 1910 when the chartered banks defeated their rivals and withstood competition from the new caisses populaires (Table 8.1).

Although the chartered banks dominated the financial system in 1870, they left significant gaps in the capital market. In particular, the chartered banks avoided long-term loans, partly because they were prohibited from lending on land as collateral (although in practice this had been circumvented during the 1860s and was a contributory factor in the bank failures of 1866–1887). On the other side of the balance sheet, the chartered banks relied on their note issue and large customers for funds, neglecting small depositors and sale of debentures as sources of funds. It was these gaps which were filled by government and post office savings banks and life insurance companies, which attracted small savers' funds (which grew in importance after 1870), and by building societies and mortgage loan companies, which made loans on security of land and raised capital outside Canada to finance the loans.

Crucial to the operation of the building societies and mortgage loan companies was 1873 legislation permitting them to issue debentures. In 1875 before the impact of the law was felt, less than 4 per cent of their liabilities were debentures payable outside Canada, but by 1880 this proportion was 33½ per cent (Neufeld, 1972, p. 206). The profitability of their business centred on the interest rate spread between England and Canada. In 1873 British government consols paid 3¼ per cent, Ontario mortgages cost 9 per cent and mortgage loan company debentures paid 6 per cent—leaving a good margin for risk to British investors and to the loan companies. The spread fell during the 1880s, but the Prairies were starting to provide new profitable opportunities for mortgage loans. By 1900 the spread had narrowed considerably: British consuls paid 2½ per cent, loan company debentures paid 4 per cent, Ontario mortgages cost 5¾ per cent and Manitoba mortgages 7½ per cent. There was less incentive for British investors to buy these debentures and declining profits to be made from farm mortgages, both of which intensified by World War I. In retrospect the fatal errors of the mortgage companies which caused their precipitous decline in relative importance after 1896 were their slowness in diversifying their liabilities from British to Canadian sources and their slowness in diversifying their assets from rural to urban loans.

The chartered banks' revival, which started in the 1890s, was not due solely to their rivals' failings but also to their own increased aggressiveness. The chartered banks began to pay more attention to attracting deposits and to that end increased their branches from 426 in 1890 to 4,676 in 1920—a number not reattained until the 1950s and representing in 1920 the very low ratio of one branch to 1,900 people (cf., the more or less stable ratio of 1:3,500 since World War II). The number of branches was clearly overexpanded between 1890 and 1920, but the expansion put great pressure on government and other savings banks which had previously benefitted from their accessibility.

A second important feature in the chartered banks' competitive position was their declining numbers. The all-time high was the fifty-one chartered banks in 1874, but failures, especially in 1879 and 1887, reduced their ranks to forty-one by the early 1890s. The number of chartered banks continued to fall to thirty in 1910 and eleven by 1925, where it has approximately remained since. The causes of increased concentration were the lack of new entrants, bank failures and mergers. The 1890 Bank Act revision increased the minimum paid-up capital for a new bank from $100,000 to $250,000, increasing barriers to entry. The 1900 revision made bank mergers easier by requiring only the approval of the Governor-in-Council instead of a special act of Parliament; the government did become worried about increased concentration, but usually agreed to a merger when one of the partners threatened failure. Finally, bank failures continued to occur, with twelve between 1890 and 1914. The situation was ripe for cartelization, and the Canadian Bankers' Association was founded in 1892 and achieved the status of a public corporation in 1900. The CBA's official aim was the improvement of banking standards and education, but it also acted in classic cartel manner to restrict competition from near substitutes for chartered banks. The bankers had long opposed the mortgage loan companies' right to accept deposits, and the CBA successfully lobbied for the withdrawal of this right, forcing the mortgage loan companies to rely increasingly for funds on their decreasingly adequate foreign sales of debentures. The CBA also lobbied for lower interest rates on government and post office savings banks' deposits, and the government was amenable to this because its financial needs were less pressing after the Canadian Pacific Railway's completion. The interest rates on the government controlled institutions fell from 4 per cent in 1890 to 2½ per cent in 1900. Meanwhile, interest rates on chartered banks' savings accounts were coordinated by the CBA and kept marginally above their competitors' rates, encouraging the transfer of deposits from government and post office savings banks to the chartered banks.

The net effect of a declining foreign debenture base for mortgage loan companies and decreased government support for its savings banks, in conjunction with increased branches and interest rates on savings accounts with chartered banks, was a significant change in the balance of assets between the chartered banks and their competitors (Table 8.1). Naylor has argued that the revived domination of the chartered banks was harmful to Canadian economic development between 1896 and 1914. Firstly, the chartered banks retained their orientation towards commerce and short-term loans, and did not channel funds to productive investment in industry or agriculture. Secondly, the bankers' cartel limited competitive bidding for Canadian savings, perhaps reducing the total amount of funds available for investment. Just how important these criticisms are is impossible to say without more detailed study, although we have already seen in chapter 7.4 that Prairie farmers suffered from inadequate credit facilities.

The rapid growth and diversification of the Canadian economy between Confederation and the First World War increased the demand for financial services and opened up possibilities for greater specialization by financial institutions. Initially, the chartered banks were slow to respond to the new situation, but once the openings had been made clear by other more innovative institutions, the banks were able through cartelization to retain their dominant position in the financial sector. Since 1910 the relative importance of the chartered banks in Canada's financial sector has continued to decline as a result of the emergence of new institutions providing specialized functions. The most important of these non-bank financial intermediaries are trust companies, consumer loan and finance companies, private and public pension funds, caisses populaires and government bodies such as the Central Mortgage and Housing Corporation. Their growth is parallelled by similar institutions in other industrial nations and has been concentrated in the post-World War II era. The chartered banks have, however, retained control of traditional banking services and continue to enjoy monopoly power in the charging for these services.

4. Central Banking

For most of Canada's history the government's role in the financial sector was restricted to setting the institutional framework, with little direct intervention to promote economic development or stability. After the adoption of responsible government during the 1840s, the idea of a provincial note issue as a means of stabilizing the currency supply and of raising government finance was posed several times, but it was strongly opposed by the chartered banks, especially the Ontario banks whose profits depended on their note issue. When in 1866 the government finally issued provincial notes, the only bank to cooperate was the government's own fiscal agent, the Bank of Montreal.

After Confederation responsibility for banking and currency was vested in the Dominion government. Legislation of 1868 and 1870 extended the principal features of the Province of Canada's financial legislation to the remainder of the Dominion. Restriction of the chartered banks' note issue to a minimum face value of $5 gave Dominion notes a monopoly of small bills. The principle that government and chartered banks' notes would circulate side by side was, however, maintained until the establishment of the Bank of Canada in 1935, and chartered banks' notes continued to circulate until after the Second World War.

Despite the establishment of a government note issue, there was little opportunity to use credit control as a policy weapon before 1914. The amount of the Dominion note issue was in principle subject to a prescribed gold backing, although the legislation was sufficiently vague to allow some latitude in the size of note issue compatible with given gold reserves (Rich, 1977). In practice, the government made little use of its limited power of monetary management. Short-term credit variations in the pre-1914 financial system were largely determined by the daily operations of the chartered banks, but these variations were in turn limited by the 1870 Dominion Notes Act's requirement that banks hold half of their cash reserves in Dominion notes, which thus linked Canada's money supply closely to her gold reserves. In the longer term, monetary policy was therefore "automatic," as in other countries on the gold standard, with the money supply determined by gold inflows and outflows.

A major change in the system was the Finance Act, introduced as a wartime measure in 1914 and made permanent in 1923. Under the Act banks could apply for Dominion notes which could be used as additional cash reserves if the banks wished to extend credit. This met the immediate objectives of preventing a bank panic in 1914 and of helping to finance the war, but it was not so suitable for peacetime conditions. By removing the relationship between gold reserves and credit, the Finance Act meant that Canada no longer had an "automatic" monetary policy, but there was no provision for management of the money supply and the terms of advances under the Act were not used as an instrument of credit control. The Finance Act allowed the chartered banks to readily expand credit during the 1926–1929 boom on the basis of Dominion notes held as reserves, and after 1929 when the reserves were no longer required, the Dominion notes were speedily returned. Thus the procyclical fluctuations in money supply were larger than they would have been in the absence of the Finance Act, which exaggerated the amplitude of the business cycle. The Finance Act also prevented a successful return to the gold standard, which had been abandoned after the outbreak of World War I. The readoption of the gold standard in 1926 was followed by an outflow of gold, and the specie-flow adjustment mechanism (reduced gold reserves produce deflation until the payments deficit is corrected) no longer worked because the domestic money supply was not determined by the size of Canada's gold reserves. The export of gold was restricted by the end of 1928, and the gold standard was legally abandoned in 1931.

The weaknesses of the Finance Act with respect to both domestic and external financial stability were emphasized by the depression of the 1930s. In 1933 a Royal Commission was appointed, and following its recommendations the government established a central bank. The Bank of Canada began operations in March 1935, at first under private ownership but after 1938 as a public institution. The central bank was given sole right of note issue, and the chartered banks' notes were gradually withdrawn during the period up to 1950. The major functions of the Bank of Canada were to regulate credit and currency to mitigate fluctuations in the economy, to control the external value of the currency and to advise the government on monetary policy. For the first time, and somewhat belatedly, monetary policy became one of the tools used by the government to influence the level of economic activity.

5. Conclusions

Early financial innovations were in response to the lack of adequate means of exchange. The preferred medium of exchange was gold and silver, but these were constantly in short supply, and the colonists had to seek alternative media of exchange. Paper currency provided the answer, but the imperial government was unwilling (especially after 1763) to authorize a permanent colonial note issue. Eventually, private banks operating under statutory charters were created to fill the need (section 1). Their banknotes were a good solution to the currency shortage problem and improved the efficient operation of an increasingly complex economy.

Although the chartered banks used their note issue to make interest-bearing loans, these were largely short-term commercial loans or to governments. The financial intermediary role was relatively unimportant before the mid-nineteenth century, and there was little demand for financial innovations to provide such services. The Bank War of the 1830s in the United States had only a feeble counterpart in Canada, where the chartered banks' position remained intact (section 2). The Canadian banks faced a more serious challenge after the 1860s, when the economic changes described earlier in chapters 6 and 7 created a demand for new financial services which the banks neither anticipated nor satisfied. The period between Confederation and the First World War saw the most rapid intensive growth of the Canadian financial sector, combined with a dramatic struggle by the chartered banks to regain lost ground and in particular to act as financial intermediaries between newly important savers and potential investors (section 3). Although the long-term trend in Canada, as in other industrial countries, has been for non-bank financial intermediaries to take a growing share of the financial sector, the Canadian chartered banks have been able to maintain a significant market share and to enjoy some monopoly power within their segment of the market.

In Canada financial innovations have generally been in response to other economic changes rather than acting as stimuli to economic development; changes in the supply of financial services have followed shifts in demand rather than vice versa. This implies a passive role, rather than the active role which banks have played in other latecomers' development (e.g., Germany). Some writers have even argued that the financial sector retarded Canadian economic development because of the continuing dominance of the conservative chartered banks, although this charge remains unproven. Evaluation of the financial sector's performance is critical to evaluation of government policy in this area. Although the government rarely intervened directly in the financial sector until after the First World War, legislation and other behaviour did favour the established banks at critical moments and provided little encouragement to competing financial institutions. The federal government has also granted protection from non-Canadian competition, e.g., by imposing citizenship requirements for bank directors and by requiring life insurance companies to balance their Canadian assets and liabilities. Only since the 1920s has the government played a more interventionist role by creating specialized public financial institutions and controlling the money supply.

Chapter 9
Business Cycles

A typical feature of modern market economies is the business cycle. In Canada since Confederation these short cycles have lasted on average just over four years from one peak to the next, although there have been considerable variations in length. In this chapter we examine the domestic causes of the Canadian business cycle and whether it coincided with other countries' cycles. In the final section one of the most dramatic cycles, that of the 1920s and 1930s, is given particular attention.

Fluctuations did of course occur in the preindustrial economy, but they differed fundamentally from the modern business cycle. Agricultural fluctuations, especially before the widespread commercialization of agriculture, were primarily related to natural conditions and were not necessarily cyclical. The early Canadian economy was also subject to fluctuations stemming from changes in staple exports, but these were usually a result of long-run shifts in demand rather than a cyclical phenomenon. Finally, in the nineteenth century a new cause of recession in the commercial economy of the St. Lawrence was bank panics, which were often transmitted from the United States (e.g., in 1837), but which did not usually have a great effect on the real sector of the economy. The modern business cycle is distinguished from these earlier fluctuations by its wave-like pattern and by its impact on the whole monetarized or market-oriented part of the economy, which in post-Confederation Canada means almost the entire economy.

1. Course of the Business Cycle and its Domestic Causes

Cyclical fluctuations in the Canadian economy have been identified and dated from 1873 (Table 9.1). Earlier cycles may have existed. For example, evidence in commodity price indices and applications for building permits indicates an October/November 1868 peak, a mid-1869 trough, a May/July 1870 peak, an August 1871 trough and a November 1873 peak. The data are, however, too sparse to consider these to be accurate reference points or to deduce the economy-wide impact of the cycle. Thus, the business cycle appears to have emerged during the late 1860s and has been a prominent feature of the Canadian economy since the 1870s.

The two most popular explanations of the business cycle are those of the Keynesian and monetarist schools. The Keynesian approach emphasizes changes in aggregate demand; increases in desired investment, exports or government expenditure have a positive effect on national income, while increases in desired saving, imports or taxation have a negative effect, and in either case the final result of the change is magnified by the multiplier. Monetarists, on the other hand, place the money

Table 9.1
Business Cycles in Canada, 1873–1939

Business Cycle Reference Dates			
Trough		Peak	
		Nov.	1873
May	1879	July	1882
Mar.	1885	Feb.	1887
Feb.	1888	July	1890
Mar.	1891	Feb.	1893
Mar.	1894	Aug.	1895
Aug.	1896	Apr.	1900
Feb.	1901	Dec.	1902
June	1904	Dec.	1906
July	1908	Mar.	1910
July	1911	Nov.	1912
Jan.	1915	Jan.	1918
Apr.	1919	June	1920
Sept.	1921	June	1923
Aug.	1924	Apr.	1929
Mar.	1933	July	1937
Oct.	1938		

Source: Chambers (1958), p. 406; Chambers (1964), p. 180; Hay (1966), p. 361.

supply in the centre of the picture, with a fall in the money supply reducing national income and an increase in the money supply either raising real output (if unemployment exists) or raising the price level.

Both Keynesians and monetarists accept that increases in the trade deficit (surplus) will have a negative (positive) impact on the level of economic activity. In practice, however, staple exports no longer dominated Canadian economic fortunes by Confederation. The impact of lumber and agricultural exports was perhaps strongest in 1874, when the lower exports resulting from reduced overseas lumber demand and good European harvests were an important cause of the downturn. When agricultural exports increased again in 1875–1876, however, they were not sufficient to turn the cycle round. Grain exports were a source of the 1894 recovery, but on many other occasions agricultural exports moved contracyclically. In sum, although changes in export demand could moderate or accentuate the business cycle, trade fluctuations were not sufficiently large relative to changes in other components of aggregate demand or other determinants of the money supply to be the prime mover of the business cycle.

The prime domestic causes of business cycles since the 1870s have been changes in investment expenditures or changes in the money supply, both of which have moved consistently with Keynesian and monetarist explanations of the business cycle. The mechanisms can be illustrated from the most severe depression of the late nineteenth century, whose downswing lasted from November 1873 until May 1879. The upturn was delayed by business uncertainty during 1878 as businessmen awaited the outcome of the general election and proof of the new government's resolve to implement its policies. This uncertainty, followed by greater business optimism in 1879, determined the time path of investment demand. The 1879 trough also featured four bank failures, which were the culmination of the monetary side of the depression. In general, however, although the money supply has tended to move pro-cyclically, Canadian cycles have not been characterized by bank panics (as in the United States) or other financial catastrophes (as in England and Europe during the 1890s).

It would be extremely difficult to discriminate between Keynesian and monetarist explanations of the Canadian business cycle, at least before the establishment of the Bank of Canada in 1935, because the principal determinant of the money supply was the demand for credit. Whether business expectations or the money supply are considered the prime mover, the implication is that Canada already had a well-developed economy; that is, output of subsistence farming, staple exports and bank panics had lost preeminence by the time of Confederation and had been replaced by forces typical of a more diversified economy, where investment in producer durables and the behaviour of financial intermediaries are important.

2. Relation to Other Countries' Business Cycles

The openness of the Canadian economy and its close connections with the British and the American economies raise the question of whether Canadian business cycles may be externally caused. A first step to answering this question is to identify whether Canadian business cycles have coincided with or regularly followed those of other countries. If such a coincidence is found, it is then necessary to identify the transmission mechanism if a causal relationship is to be shown.

Of the twelve reference dates (i.e., business cycle turning points) established by Chambers for the period 1873-1896 (Table 9.1), eight lie within a two-month zone of coincidence with their U.S. counterparts. On the other hand, the Canadian cycles fail to show any close association in timing with British cycles—and apparently with those of other European countries. Chambers concludes that his study supports "a view of the Canadian economy as being peripheral, more nearly attached to the United States than to Western Europe" (Chambers, 1964, p. 409).

In a more recent study, Hay combines Chambers' reference points with those for twentieth-century business cycles in order to extend the period of analysis. Hay concludes that a remarkable coincidence exists between American and Canadian cycles over the period 1873–1861: (1) the average U.S. cycle lasted 49 months and the average Canadian cycle 49½ months; (2) the leads or lags were very short, with on average a Canadian lead of less than one month; (3) the lead or lag was rarely more than three months. In contrast, many British cycles cannot be matched with Canadian counterparts, the average British cycle lasted 59½ months, and the average Canadian lead was two months with a large variance.

Chambers and Hay arrived at their conclusions by comparing reference dates, which specify the timing and length of cycles. The amplitude of cycles is also important, and this can be analyzed with the help of spectral analysis. Bonomo and Tanner applied this technique to Canadian and U.S. data for the period 1919–1967. They reaffirmed the close correlation between U.S. and Canadian cycles and found an average Canadian lag of half a month. Concerning amplitude, their finding was that "the cycles in Canada are damped versions of the counterparts in the U.S." (Bonomo & Tanner, 1972, p. 4). This could reflect more enlightened government policy in Canada, but this is not very plausible in view of the little countercyclical policy in either country before World War II. A more likely explanation of the more damped Canadian cycles is that as a result of her higher marginal propensity to import she has a smaller multiplier than the United States. A further explanation might lie in the greater variation of regional cycles in Canada, since if these are out of phase their averaging will dampen the estimated national business cycle; evidence on the degree of independence of the British Columbia cycle is given in Blain, et al. (1974). Finally, the differing amplitudes may reflect that the causes of the two countries' business cycles differ in nature or in magnitude.

The close similarity of the Canadian and U.S. cycles in timing and length has led to the belief that Canada's business cycle is largely imported from her southern neighbour. Possible transmission mechanisms are trade and money markets. Since a large part of Canada's commodity production is for export to the United States, and investment in the sectors producing these goods is sensitive to American conditions, a fall in U.S. demand could adversely affect both exports and investment, leading to a downturn in the Canadian economy. The connection between U.S. and Canadian money markets is reflected in the similarity of stock market behaviour in the two countries. Particularly important may be the role of U.S. transnational corporations, who may be unwilling or unable during a U.S. recession to increase their investment, including investment in Canada. There are, however, two objections to these "concrete" transmission mechanisms, one based on the close coincidence of the two countries' cycles and the other based on the constancy of the relationship before 1900. The transmission mechanisms imply that Canadian cycles are lagged versions of U.S. cycles, but Bonomo & Tanner estimated an average lag of a mere half month, while Hay even estimated a Canadian lead, and the averages are based on a mixture of lags and leads. Furthermore, Chambers found a similar coincidence between U.S. and Canadian cycles in the late nineteenth century, when Canadian trade was oriented towards Britain as much as towards the United States and direct foreign investment was minor.

A more satisfactory explanation of the two countries' similar business cycles would be to identify a common cause. The leader of the monetarist school has emphasized the central role of the U.S. money supply: "If you want to know what happens to Canadian income, you do better to know what happens to the U.S. money stock than to know what happens to the Canadian money stock" (Friedman, 1973, p. 17). A Keynesian would look to the determinants of business expectations which in turn determine the level of investment, the most volatile component of aggregate demand. These expectations have, on the whole, been similar in the United States and Canada. The similarity is perhaps, as one writer expresses it, a result of "the contagious nature of American business and financial opinion" (Bryce, 1939, pp. 383-4), or perhaps due to both business communities watching the same indicators and reading the same literature. The communality of expectations can explain the similar stock price movements and the approximate coincidence of business cycles, while variations in timing, length and amplitude of cycles reflect country-specific factors.

3. The Depression of the 1930s

The depression of the 1930s was the most severe in recent Canadian history and was also characterized by a very slow recovery. As background to the depression it is necessary to look at development during the 1920s. This has an added advantage of updating the accounts of industrial and agricultural development given in chapters 6 and 7.

After World War I there was a period of economic uncertainty, but starting in 1921 Canada enjoyed a long, more or less sustained boom, which lasted until 1929. The boom was fueled by bouyant foreign demand for Canadian exports and by the growth of major new industries, of which the most important were newsprint, automobiles, mining and utilities (especially hydroelectric power). These industries were characterized by the importation of new technology, a responsiveness to growing North American demand for consumer goods and their appropriateness to Canadian resource endowment. Most of the new industries had already begun production before World War I, but their greatest impact on Canadian income came during the 1920s.

Pulp and paper was by 1925 the largest manufacturing industry in

Canada. Its major branch was newsprint, production of which tripled between 1913 and 1920 and then tripled again between 1920 and 1929 (from less than 300,000 tons in 1913 to 867,000 tons in 1920 and 2.7 million tons in 1929). Newsprint production was export-oriented, with 90 per cent of output being exported, and Canada dominated world markets with 65 per cent of total newsprint exports in 1929. The industry's growth was largely due to rapid growth in U.S. demand for newsprint, while U.S. newsprint production remained more or less constant between 1913 and 1929. Canada was well placed to supply the American market, because she had wood, water and power located in fairly close proximity and embargoes on pulpwood exports ensured that processing remained in Canada.

The automobile industry had likewise existed in Canada before World War I, but its greatest absolute increase in production came after the war. The main growth force was the increase in domestic automobile registrations from 2,000 (1907) to 276,000 (1918) and 1.2 million (1929). Tariff protection from 1907 onwards ensured that the demand would be primarily met by Canadian production, although the industry was soon dominated by subsidiaries of U.S. corporations. Annual output rose from 94,000 units in 1920 to 263,000 in 1929, of which 102,000 were exported to British imperial preference areas. The tremendous importance of the industry lay not only in its direct economic impact, but even more in the changed lifestyles and multifarious related activities stemming from the new mode of transport. Its effect on investment was huge; investment in automobiles and highway construction accounted for 9 per cent of GNP in the years 1926-1930, compared to less than 1 per cent for 1906-1910. Two features of the automobile industry were particularly significant for the depression. Firstly, because automobiles were a consumer durable whose purchase could easily be delayed if credit conditions were poor or future income uncertain, they gave consumption demand some of the volatility associated with investment demand. Secondly, the industry's capacity in 1930 was 400,000 vehicles per year, which was well above the record 1929 output and meant that future investment would be limited until existing capacity was more fully utilized.

Without examining other growth industries in detail, an overview of Canada's economic development during the 1920s can now be presented. Economic growth in the 1920s, and particularly during the second half of the decade, was much more rapid in Canada than in most other countries. Manufacturing output increased by 37 per cent between 1923 and 1929, compared to 13 per cent in the United States and 12 per cent in Britain. Investment in manufacturing and mining rose by 80 per cent between 1926 and 1929, compared to 15 per cent in the United States (Safarian, 1970, pp. 65-6). The magnitude of the investment boom meant that if business optimism gave way to pessimism, the ensuing drop in investment demand would be large and Canada would experience a relatively severe depression. Moreover, the large and recent capital stock in many industries meant that the Canadian recovery would be slower because new investment would increase but gradually. A second source of instability which emerged during the 1920s boom was a renewed vulnerability to changes in export conditions. Much of Canadian production was export-oriented and Canada had large shares of some world markets (e.g., newsprint, aluminum, wheat, copper, lead and zinc).

Canada experienced a slowdown in demand for her exports in 1928, but what could have been a minor Canadian recession was made much more severe by two international events: the U.S. depression, which began in 1929, and the breakdown of world trade and finance between 1929 and 1931. The American depression led to lower import demand in Canada's main export market, and this was made worse when the U.S. government tried to export its unemployment by imposing the protective Smoot–Hawley tariff in 1930. At the same time, U.S. corporations cut back their investment expenditure, which included investment in Canada. The breakdown of world trade began with falling primary product prices and was made worse by the reduction in capital exports from creditor countries, which left the debtor countries facing severe debt repayment problems. World trade declined further after rounds of retaliatory tariff increases by the trading nations, and short term capital movements became a major and destabilizing component of countries' balance of payments. Flight of capital from Austria and Germany (and the failure of the largest Austrian bank in May 1931) was succeeded by doubts over British loans to Germany and capital outflows from Britain, culminating in Britain being forced to leave the gold standard. The international depression and the breakdown in world trade and finance was particularly crippling to the Canadian economy because of its export orientation.

The international depression, the large drop in investment when optimism faded and the excess capacity in 1929 combined to make the 1929–1933 downswing especially severe in Canada. National income in 1933 was only 55 per cent of its 1929 level. Unemployment rose to 30 per cent in 1933, which is perhaps the best single measure of the human suffering—although it is, if anything, an underestimate because a large number of the "employed" were working only part-time. Thompson (1970, p. 24) has estimated the gap between potential and realized output in 1933 at 38 per cent, which suggests the total underemployment of factors of production. Not all components of gross national expenditure fell equally. Investment, whether measured in current or constant dollars, was only 11 per cent of its 1929 level in 1933. The value of exports fell by 50 per cent, although their volume only fell by 25 per cent. On the other hand, consumption and government expenditures were more stable.

Although the recovery began in most industrial countries during

1932, it was delayed in North America. The Canadian depression flattened out in 1932 and exports to Britain revived, but consumption and investment responded sluggishly. The March 1933 U.S. bank crisis harmed business confidence, and Canadian investment fell again. The first quarter of 1933 was the low point, but after that exports grew and the U.S. recovery inspired greater business confidence. Between 1933 and 1937 economic recovery was substantial. The 1926 level of Gross National Expenditure was reached again, but the 1937 GNE was still 13 per cent below that of 1929—and this was in spite of a 10 per cent increase in population between 1929 and 1937. A tenth of the labour force was still unemployed in 1937. Indeed, although recovery was substantial when viewed in isolation, its most striking characteristic was its relative slowness.

Of the other major industrial nations only the United States suffered a more severe decline in national income, but she recovered more quickly than Canada so that the total effect between 1929 and 1937 was similar. The major European countries experienced less severe depressions and more rapid recoveries than Canada (Table 9.2). The difference seems due to Canada's greater vulnerability to falling export prices and to her greater reduction in investment, which was partly related to declining exports but also to the features of her 1920s boom. Although U.S. and Canadian experiences were similar in aggregate, there were significant differences in the behaviour of the components of GNE (Table 9.3). Canadian exports performed much better than U.S. exports between 1929 and 1937, which should have had a positive effect on Canada's national income relative to that of the United States; but this was offset by the inferior performance of investment and government expenditure in Canada, pointing once more to the key role of investment in the depression and recovery periods. Finally, lest these international comparisons appear too dismal from a Canadian viewpoint, it must be emphasized that even though the 1920s boom increased the length and severity of the 1930s depression, Canada still benefitted from the increased output of the boom itself. Thus, if the comparisons in Table 9.2 were made from a base in the early 1920s, Canada's economic performance would outstrip that of the other countries. This is important, because although the 1930s depression was more severe in Canada than in western Europe, it is easier to withstand fluc-

Table 9.2
Indices of National Income for Various Countries, 1929-1937 (1929 = 100)

	Canada	USA	UK	Germany	France	Japan
1933	55	48	85	59	84	84
1937	85	84	111	97	102-22	139

Source: Safarian (1970), p. 98.

Table 9.3
Changes in Components of Gross National Expenditure in Canada and
the U.S.A., 1929–1937 (1929 = 100)

	Canada	U.S.A.
Consumption	86	85
Investment	53	72
Government Expenditure	98	137
Exports	98	63
Imports	72	71
Total	87	87

Source: Safarian (1970), p. 223.

tuations with a higher income, and average Canadian living standards had surpassed those of much of western Europe by 1929.

From a post-World War II viewpoint, a glaring omission from the above account is the scant reference to government policy. In fact, little attempt was made to regulate the downswing of the depression. The effect of the commercial banks' lending was that the money supply moved with the cycle during the late 1920s and early 1930s, accentuating the cycle and forcing a de facto departure from the gold standard in 1929 (Courchene, 1969); in the absence of a central bank, a countercyclical monetary policy was non-existent. There was also no attempt to use fiscal policy to dampen the downswing; although the budget deficit did increase in 1930 and 1931, the positive effect on the level of economic activity was incidental to other goals, and at the trough of the depression in 1932 and 1933 the deficit was reduced. The only consistent countercyclical policy followed during the downswing was the tariff increases which followed the U.S. Smoot–Hawley tariff of 1930. This was far from a first-best policy, since it involved resource misallocation and redistribution of income (in particular, away from the agricultural sector), but it saved some jobs in the protected manufacturing sector.

Government policy was more consistent during the recovery phase of the cycle, although its influence was small. After the establishment of the Bank of Canada in 1935 there was some use of monetary policy. Fiscal policy in the form of increased expenditure on unemployment relief and housing subsidies was also resorted to. Despite these beginnings, management of the business cycle by monetary and fiscal policy only became a major policy consideration for Canadian governments after World War II. Commercial policy also changed in the mid-1930s with a shift from protection to freer trade, especially within the British Empire. This again is a trend which became more pronounced after World War II, when in recognition of the deficiencies of commercial policy as a countercyclical weapon, the major trading countries have, in principle at least, renounced its use for this purpose and have negotiated a series of multilateral tariff reductions.

Although Canadian government policy had little impact on the business cycle of the 1920s and 1930s, one of the main legacies of the depression was its impact on government policy. With the memories of the personal tragedies of the unemployed during the 1930s, minimizing unemployment became a major postwar policy goal; fiscal and monetary policies have been the main tools, and much of the Keynesian-monetarist debate has been over the two policies' relative merits. This is in contrast to pre-1930s policies which were intended to affect long-run economic growth and structure (cf. chapter 5) rather than cyclical fluctuations in the economy. Counterparts of the older policies have remained; in particular, there has been a continuing government involvement in infrastructure projects. There has, however, been a gradual retreat from the high tariff policy, largely as a result of the experience during the 1930s. Since old tariffs are no longer protecting infant industries, this has almost certainly benefitted most Canadians.

Chapter 10

Regional Variations in Economic Development

As in all large countries, Canadian economic development has not been identical in the various regions. The pattern of regional leadership has changed as the areas of early European settlement—the Atlantic provinces and Quebec—have fallen behind Ontario and the two far western provinces. To some extent, the declining relative economic importance of the eastern provinces has been a corollary of the westward movement of settlement since the late eighteenth century, but it also reflects the nature of economic activity in the different regions. Areas relying on staple exports have seen their economic fortunes fluctuate with the demand for their staples. The most stable regions are those in which manufacturing became firmly established, and the industrial areas have also been consistently among the most affluent parts of the nation. In order to explain the causes of regional inequality in post-industrial Canada, it is therefore necessary to analyze the determinants of industrial location. Finally, one aspect of the rapid urbanization of Canada since the mid-nineteenth century, the competition between Montreal and Toronto for metropolitan preeminence, is examined in the last section of this chapter.

1. Changing Patterns of Regional Leadership

In the preindustrial economy, regional and urban development was closely related to resource endowments or locational advantages in the transport system. The prosperity of Newfoundland was based on fish and that of New Brunswick on lumber, and both experienced relative economic stagnation when long-term shifts in demand made their exports less profitable. The position of Montreal, which rose to prominence as the centre of the fur trade, was more stable, because the commercial and financial expertise of the city could be turned to other uses when the fur trade left in 1821. Economic growth in Upper Canada, at least up to the mid-nineteenth century, was based on the existence of an agricultural frontier, and urban development was limited to political or military centres. On the west coast, British Columbia experienced economic decline as gold output fell during the 1860s, but her economy revived with the emergence of the salmon-canning and forestry industries in the late 1870s and the completion of CPR in 1885.

The changing patterns of regional leadership during the nineteenth century are reflected in the population data in chapter 2 and in Table 4.1. The earliest estimates of economic activity by provinces are those of Green (Table 10.1). In the comparison between east and west the 1890 figures capture the end of an era; the three Maritime provinces rank

Table 10.1
Gross Value Added by Provinces, 1890-1956 ($ millions)

	1890	1910	1929	1956
PEI	14.1	16.0	25.6	108.0
Nova Scotia	64.1	114.2	215.0	974.0
New Brunswick	49.1	75.7	140.0	706.0
Quebec	208.7	474.8	1,603.0	7,766.0
Ontario	391.2	845.5	2,423.0	11,732.0
Manitoba	30.3	133.1	382.0	1,440.0
Saskatchewan	9.7	121.4	415.0	1,647.0
Alberta	(a)	98.7	411.0	2,399.6
British Columbia	26.1	165.6	547.0	3,162.0

Note: (a) Alberta included with Saskatchewan in 1890.
Source: Green, 1971, pp. 85-8.

behind Ontario and Quebec, but are still more important than the western provinces in terms of output. This situation was reversed by 1929, when the gross value added (GVA) in the three Maritime provinces together was less than that of any of the four western provinces taken individually. In later decades there has been no such dramatic shifts in regional economic balance, and the position remains one of central Canadian economic preeminence with the west more important economically than the east.

Living standards have also displayed regional variations, although comparisons are made difficult by lack of regional price indices. Bearing this problem in mind, some conclusions can be drawn from nominal income statistics. Comparing Green's estimates (Table 10.1) with provincial population data (Table 4.1) reveals 1890 per capita GVA varying from $129 in Prince Edward Island to $266 in British Columbia. Manitoba and Ontario ranked behind British Columbia in 1890, and further east, Quebec ranked below New Brunswick and Nova Scotia. By 1910 British Columbia and Ontario outranked the Prairie provinces, which were followed by Quebec and then the Maritime provinces. Since 1926 statistics on provincial income per capita have become more plentiful; they reveal a continuation of the 1910 pattern, apart from Ontario overtaking British Columbia during the 1930s and some intraregional ranking changes among the Prairie and Maritime provinces (Alberta performing best among the former and Nova Scotia best among the latter).

A connection between varying rates of extensive growth and regional per capita income disparities is provided by internal migration. The primary mechanism by which Canada's economic centre of gravity moved westwards during the early twentieth century was factor movements, including substantial internal migration of labour in response to the prospect of a higher standard of living in the west than in the east. The extent of the wheat boom migrations, and of migration into British Columbia and postwar movements to Ontario and Alberta, indicate that the Canadian labour force is mobile and responsive to income differentials. Nevertheless, factor movements have not succeeded in removing regional income disparities, and the reduction of these disparities has become a goal of federal policy in the postwar era.

Explanation of the western provinces' above average per capita income and rapid extensive growth since the turn of the century can be offered in terms of the region's staple products. The growth and prosperity of the Prairie economy before 1930, and its susceptibility to severe fluctuations, reflect the prominence of wheat and the behaviour of world wheat markets. The later affluence of Alberta is based primarily on her oil resources. In British Columbia forest and mineral products have been the leading exports in the twentieth century, with hydroelectricity and recreation also assuming importance since 1945. External demand for the staples and ease of exploitation with current technology are the principal determinants of regional prosperity in these cases. The nature of the staple affects the extent to which increased prosperity promotes immigration into the region. The wheat boom was accompanied by large-scale immigration because labour was required to utilize the plentiful Prairie land. Population growth was slower in British Columbia because entry into forestry and mining was less open. Average incomes remained higher in British Columbia, however, because of the returns to owners of immobile resources. In the 1950s the situation reversed itself, with British Columbia and Alberta both experiencing rapid economic growth, but the former's population increased faster because wood industries were more labour-intensive than oil industries (Caves & Holton, 1959, pp. 218-32). The nature of the staples has also influenced the western province's roles in the Canadian economic and political system. The Prairie wheat economy retained close relations with central Canada; the public land was administered by the federal government, the CPR's head office was in Montreal and Prairie farmers were encouraged by the tariff to purchase equipment from Ontario. In consequence Prairie interests were frequently pressed in Ottawa (see chapter 7), and Prairie politicians have played a prominent role in Canadian affairs. British Columbia's exports are shipped directly from Vancouver to other countries rather than to the rest of Canada. Since the completion of the CPR, events in central Canada and decisions taken by the federal government have had little impact on British Columbia, with the possible exception of the protective tariff. In consequence, the B.C. economy's behaviour is remarkably independent from that of the national economy (Blain, et al., 1974). This may help to explain British Columbia's relative apathy towards national affairs and the absence of national political figures from that province, although other geographical and social factors clearly influence this behaviour as well.

More difficult to explain is the economic ascendancy of Ontario. Today, Ontario exceeds all other provinces in total output and in income per head. In part, Ontario's prosperity derives from her natural resources, but far more important is her position as the industrial heartland of Canada. Thus, in order to explain Ontario's economic leadership, it is necessary to account for the location of industry there rather than elsewhere in Canada. This will be done in the next section by comparing the locational advantages and disadvantages of Ontario and Quebec. Meanwhile, it is worth stressing that although nineteenth-century industrial technology was based on coal and iron, the importance of these resources in determining industrial location must not be exaggerated. Earlier writers (e.g., Easterbrook & Aitken, 1956) were led to conclude, erroneously, that since Canada was not endowed with large known coal and iron deposits before 1900, she could not have experienced substantial industrialization during the nineteenth century. Similarly faulty reasoning underlay the Nova Scotia pro-tariff lobby in 1879, which believed that because Nova Scotia had coal and an iron industry it would be the principal beneficiary of a protective tariff on manufactured goods. Some new manufacturing enterprises did open in Nova Scotia during the 1880s, but by the 1890s the industrial sector had collapsed as the locational advantages of central Canada became clear (cf., Acheson 1972, although he sees predatory behaviour by Montreal interests as the cause of collapse). The moral is clearly that a comparative advantage in coal and iron production was insufficient to outweigh the locational disadvantages of the Maritimes, with their small regional markets and isolation from larger markets.

The development of modern industry has typically been geographically concentrated in its early years (e.g., in Lancashire, in the Ruhr, in northeastern France). Regional income inequality worsened during the early stages of industrialization in the European countries and the United States, and only improved after the gradual diffusion of the fruits of industrialization. Green (1969) has traced the same U-shaped time path in Canada between 1890 and 1956; regional inequality increased rapidly between 1890 and 1910, rose more slowly between 1910 and 1929 and declined only after 1929. In view of the dating of Canada's industrial development (chapter 6.1) we might expect the period of increasing inequality to extend back to the 1860s, and to date Ontario's long-run ascendancy from that decade.

2. The Location of Industry

The interrelated questions of differing regional prosperity and industrial location have been framed most often in terms of a comparison between

Ontario and Quebec. The interprovincial comparison is slightly vitiated by the fact that provincial boundaries do not coincide with economic boundaries. Industrial development has been concentrated in southwestern Ontario, in particular around the western end of Lake Ontario and along the Grand River Valley, while the economy of eastern Ontario bore a closer resemblance to that of Quebec. Within the province of Quebec, the island of Montreal occupies a unique position as an industrial centre. Nevertheless, the differences between the two provinces' aggregate economic development are sufficiently clear to be worth analyzing.

The relative economic position of Ontario and Quebec during the nineteenth century can be judged from their population (Table 4.1). Ontario overtook Quebec in 1850 and her population continued to grow faster until 1891, but then the gap between the two provinces' population remained constant until after World War II. For much of the 1800s the more rapid growth in Ontario was due to the availability of virgin agricultural land, but the Ontario agricultural frontier was closed by the 1870s and land availability cannot explain Ontario's extensive growth in the late-nineteenth century. The difference between Ontario and Quebec during this period was that the industrial development which became significant during the 1860s was centred in Ontario. By 1891 the "manufacturing belt" of southern Ontario had already established its industrial leadership vis-à-vis other parts of Ontario (Gilmour, 1972) and other parts of Canada.

Many arguments have been advanced to explain why Canada's industrial revolution occurred in Ontario rather than Quebec. An obvious difference between the two provinces is their differing dominant cultures. Some theories have therefore emphasized the role of perceived cultural traits, such as a French orientation towards the family firm or general disdain for business. These explanations of Quebec's economic backwardness are not very satisfactory, because examples of dynamic French entrepreneurship can be found in the nineteenth century (e.g., in Tulchinsky, 1977) and because Quebec industry did expand rapidly after 1900 in the same cultural milieu. A more sophisticated explanation emphasizes the lack of access to capital for French-Canadian entrepreneurs, perhaps evolving from the emigration of the French-Canadian bourgeoisie in 1760 and the subsequent domination of the financial sector by Anglo-Canadians. This explanation is more attractive than the simple theory of cultural bias, but it has the same weaknesses, and it should also be remembered that the industries of the 1860s for the most part had low capital requirements.

Instead of seeking internal explanations for Quebec's industrial backwardness, Faucher & Lamontagne (1971) argue that central Canada's industrial development can best be understood in a continental North American context. Quebec's early economic development, centred on the ports of Montreal and Quebec, was the counterpart of the early development of the eastern United States, with its major urban centres of Boston, New York, Philadelphia and Baltimore. The crucial nineteenth-century change for both areas was the replacement of wood by iron and steel, which led to an increased importance for coal and a shift in the centre of economic gravity in North America. All of the above-mentioned port cities declined in relative importance, except for New York, which held the advantage as an Atlantic port for the midwest, and to a lesser extent Montreal, which remained the financial capital of Canada until after Confederation. The new centre of gravity was determined by the location of the Appalachian coalfields, and the new U.S. industrial axis ran between Pittsburgh and the Great Lakes. Within Canada, Ontario's advantage lay in its proximity to the Pittsburgh–Cleveland axis. Faucher & Lamontagne conclude that:

> the decadence of Quebec's economic prominence was not a regional incident. It was a much wider phenomenon which affected the whole continent and which was due to the passage from a régime of mercantilism to a system of industrialism based upon coal, steel and steam. (p. 261)

Quebec's only advantage was abundant labour, and the industries which did grow there (e.g., boots and shoes, textiles) were based on the sweatshop system. In general, however, industrial growth in Quebec was too slow to absorb the population increase; many people emigrated (half a million went to New England between 1850 and 1900) and agricultural activity spread to poor land which was later abandoned. Ontario, on the other hand, lay close to the major source of North American coal and to the area of rapid economic development in the United States, so that it is not surprising that the Canadian industry which emerged after the adoption of a protective tariff was located in southern Ontario.

Faucher & Lamontagne also explain the industrial growth which did take place in Quebec after 1900 in terms of trends in the North American economy. The important changes occurring after the turn of the century included the depletion of some resources in the United States (e.g., pulpwood, copper and iron), increased demand for new materials such as aluminum and nickel, and the substitution of other sources of power for coal. At first, Ontario benefitted more than Quebec from these changes as a result of her closer links to the U.S. economy and more active government policy. For example, the Ontario pulp and paper industry was protected by restrictions on raw material exports in 1900, whereas the Quebec government only introduced similar restrictions in 1910. Nevertheless, Quebec had specific advantages in resource endowment, particularly with respect to water which was crucial for hydroelectricity and for aluminum production, and especially after 1911 Quebec's industrial development was rapid. Most of the "counterpart" industrial development (e.g., automobile production) remained in Ontario, but as a result of her strong comparative advantage in certain key products, Quebec industry grew in a complementary role to U.S. industrial expansion.

The Faucher-Lamontagne hypothesis is a convincing explanation of the twentieth-century pattern, but with respect to the mid-1800s it is not the whole story. The weakness of their argument is that in trying to refute theories based on Quebec's internal disadvantages they ignore internal forces in Ontario which were favourable to that province's industrial development. The most important of these was agriculture. By 1850 Ontario farmers were producing a sizeable surplus over their own consumption need, while in Quebec the surplus hovered around zero (Isbister, 1977). Part of the difference is accounted for by larger farm family size in Quebec, but Isbister shows that even with Ontario-sized families (and assuming that this reduces consumption with no effect on production) the gap between the two provinces' surplus rates would only have been narrowed by 5 to 10 per cent in the nineteenth century. The greater part of Ontario's superior performance is thus due to higher output per farm, and particularly important in the nineteenth century was her higher output of field crops per farm.

A breakdown of the sources of productivity growth has not yet been attempted for nineteenth-century Canadian agriculture. Estimates for America, however, indicate that the largest source of productivity growth in mid-century grain farming was the mechanization of harvesting (Parker and Klein, 1966). As noted in chapter 6.2, the first major innovation, the mechanical reaper, was diffused in Ontario more slowly than in the United States, but by 1870 a significant number of farms had sufficiently large grain acreage to justify reaper purchase. In Quebec, farms were smaller and wages lower, and hence few farmers' grain acreage exceeded the threshold size at which mechanical harvesting became profitable.

The argument could be taken a further step back by asking why farm sizes and factor prices differed between the two provinces. In Ontario good land was still available and the acreage under small grains continued to increase until the 1870s, while in Quebec submarginal land was being brought into cultivation. The abundance of fertile land in Ontario, particularly in the southwest of the province, reduced pressures for subdivision and increased the opportunity cost of labour in Ontario. Cultural factors, such as smaller family size and prevalence of primogeniture in Ontario, worked in the same direction, but the key difference seems to have been the unequal arable land/labour ratios. Larger farms and higher wages provided greater incentives to mechanize grain harvesting, and mechanization proceeded fastest in southwestern Ontario where farms were largest and wages highest.

The importance of Ontario's higher and rising agricultural productivity for that province's economic growth lies in three interrelationships between agriculture and industry. Although labour was released from the agricultural sector in both provinces, only in Ontario was this accompanied by an ongoing capacity to produce an agricultural surplus to feed the nonagricultural population. In Quebec the labour release reflected, at least between 1860 and 1890, the negative consideration of inadequate opportunities in agriculture, and a high proportion of the released labour emigrated. The commodity exchange interrelationship was important in Ontario, not just because the nonagricultural population could be fed with home-grown produce, but also because significant backward, forward and final-demand linkage effects operated. The agricultural machinery industry became a leading manufacturing sector and, by the turn of the century, an export industry. Cheese factories and breweries, two other leading branches, which grew rapidly after the late 1860s on the basis of import substitution following the abrogation of the Reciprocity Treaty with the United States, both had forward linkages from agriculture. In general, the manufacturing sector in southern Ontario was characterized at least until the 1890s by an emphasis on consumer goods industries, for which the broadly based demand from the affluent agricultural sector must have been important. An interrelationship via export earnings was also present, in that Ontario grain and later cheese were major foreign exchange earners in the second half of the nineteenth century, and the earnings were increasingly spent on imported machinery which presumably went to the nonagricultural sector. Both the commodity exchange and the export earnings interrelationships were absent from Quebec, at least until the development of the dairy industry late in the nineteenth century. In sum, Ontario's economic development contains elements of "balanced growth" between agriculture and industry, and explanations which ignore the role of the agricultural sector are incomplete.

3. The Development of Metropolitan Centres

The industrialization in the second half of the nineteenth century was accompanied by increased urbanization. In 1860 the only large towns in Canada were the old cities of Montreal and Quebec and a rapidly growing Toronto, whose population increased from 30,775 to 44,821 during the 1850s. Some way behind these cities were the two urban centres of the Maritime colonies, Saint John and Halifax. Four Canada West towns with populations between 10,000 and 20,000 completed the number of towns in British North America with populations over 10,000 (Table 10.2). The relative population growth of these nine towns during the next thirty years reflected the location of industry. Montreal's population more than doubled, and the towns in the southern Ontario manufacturing belt, Toronto, Hamilton and London, grew even more rapidly. In contrast, the towns in regions which did not participate in the industrialization process declined in relative importance. The only exception was Ottawa, whose expansion arose from her political position as Dominion capital rather than from industrial growth. The contrast between urban development in southern Ontario and in other parts of Canada would be even clearer if account was taken of the rapid expansion of smaller towns in the manufacturing belt. The pattern of industrial urbanization had been established by 1891, and later industrial growth "changed the scale of the pattern form, rather than changed the form itself" (Gilmour, 1972, p. 146).

Table 10.2
Towns with Populations over 10,000 in 1861, and Their Population Growth,
1861–1891

	1861 census	1891 census
Montreal	90,323	216,650 (1)
Quebec	59,990	63,090 (3)
Toronto	44,821	181,220 (2)
Saint John	27,317	39,179 (6)
Halifax	25,026	38,556 (7)
Hamilton	19,096	48,980 (4)
Ottawa	14,669	44,154 (5)
Kingston	13,743	19,264 (10)
London	11,555	31,977 (8)

Note: bracketed figures indicate the city's rank in 1891.

Although it is not surprising that the location of industry in southern Ontario was associated with greater urbanization, it was not inevitable that this would be associated with the transfer of the national financial and commercial centre to that region. With few exceptions, industrial nations today have a single preeminent financial centre, which is sometimes, but not always, the political capital, and which is frequently located outside the nation's industrial heartland. One exception is Canada, where Montreal and Toronto have shared the position of the nation's financial centre.

In the first half of the nineteenth century Montreal was the Canadian metropolis. Montreal's preeminence was similar to that of New York in the United States, but whereas New York retained its financial preeminence even after the locus of U.S. industrial activity shifted farther west, Montreal encountered serious competition. Montreal's disadvantage stemmed from its reduced commercial importance after Upper Canada gained an ice-free outlet for overseas trade through the construction of the Erie Canal and of railway links from the Great Lakes to U.S. tidewater.

This disadvantage was clear by 1850, and there was scope for a commercial centre to emerge on the shores of Lake Ontario, serving as a shipment point for both the St. Lawrence and the New York route. Toronto played this role, which was reflected in her close connections with New York as well as with Montreal.

The emergence of Toronto as the Ontario metropolis is not difficult to explain (cf., Masters, 1955). The city has a good harbour and an excellent geographical location. In 1797, Toronto was selected as capital of Upper Canada in preference to somewhere on the Niagara Peninsula, which would have been less secure from U.S. attack. The population of government officials and hangers-on and the presence of a garrison provided an initial stimulus to Toronto's growth, giving the city an early advantage over its local rivals. Once Toronto's growth began, there were no obstacles to retard future expansion. The city's inhabitants were enterprising, its geographical situation vis-à-vis the interior was ideal and there were many good factory sites, especially on the waterfront. The gently sloping lakeshore permitted uninterrupted spatial expansion, in contrast with Hamilton which was hemmed in by the Niagara escarpment.

Conflict between the interests of Montreal and those of Upper Canada arose in the mid-nineteenth century when attempts by Montreal to channel Canadian exports along the St. Lawrence route were successfully withstood by Upper Canada (chapter 2.6). Conflict between Montreal and Toronto became more acute during the 1860s and 1870s when it focussed on two major issues: the transCanadian railway's eastern terminus and banking legislation. The first issue was settled in favour of Montreal, which became the terminus for the Canadian Pacific Railway. On the second issue, the growing monopoly position of the Bank of Montreal with its close government ties was reversed, and after the passing in 1871 of banking legislation favourable to the growth of Ontario banks, the Bank of Montreal's supremacy was never again so pronounced. The Toronto victory was important in reducing Montreal's financial hegemony. The Toronto defeat was not so important, because further railway links were soon developed. As the Ontario economy grew faster than that of Quebec, there was little to stop Toronto from reaching at least equality of metropolitan status with Montreal by the beginning of the twentieth century.

The fact that Montreal, unlike New York, had to face a challenge to its economic leadership can be explained in terms of geography and climate. More difficult to explain is the long period of dual leadership by Montreal and Toronto, which is in contrast to the experience of other countries. The only attempt to resolve this problem in a comparative history framework reaches no clear conclusion (Kindleberger, 1974, ch. 8). Kindleberger suggests that the federal government may have tried to maintain a balance between the two central provinces' metropolitan centres, but it is difficult to see exactly how such a policy was implemented, even if the federal government had wished to achieve this objective.

A number of subsidiary, but regionally important, metropolitan centres have developed in western Canada. Their existence as independent financial and commercial centres reflects the significantly different economic bases of the regions from each other and from central Canada, as well as the large distances (and different time zones) from Toronto and Montreal. In British Columbia, Vancouver with its mainland deep-water harbour soon reduced Victoria to an economically subsidiary position. In the Prairies, Winnipeg was from the beginning the undisputed commercial centre for the wheat economy. In Alberta, however, as the economy has diversified from wheat into livestock and oil, Calgary and Edmonton have both developed as metropolitan centres, repeating the bipolar phenomenon found in central Canada.

Table 10.3
Population by Census Metropolitan Areas, 1971 (thousands)

Montreal	2,743
Toronto	2,628
Vancouver	1,082
Ottawa	603
Winnipeg	540
Hamilton	499
Edmonton	496
Quebec	481
Calgary	403
London	286
Windsor	259
Kitchener-Waterloo	227
Halifax	223

Source: Statistics Canada: Population by Census Metropolitan Area, January 1973.

The pattern of metropolitan centres in Canada today (Table 10.3) reflects the component trends described above. Montreal and Toronto remain the two leading metropolitan centres in Canada. In the western provinces, Vancouver, Winnipeg, Edmonton and Calgary have established themselves as regional centres. The southern Ontario manufacturing belt remains strongly represented by Toronto, Hamilton, London and Kitchener-Waterloo, with the twentieth-century industrial newcomer of Windsor (the centre of Canada's automobile industry because of its location opposite Detroit). With the increased size of government bureaucracies, Ottawa and Quebec have retained importance, but other eastern cities have ceased to be counted among Canada's major urban areas.

Chapter 11
Conclusions

Our understanding of Canada's economic past is in a state of flux. During the first half of the twentieth century, Canadian economic history matured as a discipline, and some degree of agreement was reached about the course of Canada's economic development (represented, for example, by Easterbrook and Aitken's 1956 text). Since then, the methodological revolution involving more explicit use of economic theory and statistical methods has led to a questioning of the conventional wisdom. The cornerstone of "old" Canadian economic history, the staple theory, has been shown to have, at best, only partial relevance to economic development since the mid-nineteenth century. Research on specific issues has discredited old conclusions and established new ones. George's 1968 paper, for example, forced a reassessment of railway policy. In addition, an upsurge of interest by Canadian historians in economic matters has increased our understanding of government policy formation (e.g., Nelles, 1974), business history and social history. A failing of this recent activity, however, has been its inability to present a satisfactory general explanation of Canada's economic development. The theories presented in chapter 3 all have weaknesses, due to either lack of completeness or inapplicability to some periods or parts of the economy, but nothing has been established in their place.

An overall view of Canadian economic growth has emerged in the course of this book, and although eclectic, it is worth summarizing here. The staple theory remains adequate for the early centuries of European economic penetration of Canada. Fish attracted Europeans and led them into contact with Indians, who had furs to trade. The fur trade dominated the mainland Canadian economy from the early 1600s to the late 1700s; economic growth was tied to the fortunes of the fur trade, but because of its small linkage effects, economic development was limited. The most significant characteristic of the fur trade was its antagonism towards agriculture and ability to restrict settlement.

The pattern of heavy specialization and slow population growth was interrupted only by exogenous factors. The border settlement and emigration of Empire Loyalists after American Independence led speedily to the fall of the Montreal fur trade, and events in Europe led to its replacement by timber as the staple export of central and eastern Canada. Farther west, however, the fur trade retained its preeminence until the 1858 gold rush in British Columbia and until the post-Confederation expropriation of the Hudson's Bay Company's territory east of the Rockies.

The timber trade's economic characteristics explain the main economic phenomenon of the period 1821-1851. The excess capacity on returning timber ships reduced the costs of migration to Canada, and the lumber industry was complementary to, rather than antagonistic towards, agricultural settlement. Extensive growth took place, but because the timber trade had few linkages beyond sawmills and shipbuilding, general economic development did not result. The rapid population growth contained, however, the seeds of changes which would reduce the staple theory's relevance to later Canadian economic history.

The growing population and the more diversified economy led to significant political and economic changes in the Province of Canada around the middle of the nineteenth century. The changes have been variously described as a bourgeois revolution or Canada's industrial revolution, or could be likened to the beginning of Rostow's take-off. None of these labels provide explanations of why the changes occurred, but they do capture the magnitude of the changes and signify that this was an important transitional stage in the development of the modern Canadian economy. After this time, the staple theory's explanatory power is greatly reduced, because the Canadian economy becomes sufficiently diversified that the behaviour of no small number of commodities is critical to the development of the economy as a whole.

The first period of rapid manufacturing growth and the adoption of modern industrial technology on a significant scale was the 1860s, and the major unanswered question of this book concerns the reason why these changes occurred in that decade. The problem lies not in finding a plausible cause, but in determining the relative importance of agricultural growth in Ontario, increased protection (as a result of the 1858-1859 tariff, the U.S. Civil War and the end of reciprocity), booming railway construction after government policy shifted from neglect to generous assistance, inter alia.

Subsequent industrial development was strongly affected by association with more industrially advanced nations and assumed some of the latecomer characteristics predicted by Gerschenkron. Because technology developed elsewhere could be adopted at an advanced stage, new Canadian industries in the 1880s and later started operations with large units of production. The ensuing problems of overcapacity were tackled with mixed success by cartel formation, and later by mergers. The existence of more advanced economies permitted substantial use of foreign capital in Canadian economic development. Before 1900 the capital inflow consisted primarily of portfolio investment from Britain, but in the late nineteenth century, and especially after 1900, U.S. direct investment in Canada became more important. The reliance on foreign investment is common among latecomers, but the nature of the foreign investment is important because portfolio investment can be more easily liquidated later. In Germany, for example, foreign portfolio investment was large between 1850 and 1870, but after that period bonds expired and there was a policy of repatriating foreign-held shares when domestic funds became available. There was a similar reduction in the relative importance of foreign portfolio investment in Canada during the twentieth century, but it did not happen with respect to direct foreign investment where the branch plant is a permanent foreign-owned asset.

It is appropriate to emphasize that Canadian economic development since the 1850s has followed a well-trodden path: long-term intensive growth has been rapid and stable, manufacturing has grown in relative importance and has been accompanied by urbanization, the business cycle has become endemic and the geographical concentration of industry initially increased regional inequality. Resource endowment explains much of the particular structure of the Canadian economy, including the continuing importance of natural resources which makes the economy more responsive to external demand changes and more unstable than most industrial nations' economics. The salient differentiating features of Canadian industrial development, high concentration levels and the ubiquitous branch plants of U.S. corporations, can be accounted for by Canada's relative lateness in industrializing and by her proximity to the United States. The different pace of economic development in Canada and the United States also accounts for some institutional differences (e.g., Canada's retention of a more European banking system). In sum, after taking account of resource endowment, geography and the timing of the industrial revolution, Canada's post-industrial economic experience has been similar to that of other countries. The difficulty in finding a satisfactory approach to Canadian economic development is not a peculiarly Canadian failing, but reflects an inadequate understanding of the process of economic development in general.

Finally, it must be admitted that the question of economic well-being has had a subordinate position in Canadian economic history. The path of real intensive growth provides an indicator of improvements in average material living standards, but reveals nothing of the relative performance of different groups in the Canadian economy. In chapter 10.1 a U-shaped time-path of regional income equality was observed, and intercountry comparisons suggest that personal income distribution follows a similar path. There has, however, been no attempt to measure whether industrialization in Canada led to increased income inequality, at least initially. Muckraking accounts of early Canadian capitalists suggest that this occurred, but modern research on the historical behaviour of income distribution in Canada is just beginning. Perhaps this will yield the main incremental insights into Canada's past, since it is a grossly neglected area. Nevertheless, in light of the huge increases in average income variations, income distribution may be relatively unimportant.

Bibliography

Acheson, T.W. "The National Policy and the Industrialization of the Maritimes," *Acadiensis I*, Spring 1972, pp. 3-28.

Aitken, H.G.J. "Discussion" (on Buckley 1958), *Journal of Economic History 18*, Dec. 1958, pp. 451-2.

_____. "Defensive Expansion: The State and Economic Growth in Canada," in H.G.J. Aitken (ed.) *The State and Economic Growth*, New York, 1959, pp. 79-114.

_____. *American Capital and Canadian Resources*, Cambridge, Mass., 1961.

Anderson, T.L. "Economic Growth in Colonial New England: 'Statistical Renaissance,'" *Journal of Economic History 39*, March 1979, pp. 243-57.

Ankli, R.E. "The 1854 Reciprocity Treaty," *Canadian Journal of Economics IV*, Feb. 1971, pp. 1-20.

Ball, D.E., and G.M. Walton. "Agricultural Productivity Change in Eighteenth Century Pennsylvania," *Journal of Economic History 36*, March 1976, pp. 102-17.

Barnett, D.F. "The Galt Tariff: Incidental or Effective Protection," *Canadian Journal of Economics 9*, Aug. 1976, pp. 389-407.

Barsby, S.L. "Economic Backwardness and the Characteristics of Development," *Journal of Economic History 29*, Sept. 1969, pp. 449-72.

Bertram, G.W. "Economic Growth and Canadian Industry, 1870-1915: The Staple Model and the Take-off Hypothesis," *Canadian Journal of Economics and Political Science XXIX*, May 1963, pp. 162-84.

_____. "Historical Statistics on Growth and Structure of Manufacturing in Canada 1870-1957," in J. Henripin and A. Asimakopolous (ed.) *Canadian Political Science Association Conferences on Statistics 1962 and 1963*, Toronto 1964, pp. 93-146.

_____. "The Relevance of the Wheat Boom in Canadian Economic Growth," *Canadian Journal of Economics VI*, Nov. 1973, pp. 545-66.

Blain, L., D.G. Patterson and J.D. Rae. "The Regional Impact of Economic Fluctuations during the Inter-war Period: the Case of British Columbia," *Canadian Journal of Economics VII*, Aug. 1974, pp. 381-401.

Bonomo, V., and J.E. Tanner. "Canadian Sensitivity to Economic Cycles in the United States," *Review of Economics and Statistics LIV*, Feb. 1972, pp. 1-8.

Bryce, R.B. "The Effects on Canada of Industrial Fluctuations in the United States," *Canadian Journal of Economics and Political Science 5*, Aug. 1939, pp. 373-86.

Buckley, K.A.H. "Urban Building and Real Estate Fluctuations in Canada," *Canadian Journal of Economics and Political Science 18*, Feb. 1952, pp. 41-62.

———— . *Capital Formation in Canada 1896–1930*, Toronto: McClelland and Stewart, 1974 (first appeared in 1955).

———— . "The Role of Staple Industries in Canada's Economic Development," *Journal of Economic History 18*, Dec. 1958, pp. 439-50.

Caves, R.E. "Export-led Growth and the New Economic History," in J.N. Bhagwati, R.W. Jones, R.A. Mundell and J. Vanek (eds.) *Trade, Balance of Payments and Growth*, Amsterdam, 1971, pp. 403-42.

———— . "Economic Models of Political Choice: Canada's Tariff Structure," *Canadian Journal of Economics 9*, May 1976, pp. 278-300.

———— , and R. H. Holton. *The Canadian Economy: Prospect and Retrospect*, Cambridge, Mass., 1959.

Cell, G.T. *English Enterprises in Newfoundland 1577–1660*, Toronto: University of Toronto Press, 1970.

Chambers, E.J. "Canadian Business Cycles since 1919; A Progress Report," *Canadian Journal of Economics and Political Science 24*, May 1958, pp. 166-89.

———— . "Late Nineteenth Century Business Cycles in Canada," *Canadian Journal of Economics and Political Science 30*, Aug. 1964, pp. 391-412.

———— , and D.F. Gordon. "Primary Products and Economic Growth: An Empirical Measurement," *Journal of Political Economy LXXIV*, Aug. 1966, pp. 315-32.

Courchene, T.J. "An Analysis of the Canadian Money Supply: 1925–1934," *Journal of Political Economy 77*, May/June 1969, pp. 363-91.

Creighton, D.G. *The Empire of the St. Lawrence*, Toronto: Macmillan of Canada, 1956 (first appeared in 1937 under the title *The Commercial Empire of the St. Lawrence 1760–1850*).

Dales, J.H. *The Protective Tariff in Canada's Economic Development*, Toronto, 1966.

———— , J.C. McManus and M.H. Watkins. "Primary Products and Economic Growth: A Comment," *Journal of Political Economy 75*, Dec. 1967, pp. 876-80.

Donald, W.J.A. *The Canadian Iron and Steel Industry*, Boston, 1915.

Easterbrook, W.T., and H.G.J. Aitken. *Canadian Economic History*, Toronto: Macmillan of Canada, 1956.

Eastman, H.C., and S. Stykolt. *The Tariff and Competition in Canada*, Toronto: Macmillan of Canada, 1967.

Engerman, S.L. "Some Economic Issues Relating to Railroad Subsidies and the

Evaluation of Land Grants," *Journal of Economic History* 32, June 1972, pp. 443-63.

Faucher, A., and M. LaMontagne. "History of Industrial Development," in M. Rioux and Y. Martin (eds.) *French Canadian Society*, Toronto 1971.

Firestone, O.J. *Canada's Economic Development 1867-1953*, London, 1958.

_____. "Development of Canada's Economy 1850-1900," in *National Bureau of Economic Research Studies in Income and Wealth 24: Trends in the American Economy in the Nineteenth Century*, Princeton 1960, pp. 217-46.

_____. *Industry and Education: A Century of Canadian Development*, Ottawa: University of Ottawa Press, 1969.

Fogel, R.W. *The Union Pacific Railroad: A Case in Premature Enterprise*, Baltimore, 1960.

Fowke, V.C. *The National Policy and the Wheat Economy*, Toronto: University of Toronto Press, 1971 (first appeared in 1957).

Friedman, M. *Money and Economic Development*, New York, 1973.

George, P.J. "The Rates of Return in Railway Investment and Implications for Government Subsidization of the Canadian Pacific Railway: Some Preliminary Results," *Canadian Journal of Economics I*, Nov. 1968, pp. 740-62.

Gerschenkron, A. *Economic Backwardness in Historical Perspective: A Book of Essays*, Cambridge, Mass. 1962.

Gilmour, J.M. *Spatial Evolution of Manufacturing: Southern Ontario 1851-1891*, Toronto: University of Toronto Press, 1972.

Glazebrook, G.P.deT. *A History of Transportation in Canada*, Toronto: McClelland and Stewart, 1964 (originally published in 1938).

Grant, D. "The Staple Theory and its Empirical Measurement," *Journal of Political Economy 82*, Nov./Dec. 1974, pp. 1249-53.

Grant, K.G. "The Rate of Settlement of the Canadian Prairies 1870-1911; A Comment," *Journal of Economic History 38*, June 1978, pp. 471-3.

Green, A.G. "Regional Inequality, Structural Change and Economic Growth in Canada 1890-1956," *Economic Development and Cultural Change 17*, July 1969, pp. 567-83.

_____. *Regional Aspects of Canadian Economic Growth*, Toronto: University of Toronto Press, 1971.

_____, and M.C. Urquhart. "Factor and Commodity Flows in the International Economy of 1870-1914: A Multi-Country View," *Journal of Economic History 36*, March 1976, pp. 217-52.

Grubel, H.G. *International Economics*, Homewood, Ill., 1977.

Hamelin, J. *Économie et Société en Nouvelle-France*, Quebec, 1960.

Hartland, P. "Canadian Balance of Payments since 1868," in *National Bureau of Economic Research Studies in Income and Wealth 24: Trends in the American Economy in the Nineteenth Century*, Princeton 1960, pp. 717-753.

Hay, K.A.J. "Early Twentieth Century Business Cycles in Canada," *Canadian Journal of Economics and Political Science 32*, Aug. 1966, pp. 354-65.

Helleiner, G.K. "The Political Economy of Canada's Tariff Structure: An Alternative Model," *Canadian Journal of Economics 10*, May 1977, pp. 318-26.

Henripin, J. *Tendances et Facteurs de la Fécondité au Canada*, Ottawa, 1968.

Innis, H.A. *The Fur Trade in Canada: An Introduction to Canadian Economic History*, (rev. ed.), Toronto: University of Toronto Press, 1956 (first appeared in 1930).

————. *The Cod Fisheries: The History of an International Economy*, Toronto, 1940.

Isbister, J. "Agriculture, Balanced Growth, and Social Change in Central Canada since 1850; An Interpretation," *Economic Development and Cultural Change 25*, July 1977, pp. 673-97.

Johnson, H.G. "The Cost of Protection and the Scientific Tariff," *Journal of Political Economy 68*, Aug. 1960, pp. 327-45.

Jones, R.L. *History of Agriculture in Ontario 1613–1880*, Toronto: University of Toronto Press, 1974 (first appeared in 1946).

Kilbourn, W. *The Elements Combined. A History of the Steel Company of Canada*, Toronto, 1960.

Kindleberger, C.P. "The Formation of Financial Centers: A Study in Comparative Economic History," *Princeton Studies in International Finance No. 36*, Nov. 1974.

Kuznets, S. "Long-Term Trends in Capital Formation Proportions," *Economic Development and Cultural Change 9, No. 4 Pt. II*, July 1961.

————. *Modern Economic Growth; Rate, Structure and Spread*, New Haven, 1966.

Langdon, S. "The Emergence of the Canadian Working Class Movement 1845–75," *Journal of Canadian Studies 8*, May 1973, pp. 3-13, Aug. 1973, pp. 8-25.

Lewis, F. "The Canadian Wheat Boom and Per Capita Income New Estimates," *Journal of Political Economy 83*, Dec. 1975, pp. 1249-57.

Lithwick, N.H. *Economic Growth in Canada, A Quantitative Analysis*, 2nd ed., Toronto: University of Toronto Press, 1970.

Lower, A.R.M. *Colony to Nation: A History of Canada*, Toronto, 1946.

McDiarmid, O.J. *Commercial Policy in the Canadian Economy*, Cambridge, Mass., 1946.

Macdonald, L.R. "Merchants against Industry: An Idea and its Origins," *Canadian Historical Review 56*, Sept. 1975, pp. 263-81.

McDougall, D.M. "Canadian Manufactured Commodity Output 1870-1915," *Canadian Journal of Economics 4*, Feb. 1971, pp. 21-36.

_____ . "The Domestic Availability of Manufactured Commodity Output, Canada 1870-1915," *Canadian Journal of Economics 6*, May 1973, pp. 189-206.

McIvor, R.C. *Canadian Monetary Banking and Financial Development*, Toronto: Macmillan of Canada, 1958.

Mackintosh, W.A. "Economic Factors in Canadian History," *Canadian Historical Review 4*, 1923.

_____ . *The Economic Background of Dominion-Provincial Relations*, Appendix III to the Rowell-Sirois Report, Ottawa, 1939 (reprinted with an introduction by J.H. Dales, Toronto, 1964).

Maizels, A. *Industrial Growth and World Trade*, Cambridge, England, 1963.

Marr, W., and M. Percy. "The Government and the Rate of Prairie Settlement," *Canadian Journal of Economics XI*, Nov. 1978, pp. 757-67.

Martin, C. *Dominion Lands Policy*, Toronto: McClelland and Stewart, 1973 (first appeared in 1938).

Masters, D.C. *The Reciprocity Treaty of 1854*, Toronto: McClelland and Stewart, 1963.

Meier, G.M. "Economic Development and the Transfer Mechanism: Canada 1895-1913," *Canadian Journal of Economics and Political Science 19*, Feb. 1953, pp. 1-9.

Mercer, L.J. "Rates of Return and Government Subsidization of the Canadian Pacific Railway: An Alternative View," *Canadian Journal of Economics VI*, Aug. 1973, pp. 428-37.

Myers, G. *History of Canadian Wealth*, Toronto: James Lorimer, 1972 (first appeared Chicago, 1914).

Naylor, R.T. *The History of Canadian Business 1867-1914*, 2 Vols., Toronto: James Lorimer, 1976.

Nelles, H.V. *The Politics of Development*, Toronto: Macmillan of Canada, 1974.

Neufeld, E.P. *The Financial System of Canada: Its Growth and Development*, Toronto: Macmillan of Canada, 1972.

Norrie, K.H. (1974a). "Economic Opportunity and the Westward Migration of Canadians during the late Nineteenth Century: A Comment," *Canadian Journal of Economics 7*, Feb. 1974, pp. 132-5.

_____(1974b). "Agricultural Implement Tariffs, the National Policy and Income Distribution in the Wheat Economy," *Canadian Journal of Economics 7*, Aug. 1974, pp. 449-62.

_____. "The Rate of Settlement of the Canadian Prairies 1870-1911," *Journal of Economic History 35*, June 1975, pp. 410-27.

_____. "The National Policy and Prairie Economic Discrimination 1870-1930," in D.H. Akenson (ed.) *Canadian Papers in Rural History vol. 1*, Gananoque, Ont., 1978, pp. 13-32.

Officer, L., and L. Smith. "The Canadian-American Reciprocity Treaty of 1855 to 1866," *Journal of Economic History 28*, Dec. 1968, pp. 598-623.

Parker, W.N., and J.L.V. Klein. "Productivity Growth in Grain Production in the United States, 1840-60 and 1900-10," in *National Bureau of Economic Research Studies in Income and Wealth 30: Output, Employment and Productivity in the U.S. After 1800*, New York, 1966, pp. 523-80.

Paterson, D.G. *British Direct Investment in Canada, 1890-1914*, Toronto: University of Toronto Press, 1976.

Phillips, W.G. *The Agricultural Implement Industry in Canada*, Toronto, 1956.

Pickett, J. "Residential Capital Formation in Canada 1871-1921," *Canadian Journal of Economics and Political Science 29*, Feb. 1963, pp. 40-58.

Pomfret, R.W.T. "The Mechanization of Reaping in Nineteenth Century Ontario," *Journal of Economic History 36*, June 1976, pp. 399-415.

_____. "Capital Formation in Canada 1870-1900," *Explorations in Economic History*, Jan. 1981.

Ray, A.J. *Indians in the Fur Trade: Their role as trappers, hunters and middlemen in the lands southwest of Hudson Bay 1660-1870*, Toronto: University of Toronto Press, 1974.

_____, and D. Freeman. *Give us Good Measure*, Toronto, 1978.

Reid, D.J. "Company Mergers in the Fraser River Salmon Canning Industry 1885-1902," *Canadian Historical Review 56*, Sept. 1975, pp. 282-302.

Rich, E.E. "Trade Habits and Economic Motivation among the Indians of North America," *Canadian Journal of Economics and Political Science XXVI*, Feb. 1960.

Rich, G. "The Gold-Reserve Requirement under the Dominion Notes Act of 1870: How to Deceive Parliament," *Canadian Journal of Economics 10*, Aug. 1977, pp. 447-53.

Rosenbluth, G. *Concentration in Canadian Manufacturing Industries,* Princeton, 1957.

Rostow, W.W. *The Stages of Economic Growth: A Non-Communist Manifesto,* London, 1960.

Rotstein, A. "Innis: The Alchemy of Fur and Wheat," *Journal of Canadian Studies* 12, Winter 1977, pp. 6-31.

Ruddick, J.A. et al. *The Dairy Industry in Canada,* Toronto, 1937.

Ryerson, S.B. *Unequal Union: Confederation and the Roots of Conflict in the Canadas 1815-1873,* Toronto, 1968.

Safarian, A.E. *The Canadian Economy in the Great Depression,* Toronto, 1959 (reprinted Toronto: McClelland and Stewart, 1971).

Saunders, R.S. "The Political Economy of Effective Tariff Protection in Canada's Manufacturing Sector," *Canadian Journal of Economics 13,* May 1980, pp. 340-8.

Scheinberg, S. "Invitation to Empire: Tariffs and American Economic Expansion in Canada," *Business History Review 47,* Summer 1973, pp. 218-38.

Shepherd, J.F., and G.M. Walton. *Shipping, Maritime Trade and the Economic Development of Colonial North America,* New York, 1972.

Simon, M. "New Investment in Canada, 1865-1914," *Canadian Journal of Economics 4,* May 1970, pp. 238-54.

Skelton O.D. "General Economic History 1867-1912," in A. Shortt and A.G. Doughty (eds.) *Canada and its Provinces vol. IX,* Toronto, 1913, pp. 95-274.

Southey, C. "The Staples Thesis, Common Property and Homesteading," *Canadian Journal of Economics XI,* Aug. 1978, pp. 547-59.

Spelt, J. *The Urban Development in South Central Ontario,* Toronto: McClelland and Stewart, 1972 (first appeared in 1955).

Studness, C.M. "Economic Opportunity and the Westward Migration of Canadians during the Late Nineteenth Century," *Canadian Journal of Economics and Political Science 30,* Nov. 1964, pp. 570-84.

Taylor, G.R. "American Economic Growth Before 1840; An Exploratory Essay," *Journal of Economic History 24,* Dec. 1964, pp. 429.

Temin, P. *Causal Factors in American Economic Growth in the Nineteenth Century,* London, 1975.

Thompson, R.W. *International Trade and Domestic Prosperity: Canada 1926-1938,* Toronto: University of Toronto Press, 1970.

Trigger, B.G. *Children of Aataentsic: History of the Huron People to 1660*, 2 Vols., Montreal: McGill-Queen's University Press, 1976.

Tulchinsky, G.J.J. *The River Barons: Montreal Businessmen and the Growth of Industry and Transportation 1837–53*, Toronto: University of Toronto Press, 1976.

Urquhart, M.C., and K.A.H. Buckley (eds.). *Historical Statistics of Canada*, Toronto: Macmillan of Canada, 1965.

Vickery, E. "Exports and North American Economic Growth, 'Structuralist' and 'Staplist' Models in Historical Perspective," *Canadian Journal of Economics 7*, Feb. 1974, pp. 32-58.

Watkins, M.H. "A Staple Theory of Economic Growth," *Canadian Journal of Economics and Political Science 29*, May 1963, pp. 141-58.

_____ . "Canada," in I.M. Wallerstein (ed.) *World Inequality: Origins and Perspectives on the World System*, Montreal, 1975.

Weldon, J.C. "Consolidations in Canadian Industry," in L.A. Skeoch (ed.) *Restrictive Trade Practices in Canada*, Toronto, 1966, pp. 228-79.

White, D.A. "Business Cycles in Canada," *Economic Council of Canada Staff Study No. 17*, Ottawa, 1967.

Wilkins, M. *The Emergence of Multinational Enterprise: American Business Abroad from the Colonial Era to 1914*, Cambridge, Mass. 1970.

Wonnacott, R.J., and P. Wonnacott. *Free Trade between the United States and Canada*, Cambridge, Mass., 1967.

Young, J. *Canadian Commercial Policy*, Ottawa, 1967.

Index